Institute of Mathematical Statistics

LECTURE NOTES-MONOGRAPH SERIES
Shanti S. Gupta, Series Editor

Volume 3

Empirical Processes

Peter Gaenssler

Mathematical Institute
of the University of Munich

Institute of Mathematical Statistics
Hayward, California

Institute of Mathematical Statistics

Lecture Notes-Monograph Series

Series Editor, Shanti S. Gupta, Purdue University

The production of the IMS Lecture Notes-Monograph Series is managed by the IMS Business Office: Bruce E. Trumbo, Treasurer, and Jose L. Gonzalez, Business Manager.

Library of Congress Catalog Card Number: 83-82637

International Standard Book Number 0-940600-03-X

Printed in the United States of America

CONTENTS

PREFACE

The present notes are based on lectures given at the Department of Statistics, University of Washington, Spring 1982, when the author was on leave form the Mathematical Institute, University of Munich, as a Visiting Professor at the University of Washington, supported by the National Science Foundation under Grant (MCS) 81-02568.

The last section of these lecture notes is supplemented by a course on Functional Central Limit Theorems held at the University of Munich during the Summer term in 1982.

ACKNOWLEDGEMENTS

These lecture notes gained much from the extremely stimulating atmosphere at the Department of Statistics of the University of Washington in Seattle. Special thanks are due to Professors Michael Perlman, Ronald Pyke and Galen Shorack for their great hospitality and for the very helpful conversations. I want to mention here that it was Professor Ronald Pyke who gave to me the decisive impulse for studying empirical processes after having attended his beautiful lecture at the Mathematical Research Institute Oberwolfach in 1974. I also express my gratitude to Professor R.M. Dudley (MIT) for the privilege of obtaining at any time preprints of his newest results. The present notes are mainly influenced by his work and the correspondence we occasionally had on the subject.

These notes gained also from some remarks made by Professor D. Pollard (Yale) who visited the University of Washington at the same time, as well as from the careful reading of the manuscript by my assistant Dr. Erich Häusler. Finally, the contributions and critical remarks made by my students J. Schattauer and W. Schneemeier in connection with section 3 and 4 were of significant importance.

I am also very grateful to the referees for suggesting further valuable improvements for the final version.

Special thanks are due to Mrs. K. Bischof for typing the final version of the manuscript with an admirable skill.

Last not least I would like to thank Professors Michael Perlman and Shanti S. Gupta for encouraging me to publish these notes in the IMS Lecture Notes - Monograph Series.

Munich, August 1982; revised June 1983. PETER GAENSSLER

TO MY WIFE INGRID

with admiration and thanks

for her patience with me

1. Introduction and some structural properties of empirical measures.

Many standard procedures in statistics are based on a random sample $x_1,\ldots,x_n$ of i.i.d. observations, i.e., it is assumed that observations (or measurements) occur as realizations (or values) $x_i = \xi_i(\omega)$ in some sample space X of a sequence of independent and identically distributed (i.i.d.) random elements $\xi_1,\ldots,\xi_n$ defined on some basic probability space (p-space for short) $(\Omega,\mathcal{F},\mathbb{P})$; here ξ is called a RANDOM ELEMENT in X whenever there exists a $(\Omega,\mathcal{F},\mathbb{P})$ such that $\xi: \Omega \to X$ is $\mathcal{F},\mathcal{B}$-measurable for an appropriate σ-algebra $\mathcal{B}$ in X, in which case the law $\mu \equiv L\{\xi\}$ of ξ is a well defined p-measure on $\mathcal{B}$ ($\mu(B) = \mathbb{P}(\{\omega\in\Omega: \xi(\omega)\in B\}) \equiv \mathbb{P}(\xi\in B)$ for short, $B\in\mathcal{B}$).

In classical situations, the sample space X is usually the k-dimensional Euclidean space $\mathbb{R}^k$, $k\geq 1$, with the Borel σ-algebra $\mathbb{B}_k$. In the present notes, if not stated otherwise, the sample space X is always an arbitrary measurable space $(X,\mathcal{B})$.

Given then i.i.d. random elements ξ_i in $X = (X,\mathcal{B})$ with (common) law μ on $\mathcal{B}$ we can associate with each (sample size) n the so-called EMPIRICAL MEASURE

(1) $$\mu_n := \frac{1}{n}(\varepsilon_{\xi_1} + \ldots + \varepsilon_{\xi_n}) \text{ on } \mathcal{B},$$

where $$\varepsilon_x(B) := \begin{cases} 1 \text{ if } x\in B \\ 0 \text{ if } x\notin B \end{cases}, \quad B\in\mathcal{B}.$$

In other words, given the first n observations $x_i = \xi_i(\omega)$, $i=1,\ldots,n$, $\mu_n(B) \equiv \mu_n(B,\omega)$ is the average number of the first n x_i's falling into B. (The notation $\mu_n(\cdot,\omega)$ should call attention to the fact that μ_n is a random p-measure on $\mathcal{B}$.)

μ_n may be viewed as the statistical picture of μ and we are thus interested in the connection between μ_n and μ, especially when n tends to infinity.

In what follows, let $\mathcal{C}$ be some subset of $\mathcal{B}$ (e.g., $\mathcal{C} = \{(-\infty,t]: t\in\mathbb{R}^k\}$, the class of all lower left orthants in $X = \mathbb{R}^k$, or the class of all closed Euclidean balls in $\mathbb{R}^k$, to have at least two specific examples in mind). Denoting with 1_C the indicator function of a set $C\in\mathcal{C}$, $\mu_n(C)$ can be rewritten in the form

$$\mu_n(C) = \frac{1}{n} \sum_{i=1}^{n} 1_C(\xi_i).$$

Now, since the random variables $1_C(\xi_i)$, $i=1,2,\ldots$ are again i.i.d. with common mean $\mu(C)$ and variance $\mu(C)(1-\mu(C))$, it results from classical probability theory that

(2) (Strong Law of Large Numbers): For each fixed $C\in\mathcal{C}$ one has
$\mu_n(C) \to \mu(C)$ $\mathbb{P}$-almost surely ($\mathbb{P}$-a.s.)
as n tends to infinity.

(3) (Central Limit Theorem): For each fixed $C\in\mathcal{C}$ one has
$n^{1/2}(\mu_n(C) - \mu(C)) \xrightarrow{\mathcal{L}} \overline{G}_\mu(C)$ as n tends to infinity,
where $\overline{G}_\mu(C)$ is a random variable with
$\mathcal{L}\{\overline{G}_\mu(C)\} = \mathcal{N}(0,\mu(C)(1-\mu(C)))$.

(4) (Multidimensional Central Limit Theorem): For any finitely many $C_1,\ldots,C_k\in\mathcal{C}$ one has
$\{n^{1/2}(\mu_n(C_j) - \mu(C_j)) : j=1,\ldots,k\} \xrightarrow{\mathcal{L}} \{\overline{G}_\mu(C_j) : j=1,\ldots,k\}$
as n tends to infinity, where $\overline{\mathbb{G}}_\mu \equiv (\overline{G}_\mu(C))_{C\in\mathcal{C}}$ is a mean-zero Gaussian process with covariance structure
$\mathrm{cov}(\overline{G}_\mu(C), \overline{G}_\mu(D)) = \mu(C\cap D) - \mu(C)\mu(D)$, $C,D\in\mathcal{C}$.

Here, according to Kolmogorov's theorem (cf. Gaenssler-Stute (1977), 7.1.16), $\overline{\mathbb{G}}_\mu$ is viewed as a random element in $(\mathbb{R}^{\mathcal{C}},\mathbb{B}_{\mathcal{C}})$, where $\mathbb{B}_{\mathcal{C}} \equiv \bigotimes_{\mathcal{C}} \mathbb{B}$ denotes the product σ-algebra in $\mathbb{R}^{\mathcal{C}}$ of identical components $\mathbb{B}$, $\mathbb{B}$ being the σ-algebra of Borel sets in $\mathbb{R}$.

In this lecture we are going to present uniform analogues of (2) (with the uniformity being in $C\in\mathcal{C}$) known as GLIVENKO-CANTELLI THEOREMS (Section 2) and functional versions of (4), so-called FUNCTIONAL CENTRAL LIMIT THEOREMS (Section 4); an appropriate setting for the latter is presented in Section 3 which might also be of independent interest. First we want to give insight into some more or less known

STRUCTURAL PROPERTIES OF EMPIRICAL MEASURES:

For this, consider instead of μ_n the counting process

$$N_n(B) := n\mu_n(B), \quad B\in\mathcal{B}.$$

Note that $\mathcal{L}\{N_n(B)\} = \mathrm{Bin}(n,\mu(B))$ (i.e., $\mathbb{P}(N_n(B)=j) = \binom{n}{j}\mu(B)^j(1-\mu(B))^{n-j}$, $j=0,1,\ldots,n$). The following Markov and Martingale properties associated with empirical measures are well known; since however specific references are not conveniently available, and especially not in the set-indexed context of these lectures, we present detailed derivatives.

LEMMA 1 (MARKOV PROPERTY). For any $\emptyset = B_0 \subset B_1 \subset \ldots \subset B_{k-1} \subset B_k \subset B_{k+1} = X$ with $B_i \in \mathcal{B}$ such that for $D_i := B_i \setminus B_{i-1}$, $\mu(D_i) > 0$, $i=1,\ldots,k+1$, and for any $0 \leq m_1 \leq \ldots \leq m_{k-1} \leq m_k \leq n$ with $m_i \in \{0,1,\ldots,n\}$ one has

$$\mathbb{P}(N_n(B_k) = m_k \mid N_n(B_1) = m_1,\ldots,N_n(B_{k-1}) = m_{k-1})$$
$$= \mathbb{P}(N_n(B_k) = m_k \mid N_n(B_{k-1}) = m_{k-1})$$
$$= \binom{n-m_{k-1}}{m_k-m_{k-1}} \cdot \left(\frac{\mu(D_k)}{\mu(D_k\cup D_{k+1})}\right)^{m_k-m_{k-1}} \cdot \left(1-\frac{\mu(D_k)}{\mu(D_k\cup D_{k+1})}\right)^{n-m_k}.$$

Proof. $\mathbb{P}(N_n(B_k) = m_k \mid N_n(B_1) = m_1,\ldots,N_n(B_{k-1}) = m_{k-1})$

$$= \frac{\mathbb{P}(N_n(B_1)=m_1,\ldots,N_n(B_{k-1})=m_{k-1},N_n(B_k)=m_k)}{\mathbb{P}(N_n(B_1)=m_1,\ldots,N_n(B_{k-1})=m_{k-1})} =: \frac{a}{b}, \text{ say, where}$$

$$a = \mathbb{P}(N_n(D_1) = m_1,\ N_n(D_2) = m_2-m_1,\ldots,N_n(D_k) = m_k-m_{k-1},\ N_n(D_{k+1}) = n-m_k)$$

$$= \frac{n!}{m_1(m_2-m_1)!\ldots(m_k-m_{k-1})!(n-m_k)!}\,\mu(D_1)^{m_1}\mu(D_2)^{m_2-m_1}\ldots\mu(D_k)^{m_k-m_{k-1}}\mu(D_{k+1})^{n-m_k},$$

$$b = \frac{n!}{m_1!(m_2-m_1)!\ldots(m_{k-1}-m_{k-2})!(n-m_{k-1})!}\,\mu(D_1)^{m_1}\mu(D_2)^{m_2-m_1}\ldots\mu(D_{k-1})^{m_{k-1}-m_{k-2}}\times$$
$$\times\ \mu(D_k\cup D_{k+1})^{n-m_{k-1}},$$

whence $$\frac{a}{b} = \frac{(n-m_{k-1})!}{(m_k-m_{k-1})!(n-m_k)!}\cdot\frac{\mu(D_k)^{m_k-m_{k-1}}\mu(D_{k+1})^{n-m_k}}{\mu(D_k\cup D_{k+1})^{n-m_{k-1}}}$$

$$= \binom{n-m_{k-1}}{m_k-m_{k-1}} \cdot \left(\frac{\mu(D_k)}{\mu(D_k \cup D_{k+1})}\right)^{m_k-m_{k-1}} \cdot \left(1 - \frac{\mu(D_k)}{\mu(D_k \cup D_{k+1})}\right)^{n-m_k}$$ proving equality of

the first and third term in the assertion of the lemma; the other equality follows in the same way by just taking $B_1,\ldots,B_{k-2}$ out of consideration. □

<u>Corollary.</u> Let $\mathcal{C}$ be a subset of $\mathcal{B}$ which is linearly ordered by inclusion; then $(N_n(C))_{C\in\mathcal{C}}$ is a Markov process.

<u>Lemma 2.</u> Let $\overline{B}\in\mathcal{B}$ be arbitrary but fixed such that $0 < \mu(\overline{B}) < 1$ and let $\mathcal{C} \equiv \mathcal{B}(\overline{B}) \subset \mathcal{B}$ be linearly ordered by inclusion with $\overline{B}$ as its smallest element; then for $0 \leqq m \leqq n$

$$L\{(N_n(B))_{B\in\mathcal{B}(\overline{B})} \mid N_n(\overline{B}) = m\} = L\{(m + \overline{N}_{n-m}(B\setminus\overline{B}))_{B\in\mathcal{B}(\overline{B})}\},$$

where $\overline{N}_N(D) := N\,\overline{\mu}_N(D)$, $\overline{\mu}_N$ being the empirical measure pertaining to i.i.d. random elements $\overline{\xi}_i$ in $(X,\mathcal{B})$ with $L\{\overline{\xi}_i\} = \overline{\mu}$ and $\overline{\mu}(D) := \frac{\mu(D\cap \complement\overline{B})}{\mu(\complement\overline{B})}$ for $D\in\mathcal{B}$.

(Here the laws $L\{\ldots\}$ are considered to be defined on the product σ-algebra $\mathcal{B}_{\mathcal{B}(\overline{B})}$ in $\mathbb{R}^{\mathcal{B}(\overline{B})}$ and $\complement\overline{B}$ denotes the complement of $\overline{B}$ in X.)

<u>Proof.</u> It suffices to show that the finite dimensional marginal distributions coincide.

1) As to the one-dimensional marginal distributions, let $B\in\mathcal{B}$ with $\overline{B}\subset B$ be arbitrary but fixed; then it follows from Lemma 1 that for $k \geqq m$

$$\mathbb{P}(N_n(B) = k \mid N_n(\overline{B}) = m) = \binom{n-m}{k-m} \cdot \left(\frac{\mu(B\setminus\overline{B})}{\mu(\complement\overline{B})}\right)^{k-m} \cdot \left(1 - \frac{\mu(B\setminus\overline{B})}{\mu(\complement\overline{B})}\right)^{n-k}$$

$$= \binom{n-m}{k-m} \overline{\mu}(B)^{k-m}(1 - \overline{\mu}(B))^{n-k}.$$

On the other hand, taking into account that $1_B(\overline{\xi}_i) \overset{L}{=} 1_{B\setminus\overline{B}}(\overline{\xi}_i)$ (where $\overset{L}{=}$ means equality in law) and therefore $\overline{N}_N(B) \overset{L}{=} \overline{N}_N(B\setminus\overline{B})$ for any $B\in\mathcal{B}$ with $\overline{B}\subset B$, one obtains that

$$\binom{n-m}{k-m} \overline{\mu}(B)^{k-m}(1-\overline{\mu}(B))^{n-k} = \mathbb{P}(\overline{N}_{n-m}(B) = k-m)$$

$$= \mathbb{P}(\overline{N}_{n-m}(B\setminus\overline{B}) = k-m) = \mathbb{P}(m+\overline{N}_{n-m}(B\setminus\overline{B}) = k)$$

proving the coincidence of the one-dimensional marginal distributions.

2) As to higher-dimensional marginal distributions, let us consider for simplicity the two-dimensional case (the general case runs in the same way): For this, let $B_i \in \mathcal{B}$, $i=1,2$, with $\overline{B} \subset B_1 \subset B_2$ be arbitrary but fixed; then for $k_2 \geq k_1 \geq m$,

$$\mathbb{P}(N_n(B_1) = k_1,\ N_n(B_2) = k_2 \mid N_n(\overline{B}) = m)$$

$$= \frac{\mathbb{P}(N_n(\overline{B}) = m,\ N_n(B_1) = k_1,\ N_n(B_2) = k_2)}{\mathbb{P}(N_n(\overline{B}) = m)} =: \frac{a}{b}, \text{ say, where}$$

$$a = \mathbb{P}(N_n(\overline{B}) = m,\ N_n(B_1\setminus\overline{B}) = k_1-m,\ N_n(B_2\setminus B_1) = k_2-k_1,\ N_n(X\setminus B_2) = n-k_2)$$

$$= \frac{n!}{m!(k_1-m)!(k_2-k_1)!(n-k_2)!}\ \mu(\overline{B})^m \mu(B_1\setminus\overline{B})^{k_1-m}\mu(B_2\setminus B_1)^{k_2-k_1}\mu(X\setminus B_2)^{n-k_2} \quad \text{and}$$

$$b = \binom{n}{m}\mu(\overline{B})^m(1-\mu(\overline{B}))^{n-m}, \text{ whence}$$

$$\frac{a}{b} = \frac{(n-m)!}{(k_1-m)!(k_2-k_1)!(n-k_2)!}\ \frac{\mu(B_1\setminus\overline{B})^{k_1-m}\mu(B_2\setminus B_1)^{k_2-k_1}\mu(X\setminus B_2)^{n-k_2}}{\mu(\complement\overline{B})^{n-m}}$$

$$= \frac{(n-m)!}{(k_1-m)!((k_2-m)-(k_1-m))!((n-m)-(k_2-m))!} \times$$

$$\times \left(\frac{\mu(B_1\cap\complement\overline{B})}{\mu(\complement\overline{B})}\right)^{k_1-m} \cdot \left(\frac{\mu(B_2\cap\complement\overline{B})}{\mu(\complement\overline{B})} - \frac{\mu(B_1\cap\complement\overline{B})}{\mu(\complement\overline{B})}\right)^{k_2-m-(k_1-m)} \cdot \left(1 - \frac{\mu(B_2\cap\complement\overline{B})}{\mu(\complement\overline{B})}\right)^{n-m-(k_2-m)}$$

$$= \frac{(n-m)!}{(k_1-m)!((k_2-m)-(k_1-m))!((n-m)-(k_2-m))!} \times$$

$$\times\ \overline{\mu}(B_1)^{k_1-m}\overline{\mu}(B_2\setminus B_1)^{k_2-m-(k_1-m)}\overline{\mu}(\complement B_2)^{n-m-(k_2-m)}$$

$$= \frac{(n-m)!}{(k_1-m)!((k_2-m)-(k_1-m))!((n-m)-(k_2-m))!} \times$$

$$\times\ \overline{\mu}(B_1\setminus\overline{B})^{k_1-m}\overline{\mu}((B_2\setminus\overline{B})\setminus(B_1\setminus\overline{B}))^{k_2-m-(k_1-m)}\overline{\mu}(\complement(B_2\setminus\overline{B}))^{n-m-(k_2-m)}$$

$$= \mathbb{P}(\overline{N}_{n-m}(B_1\setminus\overline{B}) = k_1-m,\ \overline{N}_{n-m}(B_2\setminus\overline{B}) = k_2-m),$$

$$= \mathbb{P}(m+\overline{N}_{n-m}(B_1\setminus\overline{B}) = k_1,\ m+\overline{N}_{n-m}(B_2\setminus\overline{B}) = k_2). \quad \square$$

LEMMA 3 (MARTINGALE PROPERTY). Let $\mathcal{C}\subset\mathcal{B}$ be linearly ordered by inclusion such that $\mu(\complement B)>0$ for all $B\in\mathcal{C}$; then, for each fixed n,

$\left(\frac{N_n(B)-n\mu(B)}{\mu(\complement B)}\right)_{B\in\mathcal{C}}$ is a martingale, i.e., for each $\bar{B}$, $B\in\mathcal{C}$ with $\bar{B}\subset B$ one has

$$\mathbb{E}\left(\frac{N_n(B)-n\mu(B)}{\mu(\complement B)}\,\Big|\,N_n(D):\mathcal{C}\ni D\subset\bar{B}\right)\ \underset{\mathbb{P}\text{-a.s.}}{=}\ \frac{N_n(\bar{B})-n\mu(\bar{B})}{\mu(\complement\bar{B})}.$$

Proof. Since $(N_n(C))_{C\in\mathcal{C}}$ is a Markov process (cf. Corollary to Lemma 1), it follows that

$$\mathbb{E}\left(\frac{N_n(B)-n\mu(B)}{\mu(\complement B)}\,\Big|\,N_n(D):\mathcal{C}\ni D\subset\bar{B}\right)\ \underset{\mathbb{P}\text{-a.s.}}{=}\ \mathbb{E}\left(\frac{N_n(B)-n\mu(B)}{\mu(\complement B)}\,\Big|\,N_n(\bar{B})\right),$$

where $\mathbb{E}\left(\frac{N_n(B)-n\mu(B)}{\mu(\complement B)}\,\Big|\,N_n(\bar{B})\right)(\omega)=\mathbb{E}\left(\frac{N_n(B)-n\mu(B)}{\mu(\complement B)}\,\Big|\,N_n(\bar{B})=m\right)$

for all $\omega\in\{N_n(\bar{B})=m\}$, $m=0,1,\ldots,n$.

Now, according to Lemma 2, $\mathbb{E}\left(\frac{N_n(B)-n\mu(B)}{\mu(\complement B)}\,\Big|\,N_n(\bar{B})=m\right)$

$$=\mathbb{E}\left(\frac{m+\bar{N}_{n-m}(B\setminus\bar{B})}{\mu(\complement B)}\right)-\frac{n\mu(B)}{\mu(\complement B)}=\frac{m+(n-m)\bar{\mu}(B)}{\mu(\complement B)}-\frac{n\mu(B)}{\mu(\complement B)}$$

$$=\frac{m\mu(\complement\bar{B})+(n-m)\mu(B\cap\complement\bar{B})-n\mu(B)\mu(\complement\bar{B})}{\mu(\complement B)\mu(\complement\bar{B})}\ \underset{(\mu(B\cap\complement\bar{B})=\mu(B)-\mu(\bar{B}))}{=}$$

$$=\frac{m-m\mu(\bar{B})+n\mu(B)-m\mu(B)-n\mu(\bar{B})+m\mu(\bar{B})-n\mu(B)+n\mu(B)\mu(\bar{B})}{\mu(\complement B)\mu(\complement\bar{B})}$$

$$=\frac{(1-\mu(B))(m-n\mu(\bar{B}))}{\mu(\complement B)\mu(\complement\bar{B})}=\frac{m-n\mu(\bar{B})}{\mu(\complement\bar{B})};$$

hence $$\mathbb{E}\left(\frac{N_n(B)-n\mu(B)}{\mu(\complement B)}\,\Big|\,N_n(\bar{B})\right)=\frac{N_n(\bar{B})-n\mu(\bar{B})}{\mu(\complement\bar{B})}.\ \square$$

Let us make at this place a remark concerning the covariance structure of $(N_n(B))_{B\in\mathcal{B}}$ supplementing the properties (2)-(4) on page 2:

It is easy to check that for any $B_i \in \mathcal{B}$, $i=1,2$,

(5) $\mathbb{E}(N_n(B_1)N_n(B_2)) = n\mu(B_1 \cap B_2) + n(n-1)\mu(B_1)\mu(B_2)$,

whence $\mathbb{E}(N_n(B_1)N_n(B_2)) = n(n-1)\mu(B_1)\mu(B_2)$ if $B_1 \cap B_2 = \emptyset$;

together with $\mathbb{E}(N_n(B_1))\mathbb{E}(N_n(B_2)) = n^2\mu(B_1)\mu(B_2)$ this yields

$\text{cov}(N_n(B_1), N_n(B_2)) = -n\mu(B_1)\mu(B_2) \neq 0$ if $B_1 \cap B_2 = \emptyset$ and

$\mu(B_i) > 0$, $i=1,2$;

therefore, $B_1 \cap B_2 = \emptyset$ does not imply that $N_n(B_1)$ and $N_n(B_2)$ are independent. (For the uniform empirical process, to be considered later, this implies that it is not a process with independent increments.) This situation changes if one considers instead the following

(6) POISSONIZATION: Let ν be a Poisson random variable (defined on the same p-space as the ξ_i's) with parameter λ and let for $B \in \mathcal{B}$

$$M(B) \equiv M(B,\omega) := \sum_{i=1}^{\nu(\omega)} 1_B(\xi_i(\omega)), \quad \omega \in \Omega.$$

Assume that ν is independent of the sequence $(\xi_i)_{i \in \mathbb{N}}$.

Then, for any pairwise disjoint $B_j \in \mathcal{B}$, $j=1,\dots,s$, the random variables $M(B_j)$, $j=1,\dots,s$, are independent.

Furthermore, for any $B \in \mathcal{B}$ and any $k \in \{0,1,2,\dots\}$ one has

$$\mathbb{P}(M(B)=k) = \frac{(\lambda\mu(B))^k}{k!}\exp(-\lambda\mu(B)).$$

Proof. Let us prove first the last statement:

$$\mathbb{P}(M(B)=k) = \mathbb{P}\Big(\bigcup_{\ell \geq k}\{\sum_{i=1}^{\ell} 1_B(\xi_i)=k,\ \nu=\ell\}\Big) = \sum_{\ell \geq k}\mathbb{P}\Big(\sum_{i=1}^{\ell} 1_B(\xi_i)=k\Big)\,\mathbb{P}(\nu=\ell)$$

$$= \sum_{\ell \geq k}\binom{\ell}{k}\mu(B)^k(1-\mu(B))^{\ell-k}\frac{\lambda^\ell}{\ell!}\exp(-\lambda)$$

$$= \sum_{\ell \geq k}\frac{\ell!}{k!(\ell-k)!}\mu(B)^k(1-\mu(B))^{\ell-k}\frac{\lambda^{\ell-k}\lambda^k}{\ell!}\exp(-\lambda)$$

$$\underset{(\ell-k=:m)}{=} \frac{(\lambda\mu(B))^k}{k!}\exp(-\lambda)\left[\sum_{m\geq 0}\frac{(\lambda(1-\mu(B)))^m}{m!}\right] = \frac{(\lambda\mu(B))^k}{k!}\exp(-\lambda\mu(B)).$$

As to the independence assertion let $B_{s+1} := \complement(\bigcup_{j=1}^{s} B_j)$, $k := \sum_{j=1}^{s} k_j$, and $k_{s+1} := \ell-k$ for $\ell \geq k$. Then

$$\mathbb{P}(M(B_j) = k_j,\ j=1,\ldots,s) = \mathbb{P}\Big(\bigcup_{\ell\geq k}\{\sum_{i=1}^{\ell} 1_{B_j}(\xi_i) = k_j,\ j=1,\ldots,s+1;\ \nu=\ell\}\Big)$$

$$= \sum_{\ell\geq k} \mathbb{P}\Big(\sum_{i=1}^{\ell} 1_{B_j}(\xi_i) = k_j,\ j=1,\ldots,s+1\Big)\,\mathbb{P}(\nu=\ell)$$

$$= \sum_{\ell\geq k} \frac{\ell!}{k_1!\ldots k_s!(\ell-k)!}\,\mu(B_1)^{k_1}\ldots\mu(B_s)^{k_s}\mu(B_{s+1})^{\ell-k}\,\frac{\lambda^{k_1+\ldots+k_s}\lambda^{\ell-k}}{\ell!}\,\exp(-\lambda)$$

$$= \prod_{j=1}^{s} \frac{(\lambda\mu(B_j))^{k_j}}{k_j!}\,\exp(-\lambda)\cdot\Bigg[\sum_{m\geq 0}\frac{(\lambda\mu(B_{s+1}))^m}{m!}\Bigg]\ldots..(*), \text{ where}$$

$[\ldots.] = \exp(\lambda\mu(B_{s+1}))$, whence

$$\exp(-\lambda)\,[\ldots.] = \exp\Big(-\lambda\Big(\sum_{j=1}^{s+1}\mu(B_j)\Big)\Big)\exp(\lambda\mu(B_{s+1})) = \exp\Big(-\lambda\Big(\sum_{j=1}^{s}\mu(B_j)\Big)\Big).$$

Therefore

$$(*) = \prod_{j=1}^{s}\frac{(\lambda\mu(B_j))^{k_j}}{k_j!}\exp(-\lambda\mu(B_j)). \quad \square$$

Later we will consider for a given $\mathcal{C}\subset\mathcal{B}$ the so-called EMPIRICAL $\mathcal{C}$-PROCESS $\beta_n \equiv (\beta_n(C))_{C\in\mathcal{C}}$ defined by

$$\beta_n(C) := n^{1/2}(\mu_n(C)-\mu(C)),\ C\in\mathcal{C}.$$

Using (5) one obtains

$$\mathrm{cov}(\beta_n(C_1),\ \beta_n(C_2)) = \mu(C_1\cap C_2) - \mu(C_1)\mu(C_2),\ C_1,C_2\in\mathcal{C}.$$

Furthermore, $n^{1/2}(\beta_n(C_1) - \beta_n(C_2)) = \sum_{i=1}^{n}\eta_i(C_1,C_2)$ with

$\eta_i \equiv \eta_i(C_1,C_2) := 1_{C_1}(\xi_i) - 1_{C_2}(\xi_i) - (\mu(C_1) - \mu(C_2))$ being independent and identically distributed with $\mathbb{E}(\eta_i) = 0$ and

$\mathrm{Var}(\eta_i) = \mu(C_1\Delta C_2) - (\mu(C_1) - \mu(C_2))^2 \leq \mu(C_1\Delta C_2)$, whence the following Bernstein-type inequality applies (cf. G. Bennett (1962)):

(7) Let $\eta_1, \eta_2, \ldots$ be a sequence of independent random variables with $\mathbb{E}(\eta_i) = 0$ and $\mathrm{Var}(\eta_i) = \sigma_i^2$ and suppose that $\sup|\eta_i| \leq M$ for some constant $0<M<\infty$; let $S_n := \sum_{i=1}^{n} \eta_i$ and $\tau_n^2 := \sum_{i=1}^{n} \sigma_i^2$; then for all n and $\varepsilon>0$

$$\mathbb{P}(S_n \geqq \varepsilon) \leq \exp\left(-\frac{\varepsilon^2/2}{\tau_n^2+\varepsilon M/3}\right).$$

From (7) we obtain immediately

LEMMA 4. For every n and $a>0$ one has for any $C_i \in \mathcal{C}$, $i=1,2$,

(i) $$\mathbb{P}(|\beta_n(C_1)-\beta_n(C_2)| \geqq a) \leqq 2\exp\left(-\frac{na^2}{2n\mu(C_1 \Delta C_2)+4n^{1/2}a/3}\right)$$

and for any $C \in \mathcal{C}$

(ii) $$\mathbb{P}(|\beta_n(C)| \geqq a) \leqq 2\exp\left(-\frac{a^2}{2\mu(C)(1-\mu(C))+an^{-1/2}}\right).$$

We will conclude this section with a further fundamental property concerning the so-called EMPIRICAL $\mathcal{C}$-DISCREPANCY

$$D_n(\mathcal{C},\mu) := \sup_{C\in\mathcal{C}} |\mu_n(C)-\mu(C)|.$$

In what follows we shall write $\|\mu_n-\mu\|$ instead of $D_n(\mathcal{C},\mu)$ and we assume that $\|\mu_n-\mu\|$ is a random variable, (i.e. $\mathcal{F},\mathcal{B}$-measurable). Then:

LEMMA 5. $(\|\mu_n-\mu\|)_{n\in\mathbb{N}}$ is a REVERSED SUBMARTINGALE w.r.t. the sequence of σ-fields $\mathcal{G}_n := \sigma(\{\mu_n(B), \mu_{n+1}(B), \ldots : B\in\mathcal{B}\})$ which means that for each m, n with $m \leqq n$

$$\mathbb{E}(\|\mu_m-\mu\| \,|\, \mathcal{G}_n) \geqq \|\mu_n-\mu\| \quad \mathbb{P}\text{-a.s.}$$

Proof. As shown in Gaenssler-Stute (1977), 6.5.5(c), the following holds: For each $C\in\mathcal{C}$ the process $(\mu_n(C)-\mu(C))_{n\in\mathbb{N}}$ is a REVERSED MARTINGALE w.r.t. $\mathcal{G}_n$, i.e., for each m, n with $m\leqq n$ one has

$$\mathbb{E}((\mu_m(C)-\mu(C)) \,|\, \mathcal{G}_n) = \mu_n(C)-\mu(C);$$

therefore

$$\mathbb{E}(\sup_{C\in\mathcal{C}} |\mu_m(C)-\mu(C)| \,|\, \mathcal{G}_n)$$

$$\geq \sup_{C\in\mathcal{C}} |\mathbb{E}((\mu_m(C)-\mu(C))|\mathcal{G}_n)| = \sup_{C\in\mathcal{C}} |\mu_n(C)-\mu(C)|. \quad \square$$

Now, as in the case of submartingales, there holds an analogous CONVERGENCE THEOREM FOR REVERSED SUBMARTINGALES (cf. Gaenssler-Stute (1977), 6.5.10) stating that for any reversed submartingale $(T_n)_{n\in\mathbb{N}}$ (on some p-space $(\Omega,\mathcal{F},\mathbb{P})$) w.r.t. a monotone decreasing sequence $(\mathcal{G}_n)_{n\in\mathbb{N}}$ of sub-σ-fields of $\mathcal{F}$ satisfying the condition that $\inf_n \mathbb{E}(T_n)>-\infty$ there exists an integrable random variable T_∞ such that $T_n \to T_\infty$ $\mathbb{P}$-a.s. and in the mean.

From this and Lemma 5 one obtains a rather simple proof of the following result (cf. D. Pollard (1981)) which, in a similar form, was one of the main results in Steele's paper (cf. M. Steele (1978)) proved there with different methods based on the ergodic theory of subadditive stochastic processes.

<u>LEMMA 6.</u> Let $(\nu_n)_{n\in\mathbb{N}}$ be an arbitrary sequence of non-negative integer valued random variables on $(\Omega,\mathcal{F},\mathbb{P})$ such that $\nu_n \overset{\mathbb{P}}{\to} \infty$ (where $\overset{\mathbb{P}}{\to}$ denotes convergence in probability; also here and in the following all statements about convergence are understood to hold as n tends to infinity). Then

$$\|\mu_n-\mu\| \to 0 \ \mathbb{P}\text{-a.s. iff } \|\mu_{\nu_n}-\mu\| \overset{\mathbb{P}}{\to} 0;$$

in particular, $\|\mu_n-\mu\| \to 0$ $\mathbb{P}$-a.s. iff $\|\mu_n-\mu\| \overset{\mathbb{P}}{\to} 0$.

(Note that according to our measurability assumption on $\|\mu_n-\mu\|$ also the RANDOMIZED DISCREPANCY $\|\mu_{\nu_n}-\mu\|$ is a random variable; in fact,

$$\{\omega: \|\mu_{\nu_n(\omega)}(\cdot,\omega)-\mu\| \leq a\} = \bigcup_{j\in\mathbb{Z}_+} \{\nu_n=j\}\cap\{\|\mu_j-\mu\|\leq a\} \quad \text{for each } a\geq 0.)$$

<u>Proof.</u> 1.) Only if-part: $\nu_n \overset{\mathbb{P}}{\to} \infty$ implies that for any subsequence $(\nu_{n'})$ of (ν_n) there exists a further subsequence $(\nu_{n''})$ such that $\nu_{n''} \to \infty$ $\mathbb{P}$-a.s., whence $\|\mu_{\nu_{n''}}-\mu\| \to 0$ $\mathbb{P}$-a.s. as n'' tends to infinity, and therefore $\|\mu_{\nu_n}-\mu\| \overset{\mathbb{P}}{\to} 0$.

2.) If-part: According to Lemma 5 the process $(\|\mu_n-\mu\|,\mathcal{G}_n)_{n\in\mathbb{N}}$ is a reversed submartingale. It is uniformly bounded; therefore, by the convergence theorem for reversed submartingales mentioned before, there exists an integrable random variable T_∞ such that $||\mu_n - \mu|| \to T_\infty$ $\mathbb{P}$-a.s. From this it follows as in part 1.) of our proof that $||\mu_{\nu_n} - \mu|| \overset{\mathbb{P}}{\to} T_\infty$, whence, by assumption, it follows that $T_\infty = 0$ $\mathbb{P}$-a.s. □

2. GLIVENKO-CANTELLI-convergence: The VAPNIK-CHERVONENKIS-Theory with some extensions.

Let us start with the simplest case: Assume that $(\xi_i)_{i\in\mathbb{N}}$ is a sequence of i.i.d. random variables on some p-space $(\Omega,\mathcal{F},\mathbb{P})$ with distribution function (df) F; let F_n be the EMPIRICAL df pertaining to $\xi_1,\ldots,\xi_n$, i.e.,

$$F_n(t) := \frac{1}{n}\sum_{i=1}^{n} 1_{(-\infty,t]}(\xi_i),\quad t\in\mathbb{R}.$$

Then the classical GLIVENKO-CANTELLI Theorem states:

$$(8)\qquad D_n^F := \sup_{t\in\mathbb{R}}|F_n(t)-F(t)| \to 0 \quad \mathbb{P}\text{-a.s.}$$

(Note that D_n^F is a random variable since $D_n^F = \sup_{t\in\mathbb{Q}}|F_n(t)-F(t)|$, where $\mathbb{Q}$ denotes the rationals.)

The proof of (8) usually runs as follows:

a) One shows that (8) holds true if the ξ_i's are uniformly distributed on (0,1).

b) Using the QUANTILE TRANSFORMATION

$$s \mapsto F^{-1}(s) := \inf\{t\in\mathbb{R}: F(t)\geq s\},\ s\in(0,1)$$

and a) one obtains (8) for the SPECIAL VERSIONS

$\hat{\xi}_i := F^{-1}(\eta_i)$, where the η_i's are independent and uniformly distributed on (0,1) (and defined on the same p-space as the ξ_i's).

Note that $\mathcal{L}\{\hat{\xi}_i\} = \mathcal{L}\{\xi_i\}$ for each i; even more, by independence, one has $\mathcal{L}\{(\hat{\xi}_i)_{i\in\mathbb{N}}\} = \mathcal{L}\{(\xi_i)_{i\in\mathbb{N}}\}$.

c) Reasoning on the fact that the validity of (8) only dependes on $\mathcal{L}\{(\xi_i)_{i\in\mathbb{N}}\}$ the proof is concluded.

In view of the more general situations we shall consider later on in this section we want to clarify c) a little bit more:

c^*) (8) claims that

$$\mathbb{P}(\{\omega\in\Omega: \lim_{n\to\infty} (\sup_{t\in\mathbb{R}} |\frac{1}{n}\sum_{i=1}^{n} 1_{(-\infty,t]}(\xi_i(\omega))-F(t)|) = 0\}) = 1;$$

consider $\xi(\omega) := (\xi_1(\omega), \xi_2(\omega),\ldots)\in\mathbb{R}^{\mathbb{N}}$ and put

$$g_n(\xi(\omega)) := \sup_{t\in\mathbb{R}} |\frac{1}{n}\sum_{i=1}^{n} 1_{(-\infty,t]}(\xi_i(\omega))-F(t)|.$$

Now, <u>note</u> (<u>and remember</u>) the fact that in the present situation

(9) $$g_n : \mathbb{R}^{\mathbb{N}} \to \mathbb{R} \text{ is } \mathcal{B}_{\mathbb{N}},\mathcal{B}\text{-measurable}$$

since $g_n(\underline{x}) = \sup_{t\in\mathbb{Q}} |\frac{1}{n}\sum_{i=1}^{n} 1_{(-\infty,t]}(x_i)-F(t)|$ for $\underline{x} := (x_1,x_2,\ldots)$.

Therefore $A := \{\underline{x}\in\mathbb{R}^{\mathbb{N}} : \lim_{n\to\infty} g_n(\underline{x})=0\} \in \mathcal{B}_{\mathbb{N}}$, whence, putting

$\hat{\xi}(\omega) := (\hat{\xi}_1(\omega), \hat{\xi}_2(\omega),\ldots)$ one obtains

$$\mathbb{P}(\{\omega\in\Omega : \lim_{n\to\infty} (\sup_{t\in\mathbb{R}} |\frac{1}{n}\sum_{i=1}^{n} 1_{(-\infty,t]}(\xi_i(\omega))-F(t)|)=0\})$$

$$= \mathbb{P}(\{\omega\in\Omega : \lim_{n\to\infty} g_n(\xi(\omega))=0\}) = \mathbb{P}(\{\omega\in\Omega: \xi(\omega)\in A\})$$

$$= \mathcal{L}\{\xi\}(A) \underset{b)}{=} \mathcal{L}\{\hat{\xi}\}(A) = \mathbb{P}(\{\omega\in\Omega : \hat{\xi}(\omega)\in A\})$$

$$= \mathbb{P}(\{\omega\in\Omega : \lim_{n\to\infty} (\sup_{t\in\mathbb{R}} |\frac{1}{n}\sum_{i=1}^{n} 1_{(-\infty,t]}(\hat{\xi}_i(\omega))-F(t)|)=0\}) \underset{b)}{=} 1.$$

When taking $(X,\mathcal{B}) = (\mathbb{R},\mathcal{B})$ and $\mathcal{C} := \{(-\infty,t] : t\in\mathbb{R}\}$, then, in the setting of Section 1, the GLIVENKO-CANTELLI-convergence (8) reads as

(8^*) $$D_n(\mathcal{C},\mu) \equiv \sup_{C\in\mathcal{C}} |\mu_n(C) - \mu(C)| \to 0 \quad \mathbb{P}\text{-a.s.}$$

Concerning more general situations it turns out however that (8^*) may hold for the empirical measures obtained from one sequence $\xi_1,\xi_2,\ldots$ of independent random elements in $(X,\mathcal{B})$ each having distribution μ but <u>not</u> for the empirical measures obtained from another such sequence, say $\eta_1,\eta_2,\ldots$.

<u>EXAMPLE</u> (cf. D. Pollard (1981), Example (5.1)).

Let $(X,\mathcal{B},\mu)$ be a nonatomic p-space (i.e., $\{x\}\in\mathcal{B}$ and $\mu(\{x\})=0$ for all $x\in X$). Suppose that there exists a subset A of X with inner measure $\mu_*(A)=0$ and outer measure $\mu^*(A)=1$ (cf. P.R. Halmos (1969), Section 16, for an example). Let $\mathcal{B}_A := A\cap\mathcal{B}$ be the trace σ-algebra of $\mathcal{B}$ on A and μ_A be the p-measure defined on $\mathcal{B}_A$ by $\mu_A(A\cap B) := \mu(B)$, $B\in\mathcal{B}$; note that μ_A is well defined since $\mu^*(A)=1$. By the definition of $\mathcal{B}_A$ the embedding ξ_A of A into X is $\mathcal{B}_A,\mathcal{B}$-measurable ($\xi_A^{-1}(B) = \{x\in A\colon \xi_A(x)=x\in B\} = A\cap B\in\mathcal{B}_A$ for any $B\in\mathcal{B}$) and one has

$$\mu_A(\xi_A^{-1}(B)) = \mu(B) \quad \text{for all } B\in\mathcal{B}.$$

Consider the p-space

$$(\Omega_1,\mathcal{F}_1,\mathbb{P}_1) := (A^{\mathbb{N}}, \bigotimes_{\mathbb{N}} \mathcal{B}_A, \times_{\mathbb{N}} \mu_A)$$

and on it the random elements $\xi_i\colon \Omega_1 \to X$, defined by

$$\xi_i(\omega_1) := \xi_A(\pi_i(\omega_1)), \quad i\in\mathbb{N},\ \omega_1\in\Omega_1,$$

where $\pi_i\colon A^{\mathbb{N}} \to A$ denotes the i-th coordinate projection.

Then, by construction, the ξ_i's are independent having distribution μ ($\mathcal{L}\{\xi_i\}(B) = \mathbb{P}_1(\xi_i^{-1}(B)) = \mathbb{P}_1(\pi_i^{-1}(\xi_A^{-1}(B))) = \mu_A(\xi_A^{-1}(B)) = \mu(B)$ for each $B\in\mathcal{B}$).

Now, let $\mathcal{C}$ be the class of all finite subsets of A;

then $\mathcal{C}\subset\mathcal{B}$ and $\mu(C)=0$ for all $C\in\mathcal{C}$ since $(X,\mathcal{B},\mu)$ we assumed to be nonatomic. But since all the ξ_i's take their values in A it follows that for the empirical measures μ_n pertaining to $\xi_1,\ldots,\xi_n$ one has

$$\sup_{C\in\mathcal{C}} |\mu_n(C)-\mu(C)| \equiv 1.$$

Taking instead the p-space

$$(\Omega_2,\mathcal{F}_2,\mathbb{P}_2) := ((\complement A)^{\mathbb{N}}, \bigotimes_{\mathbb{N}} \mathcal{B}_{\complement A}, \times_{\mathbb{N}} \mu_{\complement A})$$

and on it the random elements $\eta_i\colon \Omega_2 \to X$, defined by

$$\eta_i(\omega_2) := \xi_{\complement A}(\pi_i(\omega_2)), \quad i\in\mathbb{N},\ \omega_2\in\Omega_2,$$

where here $\pi_i\colon(\complement A)^{\mathbb{N}} \to \complement A$ is again the i-th coordinate projection and where $\xi_{\complement A}$

denotes the embedding of $\complement A$ into X, it follows as before (noticing that $\mu^*(\complement A)=1$) that the η_i's are i.i.d. with distribution μ (whence $\mathcal{L}\{(\eta_i)_{i\in\mathbb{N}}\} = \mathcal{L}\{(\xi_i)_{i\in\mathbb{N}}\}$).

But, for the same class $\mathcal{C}$ as before one has now for the empirical measure μ_n pertaining to $\eta_1,\ldots,\eta_n$, $\mu_n(C)=0$ for all $C\in\mathcal{C}$, since the η_i's take their values in $\complement A$, whence

$$\sup_{C\in\mathcal{C}}|\mu_n(C)-\mu(C)| \equiv 0.$$

(Note that in both cases $D_n(\mathcal{C},\mu) \equiv \sup_{C\in\mathcal{C}}|\mu_n(C)-\mu(C)|$ is measurable.)

Finally, taking as underlying p-space the CANONICAL MODEL

$$(\Omega,\mathcal{A},\mathbb{P}) = (X^{\mathbb{N}},\mathcal{B}_{\mathbb{N}},\times_{\mathbb{N}}\mu)$$

and on it the coordinate projections ξ_i, $i\in\mathbb{N}$, being again i.i.d. with distribution μ, the above example shows that for the very same class $\mathcal{C}$ one gets e.g.,

$$\sup_{C\in\mathcal{C}}|\mu_1(C,\underline{x})-\mu(C)| = \sup_{C\in\mathcal{C}}\mu_1(C,\underline{x}) = 1_A(x_1)$$

for $\underline{x} = (x_1,x_2,\ldots) \in X^{\mathbb{N}}$, whence, since $A\notin\mathcal{B}$

$$\{\underline{x}\in X^{\mathbb{N}} : \sup_{C\in\mathcal{C}}|\mu_1(C,\underline{x})-\mu(C)| = 1\} = A\times X\times X\times\ldots\notin\mathcal{B}_{\mathbb{N}},$$

i.e., here - in contrast to (9) -

(10) $$\underline{x} \mapsto g_n(\underline{x}) := \sup_{C\in\mathcal{C}}|\mu_n(C,\underline{x})-\mu(C)|$$

is not $\mathcal{B}_{\mathbb{N}},\mathbb{B}$-measurable.

This indicates already the need for appropriate measurability assumptions to be discussed later.

Let us point out at this stage the usefulness of GLIVENKO-CANTELLI-convergence in statistics by giving only one example concerning CHERNOFF-type estimates of the mode (c.f. H. Chernoff (1964), and E.J. Wegman (1971)). For other examples, see P. Gaenssler and J.A. Wellner (1981). For the moment we anticipate the following GLIVENKO-CANTELLI-Theorem which will be proved later in this section:

(11) Let $\xi_1,\xi_2,\ldots$ be i.i.d. random vectors on some p-space $(\Omega,\mathcal{F},\mathbb{P})$ with values in $X=\mathbb{R}^k$, $k\geq 1$, having distribution μ on $\mathcal{B}=\mathcal{B}_k$. Let $\mathcal{C}\equiv\mathbb{B}_k$ be the class of all closed Euclidean balls in $\mathbb{R}^k$; then

$$\lim_{n\to\infty}\left(\sup_{C\in\mathbb{B}_k}|\mu_n(C)-\mu(C)|\right)=0 \quad \mathbb{P}\text{-a.s.}$$

Now, consider $(X,\mathcal{B})=(\mathbb{R}^k,\mathcal{B}_k)$, $k\geq 1$, and suppose that μ is "unimodal" in the following sense:

(*) there exists a $\theta\in\mathbb{R}^k$ such that for some $\delta_0>0$, $\mu(B^c(\theta,\delta_0))>\mu(B^c(x,\delta_0))$ for all $x\in\mathbb{R}^k$, $x\neq\theta$, where $B^c(x,\delta_0)$ denotes the closed Euclidean ball with center x and radius δ_0.

Facing the problem of finding a consistent sequence of estimators for the (unknown) θ, one may proceed as follows:

Suppose that $0<r_n$ with $\lim_{n\to\infty} r_n=\delta_0$ are given; then, given i.i.d. observations $x_i=\xi_i(\omega)$, $i=1,\ldots,n$, choose as estimate $\theta_n(\omega)\equiv\theta(\xi_1(\omega),\ldots,\xi_n(\omega))$ a center of a closed Euclidean ball with radius r_n which covers most of the observations, i.e. for which

(**) $\quad \mu_n(B^c(\theta_n(\omega),r_n),\omega)\geq\mu_n(B^c(x,r_n),\omega)$ for all $x\in\mathbb{R}^k$.

Then the claim is that $\lim_{n\to\infty}\theta_n=\theta$ $\mathbb{P}$-a.s.

<u>Proof.</u> Choose $M>0$ such that $\mu(\complement B^c(0,M))<\mu(B^c(\theta,\delta_0))$. According to (11) we have

$$\mathbb{P}(\Omega_o)=1 \text{ for } \Omega_o:=\{\omega\in\Omega: \lim_{n\to\infty}(\sup_{C\in\mathbb{B}_k}|\mu_n(C)-\mu(C)|)=0\}.$$

Let $\omega\in\Omega_o$ and suppose that $\theta_n(\omega)\not\to\theta$ as $n\to\infty$; then

<u>either</u> (1) $\limsup_{n\to\infty}|\theta_n(\omega)|=\infty$

<u>or</u> (2) there exists an $x\neq\theta$ such that $\lim_{j\to\infty}\theta_{n_j}(\omega)=x$ for some subsequence (n_j) of $\mathbb{N}$.

We will show that both, (1) and (2), will lead to a contradiction.

<u>ad (1):</u> $\limsup_{n\to\infty}|\theta_n(\omega)|=\infty$ implies that there exists some subsequence (n_j) of $\mathbb{N}$ such that $B^c(\theta_{n_j}(\omega),r_{n_j})\subset\complement B^c(0,M)$ for all j, whence

$$\limsup_{j\to\infty} \mu_{n_j}(B^c(\theta_{n_j}(\omega), r_{n_j}), \omega) \leq \liminf_{j\to\infty} \mu_{n_j}(\complement B^c(0,M), \omega)$$

$$= 1 - \limsup_{j\to\infty} \mu_{n_j}(\underbrace{B^c(0,M)}_{\in \mathbb{B}_k}, \omega) = 1 - \mu(B^c(0,M)) = \mu(\complement B^c(0,M))$$

$$< \mu(\underbrace{B^c(\theta,\delta_0)}_{\in \mathbb{B}_k}) = \liminf_{j\to\infty} \mu_{n_j}(B^c(\theta,\delta_0),\omega) \leq \limsup_{j\to\infty} \mu_{n_j}(B^c(\theta, r_{n_j}), \omega)$$

which is in contradiction with the choice of θ_n according to (**).

ad (2): $\lim_{j\to\infty} \theta_{n_j}(\omega) = x \neq \theta$ implies that $\liminf_{j\to\infty} \mu_{n_j}(B^c(\theta_{n_j}(\omega), r_{n_j}), \omega)$

$$\leq \underbrace{\lim_{j\to\infty} |\mu_{n_j}(B^c(\theta_{n_j}(\omega), r_{n_j}), \omega) - \mu(B^c(\theta_{n_j}(\omega), r_{n_j}))|}_{= 0 \text{ according to (11)}}$$

$$+ \limsup_{j\to\infty} \mu(B^c(\theta_{n_j}(\omega), r_{n_j})) \leq \mu(B^c(x,\delta_0)) \underset{(*)}{<} \mu(B^c(\theta,\delta_0))$$

$$= \liminf_{j\to\infty} \mu_{n_j}(B^c(\theta,\delta_0),\omega) \leq \liminf_{j\to\infty} \mu_{n_j}(B^c(\theta, r_{n_j}), \omega),$$

which again is in contradiction with the choice of θ_n according to (**). □

Before starting with the VAPNIK-CHERVONENKIS Theory we want to add here some remarks concerning the $\mathbb{P}$-a.s. limiting behaviour of so-called weighted discrepancies which are of importance in statistics as well (cf. T.W. Anderson and D.A. Darling (1952), J. Durbin (1953)).

For this, let $(X,\mathcal{B}) = (\mathbb{R},\mathcal{B})$ and $(\xi_i)_{i\in\mathbb{N}}$ be a sequence of i.i.d. random variables on some p-space $(\Omega,\mathcal{F},\mathbb{P})$ with df F; let F_n be the empirical df pertaining to $\xi_1,\ldots,\xi_n$ and define the WEIGHTED DISCREPANCY by

$$D_n^F(q) := \sup_{t\in\mathbb{R}} \frac{|F_n(t)-F(t)|}{q(F(t))}$$

where $q: [0,1] \to \mathbb{R}_+$ is some given WEIGHT FUNCTION.

(Note that $D_n^F(q) \equiv D_n^F$ for $q \equiv 1$.)

Considering instead of the ξ_i's the special versions $\hat{\xi}_i = F^{-1}(\eta_i)$, the η_i's being independent and uniformly distributed on $(0,1)$, it follows in the same way as pointed out in part c*) of the outline of the proof of (8) that w.r.t. $\mathbb{P}$-a.s. convergence of $D_n^F(q)$ for <u>continuous</u> q's one may consider w.l.o.g. instead of $D_n^F(q)$ its versions

$$\hat{D}_n^F(q) := \sup_{t\in\mathbb{R}} \frac{|\hat{F}_n(t)-F(t)|}{q(F(t))},$$

where $\hat{F}_n$ is the empirical df pertaining to $\hat{\xi}_1,\ldots,\hat{\xi}_n$.

But, due to the identity $\{\hat{\xi}_i \leq t\} = \{\eta_i \leq F(t)\}$ for all $t\in\mathbb{R}$ one has $\hat{F}_n(t) = U_n(F(t))$ for all $t\in\mathbb{R}$, where U_n is the empirical df pertaining to $\eta_1,\ldots,\eta_n$. Therefore

$$\hat{D}_n^F(q) = \sup_{t\in\mathbb{R}} \frac{|U_n(F(t))-F(t)|}{q(F(t))} \leq \sup_{s\in[0,1]} \frac{|U_n(s)-s|}{q(s)} =: D_n(q),$$

where we remark that for continuous F we have even $\hat{D}_n^F(q) = D_n(q)$, whence for continuous q's and F's one has, comparing again with part c*) of the outline of the proof of (8), that

$$D_n^F(q) \overset{L}{=} \hat{D}_n^F(q) = D_n(q)$$

showing that in this case $D_n^F(q)$ is a DISTRIBUTION-FREE STATISTIC. By the way, since for continuous q's and <u>arbitrary</u> F's $D_n^F(q) \overset{L}{=} \hat{D}_n^F(q) \leq D_n(q)$, we obtain in this case that

$$\mathbb{P}(D_n^F(q)\geq d) \leq \mathbb{P}(D_n(q)\geq d) \quad \text{for each } d\geq 0.$$

Also, the above remarks show that for continuous q's we may restrict ourselves w.l.o.g. to the case of finding conditions on q such that

$$(*) \quad \lim_{n\to\infty} D_n(q) = 0 \quad \mathbb{P}\text{-a.s.}$$

in order to get the same GLIVENKO-CANTELLI-convergence for $D_n^F(q)$.

The following theorem gives in a certain sense necessary and sufficient conditions on q for (*) to hold (cf. J.A. Wellner (1977) and (1978)).

<u>THEOREM 1.</u> Let $(\eta_i)_{i\in\mathbb{N}}$ be a sequence of independent random variables on some p-space $(\Omega,\mathcal{F},\mathbb{P})$ being uniformly distributed on $[0,1]$. Let $D_n(q)$ be defined as above with a weight function q belonging to the set

$\mathcal{Q}_1 := \{q:[0,1] \to \mathbb{R}$, q continuous, $q(0) = q(1) = 0$, $q(t) > 0$ for all $t\in(0,1)$, q monotone increasing on $[0,\delta_o]$ and monotone decreasing on $[1-\delta_1,1]$ for appropriate $\delta_i=\delta_i(q)$, $i=0,1\}$.

Then, putting $\Psi(t) := \frac{1}{q(t)}$, one has:

(i) For any $q\in\mathcal{Q}_1$ with $\int_0^1 \Psi(t)dt < \infty$ it follows that

$$\lim_{n\to\infty} D_n(q) = 0 \quad \mathbb{P}\text{-a.s.}$$

(ii) For any $q\in\mathcal{Q}_1$ with $\int_0^1 \Psi(t)dt = \infty$ it follows that

$$\limsup_{n\to\infty} D_n(q) = \infty \quad \mathbb{P}\text{-a.s.}$$

<u>Proof.(i):</u> For any $\varepsilon>0$ there exist $\theta_i>0$ such that $\theta_i<\delta_i$, $i=0,1$, with

$$\int_0^{\theta_o} \Psi(t)dt < \varepsilon/4 \quad \text{and} \quad \int_{1-\theta_1}^1 \Psi(t)dt < \varepsilon/4.$$

We have $D_n(q) = \sup_{t\in(0,1)} \Psi(t)|U_n(t)-t| \leq \sup_{0<t\leq\theta_o} \Psi(t)U_n(t)$

$$+ \sup_{0<t\leq\theta_o} \Psi(t)t + \sup_{\theta_o\leq t\leq 1-\theta_1} \Psi(t)|U_n(t)-t| + \sup_{1-\theta_1\leq t<1} \Psi(t)|U_n(t)-t|$$

$$=: I_1(n) + I_2 + I_3(n) + I_4(n), \text{ say.}$$

Now, to start with the first summand $I_1(n)$, one has

$$I_1(n) \leq \frac{1}{n} \sum_{i=1}^n \sup_{0<t\leq\theta_o} \Psi(t)\, 1_{[0,t]}(\eta_i) \leq \frac{1}{n} \sum_{i=1}^n \Psi(\eta_i)\, 1_{[0,\theta_o]}(\eta_i)$$

$\to \int_0^{\theta_o} \Psi(t)dt$ $\mathbb{P}$-a.s. by the SLLN, whence $\limsup_{n\to\infty} I_1(n) < \varepsilon/4$ $\mathbb{P}$-a.s.

Concerning I_2, note that for all $0<t\leq\theta_o$

$$\Psi(t)t \leq \int_0^t \Psi(s)ds \leq \int_0^{\theta_o} \Psi(s)ds, \text{ whence } I_2 = \sup_{0<t\leq\theta_o} \Psi(t)t < \varepsilon/4.$$

As to $I_3(n)$ we have $I_3(n) = \sup_{\theta_o\leq t\leq 1-\theta_o} \frac{1}{q(t)} |U_n(t)-t|$

$$\leq \underbrace{[\min_{\theta_o\leq t\leq 1-\theta_1} q(t)]^{-1}}_{=:\ c \text{ with } 0<c<\infty} \sup_{\theta_o\leq t\leq 1-\theta_1} |U_n(t)-t| \to 0 \quad \mathbb{P}\text{-a.s. according to (8).}$$

Therefore $\lim_{n\to\infty} I_3(n) = 0$ $\mathbb{P}$-a.s.

Finally, $I_4(n) = \sup_{1-\theta_1 \leq t < 1} \Psi(t) \left| 1 - \frac{1}{n} \sum_{i=1}^{n} 1_{(t,1]}(\eta_i) - t \right|$

$$\leq \frac{1}{n} \sum_{i=1}^{n} \sup_{1-\theta_1 \leq t<1} \Psi(t) 1_{(t,1]}(\eta_i) + \sup_{1-\theta_1 \leq t<1} \Psi(t)(1-t)$$

$\leq \frac{1}{n} \sum_{i=1}^{n} \Psi(\eta_i) 1_{(1-\theta_1,1]}(\eta_i) + \int_{1-\theta_1}^{1} \Psi(t)dt$ where again by the SLLN

$$\lim_{n\to\infty} \frac{1}{n} \sum_{i=1}^{n} \Psi(\eta_i) 1_{(1-\theta_1,1]}(\eta_i) = \int_{1-\theta_1}^{1} \Psi(t)dt \quad \mathbb{P}\text{-a.s.; thus}$$

$$\limsup_{n\to\infty} I_4(n) < \varepsilon/2 \quad \mathbb{P}\text{-a.s.}$$

So we have shown that $\limsup_{n\to\infty} D_n(q) < \varepsilon$ $\mathbb{P}$-a.s. for any $\varepsilon>0$; this proves the assertion in (i).

<u>(ii):</u> Let $N \in \mathbb{N}$ be arbitrary but fixed; we will show

$$(+) \quad \limsup_{n\to\infty} D_n(q) \geq N \quad \mathbb{P}\text{-a.s.}$$

which gives the assertion in (ii).

Now, by assumption,

$$\text{either (a)} \quad \int_0^{\delta_0} \Psi(t)dt = \infty$$

$$\text{or} \quad \text{(b)} \quad \int_{1-\delta_1}^{1} \Psi(t)dt = \infty.$$

Let us consider case (a) (case (b) can be dealt with in an analogous way), i.e., assume

$$\int_0^{\delta_0} \Psi(t)dt = \infty.$$

Then, for n sufficiently large, say $n \geq n_0$,

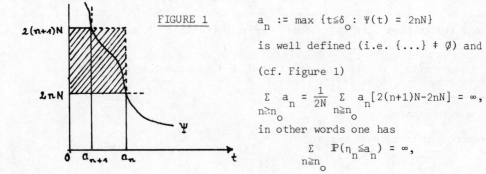

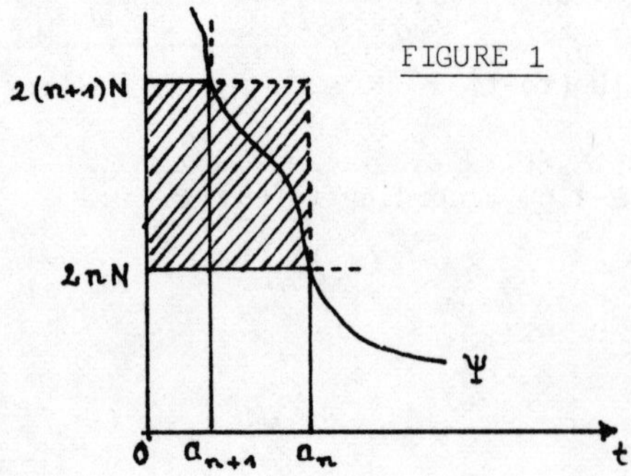

FIGURE 1

$a_n := \max\{t \leq \delta_0 : \Psi(t) = 2nN\}$ is well defined (i.e. $\{\ldots\} \neq \emptyset$) and (cf. Figure 1)

$$\sum_{n \geq n_0} a_n = \frac{1}{2N} \sum_{n\geq n_0} a_n[2(n+1)N - 2nN] = \infty,$$

in other words one has

$$\sum_{n\geq n_0} \mathbb{P}(\eta_n \leq a_n) = \infty,$$

whence by the BOREL-CANTELLI LEMMA

$$\mathbb{P}(\limsup_{n\to\infty} \{\eta_n \leq a_n\}) = 1.$$

From this we obtain, looking at the first order statistic $\eta_{n:1}$, that $\mathbb{P}$-a.s. one has $\eta_{n:1} \leq a_n$ for infinitely many n and this implies that $\mathbb{P}$-a.s.

$$\sup_{t\in(0,1)} \Psi(t)\ |U_n(t)-t| \geq \frac{1}{2}\Psi(\eta_{n:1})\ [U_n(\eta_{n:1})-U_n(\eta_{n:1}-0)]$$

$$\geq \frac{1}{2}\Psi(a_n)\ \frac{1}{n} = N \text{ for infinitely many n, which implies (+).} \quad \square$$

<u>Remark.</u> The validity of the first inequality at the end of the proof is based on the following fact which is easy to prove:

Given two df's F_1, F_2 on $\mathbb{R}$ and some strictly positive function h on some interval $(a,b)\subset\mathbb{R}$, then for any <u>continuity point</u> $t_o\in(a,b)$ <u>of F_1 and of h</u> one has

$$\sup_{a<t<b} \frac{|F_2(t)-F_1(t)|}{h(t)} \geq \frac{1}{2}\ \frac{F_2(t_o)-F_2(t_o-0)}{h(t_o)}.$$

<u>THE VAPNIK-CHERVONENKIS THEORY:</u>

There are various methods for proving GLIVENKO-CANTELLI-Theorems (i.e., a.s. convergence of empirical $\mathcal{C}$-discrepancies $D_n(\mathcal{C},\mu)$) in cases where a common geometrical structure for the sets in $\mathcal{C}$ is essentially used; see P. Gaenssler and W. Stute (1979), Section 1.1, for a survey on the results and methods of proof.

For <u>arbitrary</u> sample spaces where geometrical arguments are no longer available, perhaps the most striking method based on combinatorial arguments was developed by V.N. Vapnik and A.Ya. Chervonenkis (1971). We are going to present here their main results together with some extensions and applications.

In what follows, if not stated otherwise, let X be an arbitrary nonempty set and denote by $\mathcal{P}(X)$ the power set of X (i.e.,the class of all subsets of X). For any set A, $|A|$ denotes its cardinality.

<u>DEFINITION 1.</u> Let $\mathcal{C}$ be an arbitrary subclass of $\mathcal{P}(X)$ and, for any $F\subset X$ with $|F| < \infty$, let

$$\Delta^{\mathcal{C}}(F) := |\{F\cap C:\ C\in\mathcal{C}\}|$$

be the number of different sets of the form $F\cap C$ for $C\in\mathcal{C}$.

Furthermore, for $r=0,1,2,\ldots$ let

$$m^{\mathcal{C}}(r) := \max\{\Delta^{\mathcal{C}}(F): |F| = r\},$$

and

$$V(\mathcal{C}) := \begin{cases} \inf\{r: m^{\mathcal{C}}(r)<2^r\} \\ \infty, \text{ if } m^{\mathcal{C}}(r)=2^r \text{ for all } r. \end{cases}$$

If $m^{\mathcal{C}}(r)<2^r$ for some r, i.e., if $V(\mathcal{C})<\infty$, $\mathcal{C}$ will be called a <u>VAPNIK-CHERVONENKIS CLASS (VCC)</u>.

<u>REMARKS.</u>

a) $m^{\mathcal{C}}(\cdot)$ is called the <u>GROWTH FUNCTION pertaining to $\mathcal{C}$</u>. Note that $m^{\mathcal{C}}(r)\leq 2^r$ for all r and $m^{\mathcal{C}}(r)=2^r$ iff there exists an $F\subset X$ with $|F|=r$ such that for all $F'\subset F$ there exists a $C\in\mathcal{C}$ with $F\cap C=F'$; in other words: $m^{\mathcal{C}}(r)=2^r$ iff $\mathcal{C}$ cuts all subsets of some $F\subset X$ with $|F|=r$, saying that <u>F is shattered by $\mathcal{C}$</u>.
On the other hand, $m^{\mathcal{C}}(r)<2^r$ implies $m^{\mathcal{C}}(n)<2^n$ for all $n\geq r$.

b) <u>EXAMPLES.</u>

1) If $X=\mathbb{R}$ and $\mathcal{C} = \{(-\infty,t]: t\in\mathbb{R}\}$, then
$m^{\mathcal{C}}(r) = r+1$, whence $\mathcal{C}$ is a VCC with $V(\mathcal{C}) = 2$.

2) (cf. R.S. Wenocur and R.M. Dudley (1981)): More generally, let X be an arbitrary set with $|X|\geq 2$ and suppose that $\mathcal{C}\subset\mathcal{P}(X)$ fulfills the following condition (*):

(*) $\forall F\subset X$ with $|F|=2$ there exist $C_i\in\mathcal{C}$, $i=1,2$, such that $F\cap C_1=\emptyset$ and $F\cap C_2=F$.

(Note that (*) holds if $\{\emptyset,X\}\subset\mathcal{C}$.)

Then $\mathcal{C}$ is a VCC with $V(\mathcal{C})=2$ iff $\mathcal{C}$ is linearly ordered by inclusion.

<u>PROOF.</u> Assume to the contrary that $\mathcal{C}$ is not linearly ordered by inclusion. Then there exist $C',C''\in\mathcal{C}$ such that $C'\not\subset C''$ and $C''\not\subset C'$; choosing $x_1\in C'\setminus C''$ and $x_2\in C''\setminus C'$, it follows, together with (*), that $F := \{x_1,x_2\}$ is shattered by $\mathcal{C}$ which implies $V(\mathcal{C})>2$.

To prove the other direction, assume (cf. (*)) that $\mathcal{C}$ contains at least two elements and is linearly ordered by inclusion. Then, since $|\mathcal{C}|\geq 2$

implies $V(\mathcal{C}) \geq 2$ (note that $|\mathcal{C}|=1$ iff $V(\mathcal{C})=1$), it remains to show that $V(\mathcal{C}) \leq 2$:

For this, consider an $F \subset X$ with $|F|=2$; then, since $\mathcal{C}$ is linearly ordered by inclusion, there is at most one $F' \subset F$ with $|F'|=1$ and $F'=F\cap C$ for some $C\in\mathcal{C}$, showing that F is not shattered by $\mathcal{C}$. □

3) If $X=[0,1]$ and $\mathcal{C} := \{C\subset X: |C|<\infty\}$, then $m^{\mathcal{C}}(r)=2^r$ for all r, whence $V(\mathcal{C})=\infty$.

c) Let $\phi(v,r) := \sum_{j=0}^{v} \binom{r}{j}$, where $\binom{r}{j} := 0$ for $j>r$,

i.e.,
$$\phi(v,r) = \begin{cases} \sum_{j=0}^{v} \binom{r}{j}, & \text{if } v<r \\ 2^r, & \text{if } v\geq r. \end{cases}$$

(Note that $\phi(v,r)$ is the number of all subsets of an r-element set with at most v elements.)

Then it is easy to show that the following relations hold true:

(12)
$$\phi(v,r) = \phi(v,r-1) + \phi(v-1,r-1),$$

where $\phi(0,r) = 1$ and $\phi(v,0) = 1$;

(13)
$$\phi(v,r) \leq r^v+1 \text{ for all } v,r \geq 0.$$

The following remarks d) and e) are taken from R.M. Dudley (1978).

d) Let $\mathcal{H}_k$ be the collection of all open halfspaces in $\mathbb{R}^k$, $k\geq 1$, i.e., all sets of the form

$$\{x\in\mathbb{R}^k : (x,u)>c\} \quad \text{for} \quad 0 \neq u\in\mathbb{R}^k \text{ and some } c\in\mathbb{R},$$

and let $N_k(r)$ be the maximum number of open regions into which $\mathbb{R}^k$ is decomposed by r hyperplanes H_j

$$H_j = \{x\in\mathbb{R}^k : (x,u_j) = c_j\},\ j=1,\dots,r;$$

then the maximum number $N_k(r)$ is attained for $H_1,\dots,H_r$ in "general position" i.e. if any k or fewer of the u_j are linearly independent.

L. Schläfli (1901, posth.) showed that

(14) $$N_k(r) = \phi(k,r).$$

J. Steiner (1826) had proved this for $k \leq 3$.

e) If F is an r-element subset of $\mathbb{R}^k$, then

(15) $$\Delta^{\mathcal{H}_k}(F) \leq 2\phi(k,r-1)$$

and equality is attained if the points of F are in "general position", i.e. no k+1 of them are in any hyperplane (cf. T.M. Cover (1965); E.F. Harding (1967); D. Watson (1969)).

Therefore the growth function $m^{\mathcal{H}_k}(\cdot)$ pertaining to $\mathcal{H}_k$ satisfies

(16) $$m^{\mathcal{H}_k}(r) = 2\phi(k,r-1).$$

Without using (14)-(16), but directly from the definition of $\phi(v,r)$ and the recurrence relation (12), Vapnik and Chervonenkis ((1971), Lemma 1) proved the following lemma:

Lemma 7. If X is any set and if $\mathcal{C} \subset \mathcal{P}(X)$ is a Vapnik-Chervonenkis class (i.e., $V(\mathcal{C}) \leq v < \infty$ for some v), then

$$m^{\mathcal{C}}(r) < \phi(v,r) \text{ for all } r \geq v.$$

In view of (16) this implies that for arbitrary X one gets an upper estimate for the growth function $m^{\mathcal{C}}(\cdot)$ pertaining to a VCC $\mathcal{C} \subset \mathcal{P}(X)$ by the growth function $m^{\mathcal{H}_v}(\cdot)$ pertaining to the class $\mathcal{H}_v$ of all open halfspaces in $X = \mathbb{R}^v$, namely

(17) $$m^{\mathcal{C}}(r) < \frac{1}{2} m^{\mathcal{H}_v}(r+1) \quad \text{for all } r \geq v \geq V(\mathcal{C}).$$

Instead of Lemma 7 we shall show here a slightly sharper result whose nice proof (based on a proof of a more general result in J.M. Steele (1975)) I learned from David Pollard on occasion of one of his Seminar talks in Seattle (1982); cf. also N. Sauer (1972).

Lemma 8 (Vapnik-Chervonenkis-Lemma). Let X be any set and $\mathcal{C} \subset \mathcal{P}(X)$ be a Vapnik-Chervonenkis class (i.e., $V(\mathcal{C}) =: s < \infty$), then

$$m^{\mathcal{C}}(r) \leq \phi(s-1,r) \text{ for all } r \geq s.$$

Proof. Let $r \geq s$ be arbitrary but fixed. We have to show that for any $F \subset X$ with $|F|=r$

(a) $$\Delta^{\mathcal{C}}(F) := |\{F \cap C: C \in \mathcal{C}\}| \leq \phi(s-1,r).$$

Let $\{F_1,\ldots,F_p\}$ be the collection of all subsets of F of at least size s

(so $p = \binom{r}{s} + \binom{r}{s+1} + \ldots + \binom{r}{r}$).

Note that (a) is trivially fulfilled if

(b) $$F \cap C \neq F_i \text{ for all } i=1,\ldots,p \text{ and all } C \in \mathcal{C}.$$

Now, by assumption, we have:

(c) For each F_i there exists an $F_i^1 \subset F_i$ such that

$$F_i^1 \neq F_i \cap C \text{ for all } C \in \mathcal{C},$$

implying

(d) $$\{F \cap C: C \in \mathcal{C}\} \subset \mathcal{B}_1 := \{B \subset F: B \cap F_i \neq F_i^1 \text{ for all } i=1,\ldots,p\}.$$

In one special case the result follows readily, namely if $F_i^1 = F_i$ for all $i=1,\ldots,p$ since then $B \neq F_i$ for all $i=1,\ldots,p$ and each $B \in \mathcal{B}_1$ (which means that $\mathcal{B}_1$ cannot contain any subset of F of at least size s), so that (a) follows from (d).

We are going to show that by a successive modification of the F_i^1's the general case will reduce in a finite number of steps to this special case:

If $F_i^1 \neq F_i$ for some i, choose any $x^1 \in F$ and put

$$F_i^2 := (F_i^1 \cup \{x^1\}) \cap F_i, \quad i=1,\ldots,p,$$

and define the corresponding class

$$\mathcal{B}_2 := \{B \subset F: B \cap F_i \neq F_i^2 \text{ for all } i=1,\ldots,p\}.$$

We will show below that

(e) $$|\mathcal{B}_1| \leq |\mathcal{B}_2|.$$

If now $F_i^2 = F_i$ for all $i=1,\dots,p$, then $\mathcal{B}_2$ cannot contain any subset of F of at least size s in which case (a) follows from (d) and (e).

If $F_i^2 \neq F_i$ for some i we go once more through the same argument, i.e., we choose any $x^2 \in F$, $x^2 \neq x^1$ and put

$$F_i^3 := (F_i^2 \cup \{x^2\}) \cap F_i,\ i=1,\dots,p,$$

$$\mathcal{B}_3 := \{B \subset F : B \cap F_i \neq F_i^3 \text{ for all } i=1,\dots,p\}$$

and show as in (e) that $|\mathcal{B}_2| \leq |\mathcal{B}_3|$.

So, another n-2 ($n \leq r$) repetitions of this argument would generate classes $\mathcal{B}_4,\dots,\mathcal{B}_n$ such that

$$|\mathcal{B}_1| \leq |\mathcal{B}_2| \leq |\mathcal{B}_3| \leq \dots \leq |\mathcal{B}_n|$$

with

$$\mathcal{B}_n = \{B \subset F : B \cap F_i \neq F_i^n \text{ for all } i=1,\dots,p\}$$

and $F_i^n = F_i$ for all $i=1,\dots,p$, which is the special case implying (a).

So it remains to prove (e):

For this it suffices to show that there exists a one-to-one map, say T, from $\mathcal{B}_1 \setminus \mathcal{B}_2$ into $\mathcal{B}_2 \setminus \mathcal{B}_1$.

Our claim is that $T(B) := B \setminus \{x^1\}$ is appropriate:

Let $B \in \mathcal{B}_1 \setminus \mathcal{B}_2$; then by definition of $\mathcal{B}_i$, i=1,2,

$$B \cap F_i \neq F_i^1 \text{ for all } i=1,\dots,p$$

$$\text{and} \quad B \cap F_j = F_j^2 \text{ for at least one } j \in \{1,\dots,p\}$$

implying that $x^1 \in \complement F_j^1$ whereas, by construction, $x^1 \in F_j^2$ and therefore $x^1 \in F_j$ and $x^1 \in B$; the last makes T one-to-one. It remains to show that $B \setminus \{x^1\} \in \mathcal{B}_2 \setminus \mathcal{B}_1$ for all $B \in \mathcal{B}_1 \setminus \mathcal{B}_2$. So, let $B \in \mathcal{B}_1 \setminus \mathcal{B}_2$; then

$$(B \setminus \{x^1\}) \cap F_j = (B \cap F_j) \setminus \{x^1\} = F_j^2 \setminus \{x^1\} = F_j^1, \text{ whence}$$

$(B \setminus \{x^1\}) \notin \mathcal{B}_1$; so we must finally show that $B \setminus \{x^1\} \in \mathcal{B}_2$, i.e. that

$$(+) \quad (B \setminus \{x^1\}) \cap F_i \neq F_i^2 \text{ for all } i=1,\dots,p.$$

<u>ad (+):</u> Let $i \in \{1,\dots,p\}$ be arbitrary but fixed; if $x^1 \in F_i$, then $x^1 \in F_i^2$,

but $x^1 \notin (B\setminus\{x^1\}) \cap F_i$, implying (+) in this case. If $x^1 \in \complement F_i$, i.e., $\{x^1\} \cap F_i = \emptyset$, then $F_i^2 = F_i^1$, whence $(B\setminus\{x^1\}) \cap F_i = B \cap F_i \neq F_i^1 = F_i^2$, implying (+) also in this case. This proves Lemma 8. □

The next lemma, being a consequence of Lemma 7 or Lemma 8, respectively, will be one of the key results used below.

Lemma 9. Let X be any set and $\mathcal{C}\subset\mathcal{P}(X)$ be a Vapnik-Chervonenkis class (i.e., $V(\mathcal{C}) =: s < \infty$); then

(i) $m^{\mathcal{C}}(r) \leq r^s$ for all $r\geq 2$, and

(ii) $m^{\mathcal{C}}(r) \leq r^s+1$ for all $r\geq 0$.

Proof. According to Lemma 7 and (13) we have

$m^{\mathcal{C}}(r) < \phi(s,r) \leq r^s+1$ for all $r\geq s$, whence (note that $m^{\mathcal{C}}(\cdot)$ is integer valued)

$$m^{\mathcal{C}}(r) \leq r^s \quad \text{for all } r\geq s;$$

if $2\leq r\leq s$, it follows that $m^{\mathcal{C}}(r) \leq 2^r \leq 2^s \leq r^s$; this proves (i). Finally, for r=0 we have $m^{\mathcal{C}}(0) = 1 = 2^0$ (whence $s\geq 1$) $\leq 0^s+1$, and for r=1 we have $m^{\mathcal{C}}(1) \leq 2 = 1^s+1$, proving (ii). □

Besides Lemma 9, the following VAPNIK-CHERVONENKIS-INEQUALITIES are basic for the whole theory. We are going to present this part in a form strengthening the original bounds obtained by Vapnik and Chervonenkis. This will be done in a similar way as in a recent paper by L. Devroye (1981).

For this, let again $(X,\mathcal{B})$ be an arbitrary measurable space (Devroye (1981) considers only $(X,\mathcal{B}) = (\mathbb{R}^k,\mathcal{B}_k)$, $k\geq 1$), and let $(\xi_i)_{i\in\mathbb{N}}$ be a sequence of independent and identically distributed random elements in $(X,\mathcal{B})$, defined on some common p-space $(\Omega,\mathcal{F},\mathbb{P})$, with distribution $\mu \equiv \mathcal{L}\{\xi_i\}$ on $\mathcal{B}$.
For $n,n' \in \mathbb{N}$ let μ_n and $\nu_{n'}$ be the empirical measures based on $\xi_1,\ldots,\xi_n$ and $\xi_{n+1},\ldots,\xi_{n+n'}$, respectively.

Let $\mathcal{C}$ be an arbitrary subset of $\mathcal{B}$, and let

$$D_n(\mathcal{C},\mu) := \sup_{C\in\mathcal{C}} |\mu_n(C) - \mu(C)|,$$

$$\bar{D}_{n,n'}(\mathcal{C}) := \sup_{C\in\mathcal{C}} |\mu_n(C) - \nu_{n'}(C)|,$$

<u>where we assume that both $D_n(\mathcal{C},\mu)$ and $\bar{D}_{n,n'}(\mathcal{C})$ are measurable w.r.t. the canonical model</u> (i.e., with $(X^{\mathbb{N}}, \mathcal{B}_{\mathbb{N}}, \times_{\mathbb{N}} \mu)$ as basic p-space and with ξ_i's being the coordinate projections of $X^{\mathbb{N}}$ onto X).
(Note that then $D_n(\mathcal{C},\mu)$ and $\bar{D}_{n,n'}(\mathcal{C})$ are also measurable considered as functions on the initially given p-space $(\Omega,\mathcal{F},\mathbb{P})$, since
$\omega \mapsto \xi(\omega) := (\xi_1(\omega),\xi_2(\omega),\ldots) \in X^{\mathbb{N}}$ is $\mathcal{F},\mathcal{B}_{\mathbb{N}}$-measurable.)

The proof of the following inequalities is patterned on the proof of Vapnik and Chervonenkis (1971). As a corollary we will obtain both, the fundamental Vapnik-Chervonenkis inequality and its improvement by Devroye (1981).

<u>Lemma 10.</u> For any $\varepsilon>0$, any $0<\alpha<1$, and any $n,n' \in \mathbb{N}$ one has

(a) $$\mathbb{P}(D_n(\mathcal{C},\mu) > \varepsilon) \leq \left(1 - \frac{1}{4\alpha^2\varepsilon^2 n'}\right)^{-1} \mathbb{P}(\bar{D}_{n,n'}(\mathcal{C}) > (1-\alpha)\varepsilon),$$

and

(b) $$\mathbb{P}(\bar{D}_{n,n'}(\mathcal{C}) > (1-\alpha)\varepsilon) \leq m^{\mathcal{C}}(n+n')\cdot 2\cdot \exp\left[-2n\left(\frac{n'}{n+n'}\right)^2(1-\alpha)^2\varepsilon^2\right],$$

where $m^{\mathcal{C}}(\cdot)$ denotes the growth function pertaining to the class $\mathcal{C}$.

Before proving this lemma, let us point out the following facts:
We have that

$$\bar{D}_{n,n'}(\mathcal{C})(\omega) = \sup_{C\in\mathcal{C}} |\mu_n(C,\omega) - \nu_{n'}(C,\omega)|$$

$$= h_{n,n'}(\xi(\omega)) \text{ for } \xi(\omega) = (\xi_1(\omega),\xi_2(\omega),\ldots) \in X^{\mathbb{N}},$$

where $h_{n,n'}: X^{\mathbb{N}} \longrightarrow \mathbb{R}$, defined by

$$h_{n,n'}(\underline{x}) := \sup_{C\in\mathcal{C}} \left|\frac{1}{n}\sum_{i=1}^{n} 1_C(x_i) - \frac{1}{n'}\sum_{i=n+1}^{n+n'} 1_C(x_i)\right|,$$

for $\underline{x} = (x_1,x_2,\ldots) \in X^{\mathbb{N}}$, is, by assumption, $\mathcal{B}_{\mathbb{N}},\mathcal{B}$-measurable, whence

$$A := \{\underline{x} \in X^{\mathbb{N}} : \overline{D}_{n,n'}(C) > (1-\alpha)\varepsilon\} \in \mathcal{B}_{\mathbb{N}},$$

and therefore

$$\mathbb{P}(\{\omega \in \Omega: \overline{D}_{n,n'}(C)(\omega) > (1-\alpha)\varepsilon\}) = L\{\xi\}(A)$$

$$= \int_{X^{\mathbb{N}}} u(h_{n,n'} - (1-\alpha)\varepsilon)\, d(\times_{\mathbb{N}} \mu) \quad \text{where } u(z) := \begin{cases} 1, & \text{if } z>0 \\ 0, & \text{if } z\leq 0. \end{cases}$$

Noticing further that $h_{n,n'}$ depends only on the first n and the following n' coordinates of $\underline{x}$, we obtain using the notation

$$x^1 := (x_1,\dots,x_n),\ x^2 := (x_{n+1},\dots,x_{n+n'}),$$

$$X^1 := \times_1^n X,\ X^2 := \times_{n+1}^{n+n'} X,\ P^1 := \times_1^n \mu,\ P^2 := \times_{n+1}^{n+n'} \mu$$

and $P := P^1 \times P^2$, that

(*) $$\mathbb{P}(\overline{D}_{n,n'}(C) > (1-\alpha)\varepsilon) = \int_{X^1\times X^2} u(h_{n,n'}(x^1,x^2)-(1-\alpha)\varepsilon)\, P(dx^1,dx^2).$$

In the very same way one has

(**) $$\mathbb{P}(D_n(C,\mu) > \varepsilon) = P^1(\{x^1=(x_1,\dots,x_n) \in X^1: \sup_{C\in\mathcal{C}} |\tfrac{1}{n} \sum_{i=1}^n 1_C(x_i)-\mu(C)| > \varepsilon\}).$$

Proof of inequality (a) in Lemma 10.

According to (*) of our remarks made before, one has

$$\mathbb{P}(\overline{D}_{n,n'}(C) > (1-\alpha)\varepsilon) = \int_{X^1\times X^2} u(h_{n,n'} - (1-\alpha)\varepsilon)\, d(P^1\times P^2)$$

$$\overset{\text{(Fubini)}}{=} \int_{X^1} [\int_{X^2} u(h_{n,n'} - (1-\alpha)\varepsilon)\, dP^2]\, dP^1$$

$$\geq \text{ⓐ} := \int_{A^1} [\int_{X^2} u(h_{n,n'} - (1-\alpha)\varepsilon)\, dP^2]\, dP^1$$

with $A^1 := \{x^1 \in X^1: \sup_{C\in\mathcal{C}} |\mu_n(C,x^1)-\mu(C)| > \varepsilon\}$,

where $$\mu_n(C,x^1) = \frac{1}{n} \sum_{i=1}^n 1_C(x_i) \text{ for } x^1 = (x_1,\dots,x_n) \in X^1.$$

But for any $(x^1,x^2) \in X^1\times X^2$ with $x^1 \in A^1$ there exists a $C_{x^1} \in \mathcal{C}$

such that

$$|\mu_n(C_{x^1},x^1) - \mu(C_{x^1})| > \varepsilon,$$

whence (for $\nu_{n'}(C,x^2) = \frac{1}{n'} \sum_{i=n+1}^{n+n'} 1_C(x_i)$ with $x^2 = (x_{n+1},\ldots,x_{n+n'}) \in X^2$)

we have

$$|\mu_n(C_{x^1},x^1) - \nu_{n'}(C_{x^1},x^2)| > (1-\alpha)\varepsilon$$

$$\text{if} \qquad |\nu_{n'}(C_{x^1},x^2) - \mu(C_{x^1})| \leqq \alpha\varepsilon;$$

therefore, we obtain for all $x^1 \in A^1$ the following estimate for the inner integral in ⓐ:

$$\int_{X^2} u(h_{n,n'}(x^1,x^2) - (1-\alpha)\varepsilon)\; P^2(dx^2)$$

$$\geqq P^2(\{x^2 \in X^2\colon |\nu_{n'}(C_{x^1},x^2) - \mu(C_{x^1})| \leqq \alpha\varepsilon\}).$$

But, by Tschebyschev's inequality,

$$P^2(\{x^2 \in X^2\colon |\nu_{n'}(C_{x^1},x^2) - \mu(C_{x^1})| > \alpha\varepsilon\})$$

$$\leqq \frac{1}{\alpha^2\varepsilon^2} \cdot \frac{\mu(C_{x^1})\,(1-\mu(C_{x^1}))}{n'} \leqq \frac{1}{4\alpha^2\varepsilon^2 n'};$$

thus, summarizing we obtain

$$\mathbb{P}(\bar{D}_{n,n'}(C) > (1-\alpha)\varepsilon) \geqq P^1(A^1)\left(1 - \frac{1}{4\alpha^2\varepsilon^2 n'}\right)$$

$$\underset{(**)}{=} \mathbb{P}(D_n(C,\mu) > \varepsilon)\left(1 - \frac{1}{4\alpha^2\varepsilon^2 n'}\right)$$

which proves (a).

Proof of inequality (b) in Lemma 10.

According to our remarks preceeding the proof we may and will consider $\bar{D}_{n,n'}(C)$ as a function $h_{n,n'}$ of

$$x = (x^1,x^2) \in X^1 \times X^2 \quad \text{with} \quad x^1 = (x_1,\ldots,x_n) \text{ and } x^2 = (x_{n+1},\ldots,x_{n+n'}).$$

Due to the symmetry of $P = P^1 \times P^2$ (w.r.t. coordinate permutations) one has for each $f \in L^1(X^1 \times X^2, \bigotimes_1^{n+n'} B, P)$

$$\int_{X^1 \times X^2} f(x)\, P(dx) = \int_{X^1 \times X^2} f(T_i x) P(dx)$$

for every permutation $T_i x$ of x (which means that $T_i x$ is the image of x when applying a permutation T_i to the $n+n'$ components of x).

Therefore,

$$\mathbb{P}(\overline{D}_{n,n'}(C) > (1-\alpha)\varepsilon) = \int_{X^1 \times X^2} u(h_{n,n'}(x) - (1-\alpha)\varepsilon)\, P(dx)$$

$$= \int_{X^1 \times X^2} \left[\frac{1}{(n+n')!} \sum_i u(h_{n,n'}(T_i x) - (1-\alpha)\varepsilon)\right] P(dx),$$

where the summation w.r.t. i is over all $(n+n')!$ permutations T_i.

We also remark here for later use in the proof that

$$u(h_{n,n'} - (1-\alpha)\varepsilon) = \sup_{C \in \mathcal{C}} u(h^C_{n,n'} - (1-\alpha)\varepsilon),$$

where $h^C_{n,n'}(x) := |\mu_n(C,x^1) - \nu_{n'}(C,x^2)|$ for

$x = (x^1,x^2) \in X^1 \times X^2$.

Next, let $x = (x^1,x^2) \in X^1 \times X^2$ (with $x^1 = (x_1,\dots,x_n)$ and $x^2 = (x_{n+1},\dots,x_{n+n'})$) be arbitrary but fixed and put $F_x := \{x_1,\dots,x_n,x_{n+1},\dots,x_{n+n'}\}$; then for any $C_1,C_2 \in \mathcal{C}$ one has that

$F_x \cap C_1 = F_x \cap C_2$ implies $h^{C_1}_{n,n'}(T_i x) = h^{C_2}_{n,n'}(T_i x)$ for all T_i.

Hence, denoting with $\mathcal{C}_x$ a subclass of $\mathcal{C}$ such that for any two $C_1,C_2 \in \mathcal{C}_x$, $F_x \cap C_1 \neq F_x \cap C_2$, and such that at the same time for any $C \in \mathcal{C}$ there exists a $C_x \in \mathcal{C}_x$ with $F_x \cap C_x = F_x \cap C$, we obtain for all T_i

$$\sup_{C \in \mathcal{C}} u(h^C_{n,n'}(T_i x) - (1-\alpha)\varepsilon) = \sup_{C \in \mathcal{C}_x} u(h^C_{n,n'}(T_i x) - (1-\alpha)\varepsilon)$$

$$\leq \sum_{C\in\mathcal{C}_x} u(h^C_{n,n'}(T_i x) - (1-\alpha)\varepsilon).$$

For later use in the proof we note here also that

$$|\mathcal{C}_x| = \Delta^{\mathcal{C}}(F_x) \quad \text{(cf. DEFINITION 1)}$$

$$\text{for every } x = (x^1,x^2) \in X^1 \times X^2.$$

It follows that

$$\frac{1}{(n+n')!} \sum_{i=1}^{(n+n')!} u(h_{n,n'}(T_i x) - (1-\alpha)\varepsilon)$$

$$= \frac{1}{(n+n')!} \sum_{i=1}^{(n+n')!} \sup_{C\in\mathcal{C}} u(h^C_{n,n'}(T_i x) - (1-\alpha)\varepsilon)$$

$$\leq \sum_{C\in\mathcal{C}_x} \left[\frac{1}{(n+n')!} \sum_{i=1}^{(n+n')!} u(h^C_{n,n'}(T_i x) - (1-\alpha)\varepsilon)\right].$$

Note that for each fixed x and C

$$\frac{1}{(n+n')!} \sum_{i=1}^{(n+n')!} u(h^C_{n,n'}(T_i x) - (1-\alpha)\varepsilon)$$

is the fraction of all $(n+n')!$ permutations $T_i x$ of x for which

$$|\mu_n(C,(T_i x)^1) - \nu_{n'}(C,(T_i x)^2)| > (1-\alpha)\varepsilon.$$

Now, for x and C being arbitrary but fixed, put

$$\eta_j := \begin{cases} 1, & \text{if } x_j \in C \\ 0, & \text{if } x_j \in \complement C \end{cases}, \quad j=1,\ldots,n+n', \text{ and denote by}$$

$(\eta_1^{(i)},\ldots,\eta_{n+n'}^{(i)})$ the vector $T_i\eta$ for $\eta = (\eta_1,\ldots,\eta_{n+n'})$.

Consider then the p-space $(\Omega_o,\mathcal{A}_o,\mathbb{P}_o)$ with Ω_o being the set of all $(n+n')!$ permutations T_i, $\mathcal{A}_o := \mathcal{P}(\Omega_o)$, and

$$\mathbb{P}_o(A) := \frac{|A|}{(n+n')!}, \quad A \in \mathcal{A}_o.$$

Then, using the random variables $\zeta_j : \Omega_o \longrightarrow \{0,1\}$, defined by $\zeta_j(T_i) := \eta_j^{(i)}$, $T_i \in \Omega_o$, $j=1,\dots,n+n'$, we obtain

$$\frac{1}{(n+n')!} \sum_{i=1}^{n} u(h^C_{n,n'}(T_i x) - (1-\alpha)\varepsilon)$$

$$= \mathbb{P}_o(|\frac{1}{n} \sum_{j=1}^{n} \zeta_j - \frac{1}{n'} \sum_{j=1}^{n'} \zeta_{n+j}| > (1-\alpha)\varepsilon)$$

$$= \mathbb{P}_o(|\frac{1}{n} \sum_{j=1}^{n} \zeta_j - \frac{1}{n'} [(n+n')\mu_{n+n'}(C,x) - \sum_{j=1}^{n} \zeta_j]| > (1-\alpha)\varepsilon)$$

$$= \mathbb{P}_o(|\frac{n'}{n} \sum_{j=1}^{n} \zeta_j - (n+n')\mu_{n+n'}(C,x) + \frac{n}{n} \sum_{j=1}^{n} \zeta_j| > (1-\alpha)\varepsilon)$$

$$= \mathbb{P}_o(|\frac{1}{n} \sum_{j=1}^{n} \zeta_j - \mu_{n+n'}(C,x)| > \frac{n'}{n+n'} (1-\alpha)\varepsilon)$$

$$\leq 2 \cdot \exp [-2n (\frac{n'}{n+n'})^2 (1-\alpha)^2 \varepsilon^2],$$

using Hoeffding's inequality for sampling without replacement from n+n' binary-valued random variables with sum $(n+n')\mu_{n+n'}(C,x)$; cf. W. Hoeffding (1963) and R.J. Serfling (1974).

Summarizing we thus obtain for every $x = (x^1,x^2) \in X^1 \times X^2$

$$\sum_{C \in \mathcal{C}} [\frac{1}{(n+n')!} \sum_{i=1}^{(n+n')!} u(h^C_{n,n'}(T_i x) - (1-\alpha)\varepsilon)]$$

$$\leq |\mathcal{C}_x| \cdot (2 \cdot \exp [-2n(\frac{n'}{n+n'})^2 (1-\alpha)^2 \varepsilon^2]) = \Delta^{\mathcal{C}}(F_x) \cdot (\dots\dots.)$$

$$\leq m^{\mathcal{C}}(n+n') \cdot (\dots\dots.), \text{ and therefore}$$

$$\mathbb{P}(\overline{D}_{n,n'}(\mathcal{C}) > (1-\alpha)\varepsilon) = \int_{X^1 \times X^2} [\frac{1}{(n+n')!} \sum_{i=1}^{(n+n')!} u(h_{n,n'}(T_i x) - (1-\alpha)\varepsilon)] \, P(dx)$$

$$\leq \int_{X^1 \times X^2} (\sum_{C \in \mathcal{C}_x} [\frac{1}{(n+n')!} \sum_{i=1}^{(n+n')!} u(h^C_{n,n'}(T_i x) - (1-\alpha)\varepsilon)]) \, P(dx)$$

$$\leq m^{\mathcal{C}}(n+n')\cdot 2\cdot \exp\left[-2n\left(\frac{n'}{n+n'}\right)^2(1-\alpha)^2\varepsilon^2\right]$$

which concludes the proof of (b). □

NOTE: We have in fact shown, assuming measurability of

$$\Delta^{\mathcal{C}}(\{\xi_1,\ldots,\xi_n,\xi_{n+1},\ldots,\xi_{n+n'}\}),\ \text{that}$$

$$\mathbb{P}(\overline{D}_{n,n'}(\mathcal{C}) > (1-\alpha)\varepsilon) \leq 2\cdot\exp\left[-2n\left(\frac{n'}{n+n'}\right)^2(1-\alpha)^2\varepsilon^2\right] \mathbb{E}(\Delta^{\mathcal{C}}(\{\xi_1,\ldots,\xi_{n+n'}\}));$$

in many cases this bound is considerably smaller than the r.h.s. of (b).

<u>COROLLARY.</u>

(i) <u>Vapnik-Chervonenkis (1971).</u>

Taking $\alpha = \frac{1}{2}$ and $n' = n$, one gets

$$\mathbb{P}(D_n(\mathcal{C},\mu) > \varepsilon) \leq 4\cdot m^{\mathcal{C}}(2n)\cdot\exp\left(-\frac{\varepsilon^2 n}{8}\right) \text{ for all } n \geq 2/\varepsilon^2.$$

(ii) <u>Devroye (1981).</u>

Taking $\alpha = \frac{1}{n\varepsilon}$ and $n' = n^2-n$, one gets

$$\mathbb{P}(D_n(\mathcal{C},\mu) > \varepsilon) \leq 4\cdot\exp(4\varepsilon + 4\varepsilon^2)\cdot m^{\mathcal{C}}(n^2)\cdot\exp(-2n\varepsilon^2)$$

for all $n > \max(\frac{1}{\varepsilon},2)$.

<u>Proof.</u> <u>(i):</u> It follows from (a) and (b) in Lemma 10 that in the present case

$$\mathbb{P}(D_n(\mathcal{C},\mu) > \varepsilon) \leq \left(1 - \frac{1}{\varepsilon^2 n}\right)^{-1}\cdot m^{\mathcal{C}}(2n)\cdot 2\cdot\exp\left[-2n\cdot\frac{1}{4}\cdot\frac{1}{4}\,\varepsilon^2\right]$$

$$\underset{(n\varepsilon^2\geq 2)}{\leq} 4\cdot m^{\mathcal{C}}(2n)\exp\left(-\frac{\varepsilon^2 n}{8}\right).$$

<u>(ii):</u> Again (a) and (b) in Lemma 10 yield in the present case

$$\mathbb{P}(D_n(\mathcal{C},\mu) > \varepsilon) \leq \left(1 - \frac{n^2}{4(n^2-n)}\right)^{-1}\cdot m^{\mathcal{C}}(n^2)2\exp\left[-2n\left(\frac{n-1}{n}\right)^2(\varepsilon^2-2\alpha\varepsilon^2+\alpha^2\varepsilon^2)\right]$$

$$\underset{((\frac{n-1}{n})^2 \geqq 1-\frac{2}{n})}{\leqq} \frac{4(n-1)}{3n-4} \cdot m^{\mathcal{C}}(n^2) \times$$

$$\times\ 2\exp\left[-2n(\varepsilon^2-2\alpha\varepsilon^2+\alpha^2\varepsilon^2)+4(\varepsilon^2-2\alpha\varepsilon^2+\alpha^2\varepsilon^2)\right]$$

$$\underset{(n\geqq 2)}{\leqq} 4\cdot m^{\mathcal{C}}(n^2)\cdot\exp[-2n\varepsilon^2+4\alpha n\varepsilon^2-2n\alpha^2\varepsilon^2+4\varepsilon^2+4\alpha^2\varepsilon^2]$$

$$\underset{(n\geqq 2)}{\leqq} 4\cdot m^{\mathcal{C}}(n^2)\exp[-2n\varepsilon^2+4\varepsilon+4\varepsilon^2]$$

$$= 4\cdot\exp(4\varepsilon+4\varepsilon^2)m^{\mathcal{C}}(n^2)\exp(-2n\varepsilon^2). \quad \square$$

Based on Lemma 9 (i) and on part (i) of the corollary to Lemma 10 we now obtain the main result of Vapnik and Chervonenkis concerning almost sure convergence of empirical $\mathcal{C}$-discrepancies in arbitrary sample spaces.

THEOREM 2. Let $(X,\mathcal{B})$ be an arbitrary measurable space and let $(\xi_i)_{i\in\mathbb{N}}$ be a sequence of independent and identically distributed random elements in $(X,\mathcal{B})$, defined on some common p-space $(\Omega,\mathcal{F},\mathbb{P})$, with distribution $\mu \equiv \mathcal{L}\{\xi_i\}$ on $\mathcal{B}$.

For $n\in\mathbb{N}$ let μ_n and ν_n be the empirical measures based on $\xi_1,\ldots,\xi_n$ and $\xi_{n+1},\ldots,\xi_{2n}$, respectively.

Let $\mathcal{C}\subset\mathcal{B}$ be a VCC such that both $D_n(\mathcal{C},\mu)$ as well as $\overline{D}_{n,n}(\mathcal{C})$ are measurable w.r.t. the canonical model; then

$$\lim_{n\to\infty} D_n(\mathcal{C},\mu) = 0 \quad \mathbb{P}\text{-a.s.}$$

Proof. Of course, it suffices to show that

$$(*) \qquad \limsup_{n\to\infty} D_n(\mathcal{C},\mu) \leqq \varepsilon \quad \mathbb{P}\text{-a.s. for every } \varepsilon>0;$$

according to the Borel-Cantelli Lemma, (*) is implied by

$$(**) \qquad \sum_{n\in\mathbb{N}} \mathbb{P}(D_n(\mathcal{C},\mu) > \varepsilon) < \infty \text{ for every } \varepsilon>0,$$

whence the proof will be concluded by showing that (**) holds true.

ad (**): Given any $\varepsilon>0$, we obtain from part (i) of the corollary to Lemma 10 that for all $n \geqq 2/\varepsilon^2$

$$\mathbb{P}(D_n(\mathcal{C},\mu) > \varepsilon) \leqq 4m^{\mathcal{C}}(2n)\cdot\exp(-\frac{\varepsilon^2 n}{8}).$$

Since, by assumption, $\mathcal{C}$ is a VCC, we have $V(\mathcal{C}) =: s < \infty$, whence by Lemma 9 (i)

$$\sum_{n\in\mathbb{N}} \mathbb{P}(D_n(\mathcal{C},\mu) > \varepsilon) \leqq \sum_{n<2/\varepsilon^2} \mathbb{P}(D_n(\mathcal{C},\mu) > \varepsilon) +$$

$$+ 4\cdot \sum_{n\geqq 2/\varepsilon^2} (2n)^s\cdot\exp(-\frac{\varepsilon^2 n}{8}) < \infty. \quad \square$$

The proof shows that the assumption of $\mathcal{C}$ being a VCC was essentially used to the amount that in this case the growth function $m^{\mathcal{C}}(r)$ is majorized by r^s for $r \geqq 2$ (with s being the minimal r for which $m^{\mathcal{C}}(r) < 2^r$); without this assumption, i.e., in case that $m^{\mathcal{C}}(r) = 2^r$ for all r, we would have arrived at

$$4\cdot \sum_{n\geqq 2/\varepsilon^2} 2^{2n} \exp(-\frac{\varepsilon^2 n}{8}) = \infty.$$

Thus, Theorem 2 can be restated as follows:

(18) If for a given $\mathcal{C}\subset\mathcal{B}$ there exists an $s<\infty$ such that $\mathcal{C}$ does not shatter any $F\subset X$ with $|F|=s$ (i.e., for any $F\subset X$ with $|F|=s$ there exists an $F'\subset F$ s.t. $F' \neq F \cap C$ for all $C \in \mathcal{C}$), then $\mathcal{C}$ is a GLIVENKO-CANTELLI-class (i.e., $\lim_{n\to\infty} D_n(\mathcal{C},\mu) = 0$ $\mathbb{P}$-a.s.), provided that the measurability assumptions stated in Theorem 2 are fulfilled.

The following example shows that these measurability assumptions cannot be dispensed with, in general.

(19) EXAMPLE (cf. M. Durst and R.M. Dudley (1980)).

Let $X = (X,<)$ be an uncountable wellordered set such that all its initial segments $\{x \in X: x < y\}$, $y \in X$, are countable (cf. J. Kelley

(1961), p. 29 -).

Then $\mathcal{C} := \{\{x \in X: x < y\}, y \in X\}$ does not shatter any $F \subset X$ with $|F| = 2$ (in fact: for any $F = \{x_1,x_2\} \subset X$ with $x_1 < x_2$ we have $\{x_2\} \neq F \cap C$ for all $C \in \mathcal{C}$, since $x_2 \in C$ would necessarily imply that $x_1 \in C$ for all $C \in \mathcal{C}$).

Note that $\mathcal{C}$ is linearly ordered by inclusion! To complete the example, let $\mathcal{B} := \{A \subset X: A \text{ countable or } \complement A \text{ countable}\}$, and let μ on $\mathcal{B}$ be defined by

$$\mu(A) := \begin{cases} 0, & \text{if } A \text{ is countable} \\ 1, & \text{if } \complement A \text{ is countable.} \end{cases}$$

Then $\mathcal{C} \subset \mathcal{B}$ and $\mu(C) = 0$ for all $C \in \mathcal{C}$; on the other hand, given any observations x_i, $i=1,\ldots,n$, of i.i.d. random elements ξ_i in $(X,\mathcal{B})$ with distribution μ, there exists a $C \in \mathcal{C}$ s.t. $x_i \in C$ for all $i=1,\ldots,n$, whence $D_n(\mathcal{C},\mu) \equiv 1$.

Note that in the present situation $\overline{D}_{n,n}(\mathcal{C})$ <u>fails</u> to be measurable w.r.t. the canonical model (cf. Theorem 2). In fact, consider for simplicity $n=1$, i.e., $\Omega = X \times X$, $\mathcal{F} = \mathcal{B} \otimes \mathcal{B}$, $\mathbb{P} = \mu \times \mu$ with ξ_1 and ξ_2 being the projections of Ω onto the first and second coordinate, respectively. Then

$$\overline{D}_{1,1}(\mathcal{C}) = \sup_{C \in \mathcal{C}} |\mu_1(C) - \nu_1(C)| = 1_{\complement\Delta},$$

where Δ denotes the diagonal in $X \times X$ which is <u>not</u> contained in $\mathcal{F}$: note that $\Delta \in \mathcal{B} \otimes \mathcal{B}$ iff there exists a countable subsystem $\mathcal{E}$ of $\mathcal{B}$ which is separating in the sense that

(+) for any $x,y \in X$ with $x \neq y$ there exists an $E \in \mathcal{E}$ such that $1_E(x) \neq 1_E(y)$; but in the present situation it can easily be shown that any countable subsystem $\mathcal{E}$ of $\mathcal{B}$ does <u>not</u> have the property (+) which implies that

$$\Delta \notin \mathcal{B} \otimes \mathcal{B} = \mathcal{F}.$$

Thus, although $D_n(\mathcal{C},\mu) \equiv 1$ is measurable w.r.t. the canonical model, $\bar{D}_{n,n}(\mathcal{C})$ is <u>not</u> in the present case.

We will show later (Section 4) that in $X = \mathbb{R}^k$, $k \geq 1$, the class $\mathbb{B}_k$ of all closed Euclidean balls fulfills the measurability assumptions made in Theorem 2. As shown by R.M. Dudley (1979) one has $V(\mathbb{B}_k) = k+2$, implying that $\mathbb{B}_k$ is a VCC; therefore, by (18) with $s = k+2$, we obtain the GLIVENKO-CANTELLI result (11) stated earlier without proof.

We are going to present here an independent nice proof of (11) which I learned from F. Topsøe ((1976), personal communication); this proof is based on the following two auxiliary results (20) and (21).

(20) <u>RADON'S THEOREM</u> (cf. F. Valentine (1964), Theorem 1.26).

Any $F \subset \mathbb{R}^k$, $k \geq 1$, with $|F| \geq k+2$, can be decomposed into two (disjoint) subsets F_i, i=1,2, such that

$$co(F_1) \cap co(F_2) \neq \emptyset,$$

where $co(F_i)$ denotes the convex hull of F_i.

(21) <u>(SEPARATION PROPERTY).</u> For any two $C_1, C_2 \in \mathbb{B}_k$ one has

$$co(C_1 \setminus C_2) \cap co(C_2 \setminus C_1) = \emptyset.$$

Now, according to (18), in order to prove (11) it suffices to show that $\mathbb{B}_k$ does not shatter any $F \subset \mathbb{R}^k$ with $|F| = s := k+2$.
Suppose to the contrary that there exists an $F \subset \mathbb{R}^k$ with $|F| = k+2$ such that for every $F_o \subset F$ there exists a $C \in \mathbb{B}_k$ with $F \cap C = F_o$.
This implies that for the F_i's of (20) which decompose a given $F \subset \mathbb{R}^k$ with $|F| = k+2$, there exist $C_i \in \mathbb{B}_k$ such that $F_i = F \cap C_i$, i=1,2.
Since $F_1 \cap F_2 = \emptyset$, we have

$$F_1 \subset C_1 \setminus C_2 \text{ and } F_2 \subset C_2 \setminus C_1,$$

and therefore

$$co(C_1 \setminus C_2) \cap co(C_2 \setminus C_1) \supset co(F_1) \cap co(F_2) \neq \emptyset \text{ (by (20))}$$

which contradicts (21). □

As the proof has shown, the separation property of the class $\mathcal{C} = \mathbb{B}_k$ was essential; at the same time the proof has shown that in general one has the following result (again under appropriate measurability assumptions as in Theorem 2):

(22) If a given class $\mathcal{C} \subset \mathcal{B}_k$ in $X = \mathbb{R}^k$, $k \geq 1$, fulfills the separation property, then $\mathcal{C}$ is a VCC and therefore also a GLIVENKO-CANTELLI class.

Let me conclude this section with the following

CONJECTURE: The class of all translates of a fixed convex set in $X = \mathbb{R}^k$, $k \geq k_o$, is, in general, not a VCC; at least it does not fulfill the separation property: in fact, consider the class of all translates of a tetrahedron C in $\mathbb{R}^3$, then the situation looks like this where you (hopefully) can see that for $C_z := C + z$ one has $C \setminus C_z = C \setminus \{x\}$ and $C_z \setminus C = C_z \setminus \{x\}$, whence

$$co(C \setminus C_z) \cap co(C_z \setminus C) = \{x\} \text{ (cf. Figure 2);}$$

I am grateful to Professors K. Seebach and R. Fritsch (Munich) for pointing out to me this example.

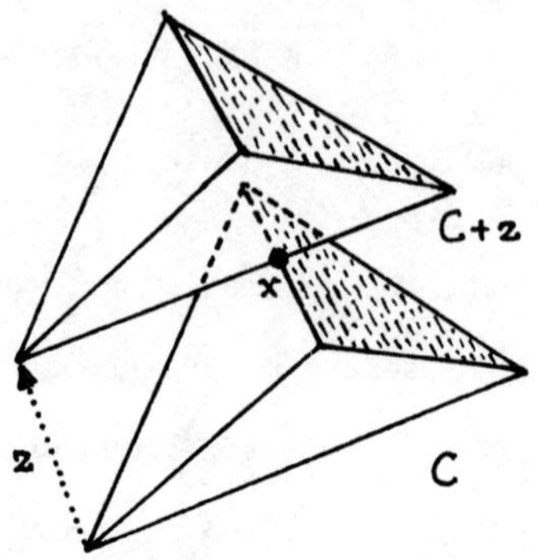

FIGURE 2

Note added in proof: As pointed out by a referee, translates of multiples of a fixed convex set need not be a GCC nor VCC: cf. Elker, Pollard and Stute (1979), Adv. Appl. Prob. 11, p. 830.

3. Weak convergence of non-BOREL measures on a metric space.*)

Let $S = (S,d)$ be a metric space with metric d and let $\mathcal{B}_b(S) \equiv \mathcal{B}_b(S,d)$ be the σ-algebra in S generated by the open (d-) balls

$$B_d(x,r) \equiv B(x,r) := \{y \in S: d(x,y)<r\}, \; x \in S, \; r>0.$$

Clearly, $\mathcal{B}_b(S)$ is a sub-σ-algebra of the Borel σ-algebra $\mathcal{B}(S)$ in S (generated by all open subsets of S).

In this section we will study a mode of weak convergence for nets of finite measures which are defined at least on $\mathcal{B}_b(S)$. Our formulation is a slight modification of a concept which was introduced by R.M. Dudley (1966) and further studied and extended by M.J. Wichura (1968); cf. also D. Pollard (1979), where it is shown that some of the key results in that theory can be deduced directly from the better known weak convergence theory for Borel measures.

As in Wichura, our presentation here is made roughly along the lines of Chapter I of Billingsley (1968) (see also P. Billingsley (1971), S I A M No. 5) which treats similar aspects of the theory of weak convergence of probabilities defined on all of $\mathcal{B}(S)$. The present theory is especially suited to cope with measurability problems arising in the theory of empirical processes as well as to allow for a proper formulation of functional central limit theorems for empirical $\mathcal{C}$-processes (cf. Section 4).

To start with, let us first establish some notation and terminology to be

---

*) This section represents and extends parts of a first draft of a "Diplomarbeit" by J. Schattauer, University of Munich, 1981.

used throughout this section.

If not stated otherwise, $S = (S,d)$ is always a (possibly non-separable) metric space. Let $\mathcal{A}$ be a σ-algebra of subsets of S such that $\mathcal{B}_b(S) \subset \mathcal{A} \subset \mathcal{B}(S)$; then the following spaces of real valued functions on S will be considered:

$\mathfrak{F}_a(S) := \{f: S \to \mathbb{R},\ f\ \mathcal{A},\mathcal{B}\text{-measurable}\}$

$C^b(S) := \{f: S \to \mathbb{R},\ f \text{ bounded and continuous}\}$

$C_a^b(S) := \mathfrak{F}_a(S) \cap C^b(S)$

$U^b(S) := \{f: S \to \mathbb{R},\ f \text{ bounded and uniformly continuous}\}$

$U_a^b(S) := \mathfrak{F}_a(S) \cap U^b(S)$.

In case of $\mathcal{B}_b(S)$ instead of $\mathcal{A}$ we shall write $\mathfrak{F}_b(S)$, $C_b^b(S)$ and $U_b^b(S)$ instead of $\mathfrak{F}_a(S)$, $C_a^b(S)$ and $U_a^b(S)$, respectively.

The following figure may help to visualize the different spaces, where the largest box represents the class of all $\mathcal{B}(S)$, $\mathcal{B}$-measurable functions $f: S \to \mathbb{R}$ and where the smallest class $U_b^b(S)$ is represented by the shaded area:

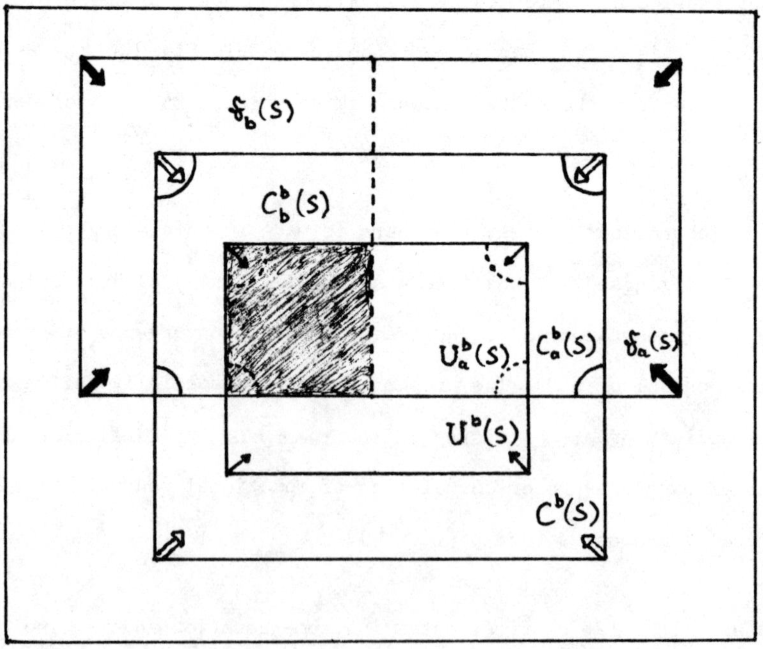

FIGURE 3 ($\mathfrak{F}_b(S)$ for example is represented as that part of the $\mathfrak{F}_a(S)$-box (marked by the bold arrows) which is left to the dotted line.)

Furthermore, let $M_a(S)$ be the space of all nonnegative finite measures defined on $\mathcal{A}$ and write $M_b(S)$ for the space of all nonnegative finite measures on $\mathcal{B}_b(S)$.

For $f: S \to \mathbb{R}$, we denote by $D(f)$ the set of discontinuity points of f.

Finally, given any $\mu \in M_a(S)$ and any bounded f or $A \subset S$, respectively, let

$$\int^* f\, d\mu := \inf\{\int g\, d\mu: g \geq f,\ g \in \mathcal{F}_a(S) \text{ and } g \text{ bounded}\},$$

$$\int_* f\, d\mu := \sup\{\int g\, d\mu: g \leq f,\ g \in \mathcal{F}_a(S) \text{ and } g \text{ bounded}\},$$

$$\mu_*(A) := \int_* 1_A d\mu, \text{ and } \mu^*(A) := \int^* 1_A d\mu.$$

Note that μ_* and μ^* are inner and outer measures, respectively, i.e., one has for every $A \subset S$

(23) $\mu^*(A) = \inf\{\mu(B): B \supset A,\ B \in \mathcal{A}\}$ and $\mu_*(A) = \sup\{\mu(B): B \subset A,\ B \in \mathcal{A}\}$.

(In fact, as to the first equality in (23), "$\leq$" is obvious, since for any $B \supset A$, $B \in \mathcal{A}$, $g := 1_B \geq 1_A$, $g \in \mathcal{F}_a(S)$ and g bounded; as to the other inequality, given any $g \geq 1_A$, $g \in \mathcal{F}_a(S)$ and g bounded, choose for each $\varepsilon > 0$ $B_\varepsilon := \{g \geq 1-\varepsilon\}$ to get $B_\varepsilon \in \mathcal{A}$ with $B_\varepsilon \supset A$ and $\mu(B_\varepsilon) \leq \int_{B_\varepsilon} (g+\varepsilon) d\mu \leq \int g d\mu + \varepsilon\mu(S)$; since $\mu(S) < \infty$, we obtain, taking $\varepsilon = \frac{1}{n}$ and letting $n \to \infty$, $B := \bigcap_{n \in \mathbb{N}} B_{1/n} \in \mathcal{A}$ with $B \supset A$ and $\mu(B) \leq \int g d\mu$, which proves the other inequality.)

The following lemma comprises some simple but still essential facts to be used later on.

<u>LEMMA 11.</u> (i) $\mathcal{B}_b(S) = \sigma(\{d(\cdot,x): x \in S\})$, where $\sigma(\{d(\cdot,x): x \in S\})$ denotes the smallest σ-algebra in S w.r.t. which all of the functions $d(\cdot,x)$, for each fixed $x \in S$, are measurable.

(ii) Let $S_o \subset S$ be such that $S_o = (S_o, d)$ is a separable metric space, then for $d(\cdot, S_o) := \inf\{d(\cdot,x): x \in S_o\}$ we have $\min(d(\cdot,S_o), n) \in U_b^b(S)$ for each n; in this case also $S_o^\delta := \{x \in S: d(x,S_o) < \delta\} \in \mathcal{B}_b(S)$ for every $\delta > 0$, and $S_o^c \in \mathcal{B}_b(S)$, where S_o^c denotes the closure of S_o in (S,d).

(iii) $K(S) \subset \mathcal{B}_b(S)$, where $K(S)$ denotes the class of all compact subsets of (S,d).

(iv) If (S,d) is separable, then $\mathcal{B}_b(S) = \mathcal{B}(S)$.

Proof. (i) is an immediate consequence of the identity $B(x,r) = \{y\in S: d(y,x)<r\}$, $x\in S$, $r>0$. To verify (ii), since $d(\cdot,A)$ is uniformly continuous for each $A\subset S$, it suffices to show that $d(\cdot,S_o) \in \mathcal{F}_b(S)$; for this, let T_o be a countable dense subset of S_o. Then, since $d(x,S_o) = d(x,T_o) = \inf\{d(x,y): y\in T_o\}$, $d(x,S_o)$ is a countable infimum of $\mathcal{B}_b$, $\mathcal{B}$-measurable functions, hence $d(\cdot,S_o) \in \mathcal{F}_b(S)$. This also shows that $S_o^\delta \in \mathcal{B}_b(S)$ implying that $S_o^c = \bigcap_{n\in\mathbb{N}} S_o^{1/n} \in \mathcal{B}_b(S)$. Since each compact subset of S is closed and separable, (iii) is just a particular case of (ii). Finally, if (S,d) is separable, then (S_o,d) is separable for each $S_o\subset S$, especially for all closed subsets F of S, whence, by (ii), $F\in\mathcal{B}_b(S)$ for all closed $F\subset S$ and therefore $\mathcal{B}(S)\subset\mathcal{B}_b(S)$ which proves (iv). □

Remark. The converse of (iv) is not true, in general: Talagrand (1978) has constructed an example of a non-separable metric space S for which $\mathcal{B}_b(S)$ coincides with $\mathcal{B}(S)$.

Now, our first subsection will be concerned with

SEPARABLE AND TIGHT MEASURES ON $\mathcal{B}_b(S)$:

DEFINITION 2. $\mu\in M_b(S)$ is called separable iff there exists a separable subset S_o of S (i.e., an $S_o\subset S$ s.t. $S_o = (S_o,d)$ is a separable metric space) with $\mu(S_o^c) = \mu(S)$.

(Note that the closure S_o^c of a separable S_o is also separable.)

(24) REMARK. Let $\mu\in M_b(S)$ be separable; then there exists a unique extension of μ to an (even τ-smooth) Borel measure $\tilde{\mu}$ on $\mathcal{B}(S)$.

Proof. By assumption there exists a closed and separable $A_o\subset S$ such that $\mu(A_o) = \mu(S)$, where $A_o\in\mathcal{B}_b(S)$ by Lemma 11 (ii). Let $\mathcal{D} := \{B\in\mathcal{B}(S): B\cap A_o\in\mathcal{B}_b(S)\}$; then $\mathcal{D}$ is a σ-algebra in S. But, since each closed subset belongs to $\mathcal{D}$ (cf. Lemma 11 (ii) and notice that $F\cap A_o$ is again closed and separable),

$\mathcal{D}$ equals $\mathcal{B}(S)$ and therefore $\tilde{\mu}(B) := \mu(B\cap A_o)$ is well defined for all $B\in\mathcal{B}(S)$. Furthermore, for every $B\in\mathcal{B}(S)$, $\tilde{\mu}(B) = \mu(B\cap A_o) = \mu(B)-\mu(B\setminus A_o) = \mu(B)$, since $\mu(B\setminus A_o) = 0$ according to $\mu(A_o) = \mu(S)$, showing that $\tilde{\mu}$ is a Borel extension of μ (being even τ-smooth since $\tilde{\mu}$ concentrates on the separable subset A_o of S). As to the uniqueness of $\tilde{\mu}$, suppose that $\tilde{\mu}_i$ are finite measures on $\mathcal{B}(S)$ with $\text{rest}_{\mathcal{B}_b(S)}\tilde{\mu}_i = \mu$, $i=1,2$; then $\tilde{\mu}_1(A_o) = \tilde{\mu}_2(A_o) = \mu(A_o) = \mu(S)$ and therefore $\tilde{\mu}_1(B) = \tilde{\mu}_1(B\cap A_o) = \mu(B\cap A_o) = \tilde{\mu}_2(B\cap A_o) = \tilde{\mu}_2(B)$ for all $B\in\mathcal{B}(S)$ showing that $\tilde{\mu}_1 = \tilde{\mu}_2$. □

(<u>Note:</u> It can be shown by examples that the assumption in (24) of μ being separable cannot be dispensed with, in general.)

<u>DEFINITION 3.</u> $\mu\in M_b(S)$ is called <u>tight</u> iff $\sup\{\mu(K): K\in\mathcal{K}(S)\} = \mu(S)$. (Note that $\mathcal{K}(S)\subset\mathcal{B}_b(S)$ according to Lemma 11 (iii).)

(25) <u>REMARK.</u> Any tight $\mu\in M_b(S)$ is separable.

<u>Proof.</u> Note first that any $K\in\mathcal{K}(S)$ is separable; now, since μ is tight, there exists for every n a $K_n\in\mathcal{K}(S)$ s.t. $\mu(K_n)>\mu(S) - \frac{1}{n}$; then $S_o := \bigcup_{n\in\mathbb{N}} K_n$ is separable and $\mu(S_o^c) \geq \mu(S_o) \geq \mu(K_n) > \mu(S) - \frac{1}{n}$ for all n, whence $\mu(S_o^c)=\mu(S)$. □

As to the converse of (25) one has

(26) <u>REMARK.</u> If $\mu\in M_b(S)$ is separable and if S is topologically complete, then μ is tight.

<u>Proof.</u> Use (24) to get the unique Borel extension $\tilde{\mu}$ of μ and apply Theorem 1, Appendix III, p. 234, in Billingsley (1968). □

(<u>Note:</u> As shown by Billingsley (1968), Remark 2, p. 234, the hypothesis of topological completeness cannot be suppressed in (26).)

WEAK CONVERGENCE/PORTMANTEAU-THEOREM:

As before, let S = (S,d) be a (possibly non-separable) metric space, let $M_a(S)$ be the space of all nonnegative finite measures on a σ-algebra A with $B_b(S)\subset A\subset B(S)$ and let $M_b(S)$ be the space of all nonnegative finite measures on $B_b(S)$.

Then, given a net $(\mu_\alpha)_{\alpha\in A}$ in $M_a(S)$ and a $\mu\in M_b(S)$, we define:

DEFINITION 4. (μ_α) converges weakly to μ (denoted by $\mu_\alpha \xrightarrow[b]{} \mu$) if

(i) μ is separable

(ii) $\lim_\alpha \int f d\mu_\alpha = \int f d\tilde{\mu}$ for all $f\in C_a^b(S)$

(where again $\tilde{\mu}$ is the unique Borel extension of μ, according to (24)).

(27) REMARKS. a) If (S,d) is a separable metric space, then Definition 4 coincides with the usual definition of weak convergence of Borel measures (cf. Lemma 11 (iv)).

b) If (μ_α) converges weakly in the sense of Wichura's (1968) definition, then (μ_α) converges in the sense of our Definition 4 but not vice versa; both definitions are equivalent if (S,d) is topologically complete (cf. (26) and our Portmanteau-Theorem below).

LEMMA 12. Let $f: S \to \mathbb{R}$ be such that $0\leq f<n$ for some $n\in\mathbb{N}$; then, for every $\mu\in M_a(S)$,

$$\int^* f d\mu \leq \mu(S) + \sum_{k=1}^{n} \mu^*(\{f\geq k\}).$$

Proof. Since by (23), for every $A\subset S$, $\mu^*(A) = \inf\{\mu(B): B\supset A, B\in A\}$, it follows that for every ε>0 and every $1\leq k\leq n$ there exists a $B_{\varepsilon,k}\in A$ s.t. $B_{\varepsilon,k}\supset\{f\leq k\}$ and $\mu^*(\{f\geq k\}) \geq \mu(B_{\varepsilon,k}) - \frac{\varepsilon}{n}$. Put $f_\varepsilon := 1_S + \sum_{k=1}^{n} 1_{B_{\varepsilon,k}}$ to get a bounded function belonging to $F_a(S)$ and dominating f ($f \leq \sum_{k=0}^{n} 1_{\{f\geq k\}} \leq 1_S + \sum_{k=1}^{n} 1_{B_{\varepsilon,k}} = f_\varepsilon$), whence

$$\int^* f d\mu = \inf\{\int g d\mu : g \geq f,\ g \in \mathfrak{F}_a(S) \text{ and } g \text{ bounded}\} \leq \int f_\varepsilon d\mu$$

$$= \mu(S) + \sum_{k=1}^{n} \mu(B_{\varepsilon,k}) \leq \mu(S) + \sum_{k=1}^{n} [\mu^*(\{f \geq k\}) + \frac{\varepsilon}{n}]$$

$$= \mu(S) + \sum_{k=1}^{n} \mu^*(\{f \geq k\}) + \varepsilon,$$

which implies the assertion since $\varepsilon > 0$ was chosen arbitrary. □

In what follows, let $\mathcal{G}(S)$, resp. $\mathcal{F}(S)$, denote the class of all open, resp. closed, subsets of S; also for $A \subset S$ let A^o, A^c and ∂A denote the interior, closure and boundary of A, respectively.

(28) PORTMANTEAU-THEOREM.

Let (μ_α) be a net in $M_a(S)$ and let $\mu \in M_b(S)$ be separable with $\tilde{\mu}$ being its unique Borel extension (cf. (24)).

Then the following assertions (a) - (h') are all equivalent:

(a) $\lim_\alpha \mu_\alpha(S) = \mu(S)$ and $\liminf_\alpha (\mu_\alpha)_*(G) \geq \tilde{\mu}(G)$ for all $G \in \mathcal{G}(S)$

(a') $\lim_\alpha \mu_\alpha(S) = \mu(S)$ and $\liminf_\alpha \mu_\alpha(G) \geq \tilde{\mu}(G)$ for all $G \in \mathcal{G}(S) \cap \mathcal{A}$

(b) $\lim_\alpha \mu_\alpha(S) = \mu(S)$ and $\limsup_\alpha \mu_\alpha^*(F) \leq \tilde{\mu}(F)$ for all $F \in \mathcal{F}(S)$

(b') $\lim_\alpha \mu_\alpha(S) = \mu(S)$ and $\limsup_\alpha \mu_\alpha(F) \leq \tilde{\mu}(F)$ for all $F \in \mathcal{F}(S) \cap \mathcal{A}$

(c) $\liminf_\alpha \int_* f d\mu_\alpha \geq \int f d\tilde{\mu}$ for all bounded lower semicontinuous $f: S \to \mathbb{R}$

(c') $\liminf_\alpha \int f d\mu_\alpha \geq \int f d\tilde{\mu}$ for all bounded lower semicontinuous $f \in \mathfrak{F}_a(S)$

(d) $\limsup_\alpha \int^* f d\mu_\alpha \leq \int f d\tilde{\mu}$ for all bounded upper semicontinuous $f: S \to \mathbb{R}$

(d') $\limsup_\alpha \int f d\mu_\alpha \leq \int f d\tilde{\mu}$ for all bounded upper semicontinuous $f \in \mathfrak{F}_a(S)$

(e) $\lim_\alpha \int^* f d\mu_\alpha = \lim_\alpha \int_* f d\mu_\alpha = \int f d\tilde{\mu}$ for all bounded $\mathcal{B}(S)$, $\mathbb{B}$-measurable $f: S \to \mathbb{R}$ which are $\tilde{\mu}$-almost everywhere ($\tilde{\mu}$-a.e.) continuous

(e') $\lim_\alpha \int f d\mu_\alpha = \int f d\tilde{\mu}$ for all bounded $f \in \mathfrak{F}_a(S)$ which are $\tilde{\mu}$-a.e. continuous

(f) $\lim_\alpha (\mu_\alpha)_*(A) = \lim_\alpha \mu_\alpha^*(A) = \tilde{\mu}(A)$ for all $A \in \mathcal{B}(S)$ with $\tilde{\mu}(\partial A) = 0$

(f') $\lim_\alpha \mu_\alpha(A) = \tilde{\mu}(A)$ for all $A \in \mathcal{A}$ with $\tilde{\mu}(\partial A) = 0$

(g) $\lim_\alpha \int^* f d\mu_\alpha = \lim_\alpha \int_* f d\mu_\alpha = \int f d\tilde{\mu}$ for all $f \in C^b(S)$

(g') $\lim_\alpha \int f d\mu_\alpha = \int f d\tilde{\mu}$ for all $f \in C_a^b(S)$ (cf. Definition 4, (ii))

(h) $\lim_\alpha \int^* f d\mu_\alpha = \lim_\alpha \int_* f d\mu_\alpha = \int f d\tilde{\mu}$ for all $f \in U^b(S)$

(h') $\lim_\alpha \int f d\mu_\alpha = \int f d\mu$ for all $f \in U_b^b(S)$.

<u>Proof.</u> The proof may be divided into 4 steps showing that the following implications hold true, where "➡" indicates the non-trivial parts.

<u>STEP 1:</u> (a) $\Leftrightarrow$ (b) ➡ (d); (c) $\Rightarrow$ (a); (c) $\Leftrightarrow$ (d); {(a), (b), (c), (d)} ➡ (e) $\Rightarrow$ (e') $\Rightarrow$ (f') ➡ (g') $\Rightarrow$ (h') ➡ (b)

<u>STEP 2:</u> (d) $\Rightarrow$ (d') $\Rightarrow$ (c') $\Rightarrow$ (a') $\Rightarrow$ (b') ➡ (b) ($\Rightarrow$ (d) by STEP 1)

<u>STEP 3:</u> (a) and (b) ➡ (f) $\Rightarrow$ (f') ($\Rightarrow$ (a) by STEP 1)

<u>STEP 4:</u> (e) $\Rightarrow$ (g) $\Rightarrow$ (h) $\Rightarrow$ (h') ($\Rightarrow$ (e) by STEP 1).

We are going to prove the "➡" parts; the others are either immediate or easy to prove.

<u>(b) ➡ (d):</u> 1. Let $f: S \to \mathbb{R}$ be upper semicontinuous and assume for the moment that $0<f<1$; then, by Lemma 12, we have for every $n \in \mathbb{N}$

$$\limsup_\alpha \int^* nf\, d\mu_\alpha \leq \limsup_\alpha [\mu_\alpha(S) + \sum_{k=1}^n \mu_\alpha^*(\{nf \geq k\})]$$

$$\leq \limsup_\alpha \mu_\alpha(S) + \sum_{k=1}^n \limsup_\alpha \mu_\alpha^*(\{nf \geq k\}) \underset{(b)}{\leq} \mu(S) + \sum_{k=1}^n \tilde{\mu}(\{nf \geq k\})$$

$$\leq \mu(S) + \int nf d\tilde{\mu},$$

whence

$$\limsup_\alpha \int^* f d\mu_\alpha \leq \frac{\mu(S)}{n} + \int f d\tilde{\mu};$$

thus (for $n \to \infty$) we obtain (d) for all upper semicontinuous f with $0<f<1$.

2. Let $f: S \to \mathbb{R}$ be upper semicontinuous and bounded, say $a<f<b$ for some $-\infty<a<b<\infty$; then $0 < \frac{f-a}{b-a} < 1$, and therefore it follows from part 1 that

$$\limsup_{\alpha} \int^{*} \frac{f-a}{b-a}\, d\mu_{\alpha} \leq \int \frac{f-a}{b-a}\, d\tilde{\mu},$$

which implies (d), since $\lim_{\alpha} \mu_{\alpha}(S) = \mu(S) = \tilde{\mu}(S)$.

<u>[(a)-(d)] ⟹ (e):</u> Let $f: S \to \mathbb{R}$ be bounded, $\mathcal{B}(S)$, $\mathbb{B}$-measurable and $\tilde{\mu}$-a.e. continuous. It follows (cf. Gaenssler-Stute (1977), Satz 8.4.3) that

$$\tilde{\mu}(\{f_{*}<f^{*}\}) = 0,$$

where $f_{*} := \sup\{g: g \leqq f,\ g \text{ lower semicontinuous}\}$ and

$f^{*} := \inf\{g: g \geqq f,\ g \text{ upper semicontinuous}\}$;

therefore, since $f_{*} \leqq f \leq f^{*}$, we obtain

$$(+) \quad \int f_{*}\, d\tilde{\mu} = \int f\, d\tilde{\mu} = \int f^{*}\, d\tilde{\mu}.$$

Furthermore, since f_{*} and f^{*} are also bounded with f_{*} being lower semicontinuous and f^{*} being upper semicontinuous, respectively, we obtain

$$\int f_{*}\, d\tilde{\mu} \underset{(c)}{\leqq} \liminf_{\alpha} \int_{*} f_{*}\, d\mu_{\alpha} \leqq \liminf_{\alpha} \int_{*} f\, d\mu_{\alpha}$$

$$\leqq \liminf_{\alpha} \int^{*} f\, d\mu_{\alpha} \leqq \limsup_{\alpha} \int^{*} f\, d\mu_{\alpha} \leqq \limsup_{\alpha} \int^{*} f^{*}\, d\mu_{\alpha} \underset{(d)}{\leqq} \int f^{*}\, d\tilde{\mu},$$

whence, by (+),
$$\lim_{\alpha} \int^{*} f\, d\mu_{\alpha} = \int f\, d\mu.$$

On the other hand, one obtains in the same way that

$$\int f_{*}\, d\tilde{\mu} \leqq \liminf_{\alpha} \int_{*} f_{*}\, d\mu_{\alpha} \leqq \limsup_{\alpha} \int_{*} f\, d\mu_{\alpha}$$

$$\leqq \limsup_{\alpha} \int^{*} f\, d\mu_{\alpha} \leqq \limsup_{\alpha} \int^{*} f^{*}\, d\mu_{\alpha} \leqq \int f^{*}\, d\tilde{\mu},$$ whence, again by (+),

$\lim_{\alpha} \int_{*} f\, d\mu_{\alpha} = \int f\, d\tilde{\mu}$, which proves (e).

<u>(f') ⟹ (g'):</u> Given $f \in C_a^b(S)$, let $f\tilde{\mu}$ ($\equiv \tilde{\mu} \circ f^{-1}$) be the image measure that f induces on $\mathbb{B}$ in $\mathbb{R}$ from $\tilde{\mu}$ (i.e., $f\tilde{\mu}(B) = \tilde{\mu}(\{f \in B\}), B \in \mathbb{B}$). Since f is bounded, we have $f\tilde{\mu}([a,b]) = \tilde{\mu}(S)$ for some $-\infty<a<b<\infty$; furthermore, since $\tilde{\mu}(S)<\infty$, we

have $f\tilde{\mu}(\{t\})>0$ for at most countable many $t\in[a,b]$. Therefore, it follows that for every $\varepsilon>0$ there exist $t_o, t_1,\ldots,t_m$ such that

(1) $a = t_o < t_1 < \ldots < t_m = b$

(2) $a < f(x) < b$ for all $x\in S$

(3) $t_j-t_{j-1} < \varepsilon$ for all $j=1,\ldots,m$

and (4) $\tilde{\mu}(\{x\in S: f(x) = t_j\}) = 0$ for all $j=0,1,\ldots,m$.

Now, let $A_j := \{x\in S: t_{j-1}\leq f(x) < t_j\}$; then $A_j\in\mathcal{A}$, the A_j's being pairwise disjoint with union S, and $\partial A_j\subset\{x\in S: f(x)\in\{t_{j-1},t_j\}\}$, whence (by (4)) $\tilde{\mu}(\partial A_j) = 0$, $j=1,\ldots,m$.

Therefore it follows by (f') that

$$(+)\quad \lim_\alpha \mu_\alpha(A_j) = \tilde{\mu}(A_j) \quad \text{for } j=1,\ldots,m.$$

Now, put $g := \sum_{j=1}^{m} t_{j-1} 1_{A_j}$ to get a bounded function $g\in\mathcal{F}_a(S)$ for which (by (3))

$$(++)\quad \sup_{x\in S} |f(x) - g(x)| < \varepsilon.$$

Then, it follows that

$$\begin{aligned}|\int f d\mu_\alpha - \int f d\tilde{\mu}| &= |\int(f-g)d\mu_\alpha + \int g d\mu_\alpha - \int(f-g)d\tilde{\mu} - \int g d\tilde{\mu}| \\ &\leq \int|f-g|d\mu_\alpha + \int|f-g|d\tilde{\mu} + |\int g d\mu_\alpha - \int g d\tilde{\mu}| \\ &\underset{(++)}{\leq} \varepsilon\mu_\alpha(S) + \varepsilon\tilde{\mu}(S) + \sum_{j=1}^{m} |t_{j-1}||\mu_\alpha(A_j) - \tilde{\mu}(A_j)|,\end{aligned}$$

whence, by (+),

$$\limsup_\alpha |\int f d\mu_\alpha - \int f d\tilde{\mu}| \leq 2\varepsilon\mu(S)$$

(note that $S\in\mathcal{A}$ with $\tilde{\mu}(\partial S) = \tilde{\mu}(\emptyset) = 0$, and $\tilde{\mu}(S) = \mu(S)$).

Thus (for $\varepsilon\to 0$) we have shown (g').

<u>(h') ⟹ (b):</u> Since $f \equiv 1\in U_b^b(S)$, we obtain from (h') at once $\lim_\alpha \mu_\alpha(S) = \mu(S)$. Next, given an arbitrary $F\in\mathcal{F}(S)$ and $\varepsilon>0$, let

$$F^\varepsilon := \{x\in S: d(x,F)<\varepsilon\};$$

then $F^{\varepsilon} \downarrow F$ as $\varepsilon \downarrow 0$, and therefore, for every $n \in \mathbb{N}$ there exists an $F^{\varepsilon_n} \in \mathcal{G}(S)$ such that $\tilde{\mu}(F^{\varepsilon_n}) \leq \tilde{\mu}(F) + \frac{1}{n}$.

Now, since by assumption μ is separable, there exists a separable $S_o \subset S$ with $\mu(S_o^c) = \mu(S)$; put, for each $x \in S$,

$$f_n(x) := \begin{cases} d(x, S_o^c \cap \complement F^{\varepsilon_n})/\varepsilon_n, & \text{if } S_o^c \cap \complement F^{\varepsilon_n} \neq \emptyset \\ 1, & \text{if } S_o^c \cap \complement F^{\varepsilon_n} = \emptyset; \end{cases}$$

then the function $g_n := \min(f_n, 1)$ has the following properties for every $n \in \mathbb{N}$:

(1) $g_n \in U_b^b(S)$ (cf. Lemma 11 (ii) and note that $S_o^c \cap \complement F^{\varepsilon_n}$ is separable),

(2) $\text{rest}_{S_o^c \cap \complement F^{\varepsilon_n}} \, g_n \equiv 0$,

and (3) $\text{rest}_F \, g_n \equiv 1$.

Therefore, for every $n \in \mathbb{N}$ we obtain

$$\limsup_{\alpha} \mu_\alpha^*(F) = \limsup_{\alpha} \int^* 1_F d\mu_\alpha \underset{(3),(1)}{\leq} \limsup_{\alpha} \int g_n d\mu_\alpha$$

$$\underset{(h'),(1)}{=} \int g_n d\mu = \int_{S_o^c} g_n d\mu = \int_{S_o^c \cap \complement F^{\varepsilon_n}} g_n d\mu + \int_{S_c^o \cap F^{\varepsilon_n}} g_n d\mu \underset{(2)}{=} \int_{S_c^o \cap F^{\varepsilon_n}} g_n d\mu$$

$$\underset{(g_n \leq 1)}{\leq} \tilde{\mu}(S_o^c \cap F^{\varepsilon_n}) = \tilde{\mu}(F^{\varepsilon_n}) \leq \tilde{\mu}(F) + \frac{1}{n},$$

whence (for $n \to \infty$) we obtain $\limsup_{\alpha} \mu_\alpha^*(F) \leq \tilde{\mu}(F)$, which proves (b).

<u>(b') ➡ (b):</u> Given an arbitrary $F \in \mathcal{F}(S)$, we have as before that for every $n \in \mathbb{N}$ there exists an $F^{\varepsilon_n} \in \mathcal{G}(S)$ s.t. $\tilde{\mu}(F^{\varepsilon_n}) \leq \tilde{\mu}(F) + \frac{1}{n}$.

Let g_n be defined as before and put $F_n := \{x \in S \colon g_n(x) \in [\frac{1}{2}, 1]\}$; then

$$F_n \in \mathcal{F}(S) \cap \mathcal{B}_b(S), \; F_n \supset F \text{ for all } n \in \mathbb{N}, \text{ and}$$

$$(+) \quad F_n \cap S_o^c \subset F^{\varepsilon_n} \cap S_o^c \text{ for all } n \in \mathbb{N}.$$

(As to (+), let $x \in F_n \cap S_c^o$; then, if $S_o^c \cap \complement F^{\varepsilon_n} \neq \emptyset$, we have by construction of g_n, $d(x, S_o^c \cap \complement F^{\varepsilon_n}) \geq \frac{\varepsilon_n}{2} > 0$, whence $x \notin S_o^c \cap \complement F^{\varepsilon_n}$, and therefore $x \in F^{\varepsilon_n} \cap S_o^c$; if $S_o^c \cap \complement F^{\varepsilon_n} = \emptyset$

(and therefore $g_n \equiv 1$), it follows that $F^{\varepsilon_n} \cap S_c^o = S_o^c$ and therefore $F_n \cap S_o^c \subset S_o^c = F^{\varepsilon_n} \cap S_o^c$.)

We thus obtain

$$\limsup_\alpha \mu_\alpha^*(F) \leq \limsup_\alpha \mu_\alpha(F_n) \underset{(b')}{\leq} \mu(F_n)$$

$$= \mu(F_n \cap S_o^c) \underset{(+)}{\leq} \tilde{\mu}(F^{\varepsilon_n} \cap S_o^c) = \tilde{\mu}(F^{\varepsilon_n}) \leq \tilde{\mu}(F) + \frac{1}{n},$$

whence (for $n \to \infty$) $\limsup_\alpha \mu_\alpha^*(F) \leq \tilde{\mu}(F)$, which proves (b).

<u>(a) and (b) ⟹ (f):</u> Given an $A \in \mathcal{B}(S)$ with $\tilde{\mu}(\partial A) = 0$, we have

$$\tilde{\mu}(A^o) \underset{(a)}{\leq} \liminf_\alpha (\mu_\alpha)_*(A^o) \leq \liminf_\alpha (\mu_\alpha)_*(A) \leq \liminf_\alpha \mu_\alpha^*(A)$$

$$\leq \limsup_\alpha \mu_\alpha^*(A) \leq \limsup_\alpha \mu_\alpha^*(A^c) \underset{(b)}{\leq} \tilde{\mu}(A^c) = \tilde{\mu}(A^o), \text{ whence}$$

$$\lim_\alpha \mu_\alpha^*(A) = \tilde{\mu}(A).$$

On the other hand, one obtains in the same way that

$$\tilde{\mu}(A^o) \leq \liminf_\alpha (\mu_\alpha)_*(A) \leq \limsup_\alpha (\mu_\alpha)_*(A) \leq \limsup_\alpha \mu_\alpha^*(A^c)$$

$\leq \tilde{\mu}(A^c) = \tilde{\mu}(A^o)$, whence also $\lim_\alpha (\mu_\alpha)_*(A) = \tilde{\mu}(A)$, which proves (f).

This concludes the proof of the Portmanteau theorem. □

<u>IDENTIFICATION OF LIMITS:</u>

Let $\mathcal{C}$ be the set of all closed balls in $S = (S,d)$ and let $\mathcal{C}^{\cap f}$ denote the class of all subsets of S which are finite intersections of sets in $\mathcal{C}$. Then, since $\mathcal{C}^{\cap f}$ is a $\cap$-closed generator of $\mathcal{B}_b(S)$, we have for any two $\mu_i \in \mathcal{M}_b(S)$, $i=1,2$, that $\mu_1 = \mu_2$ if $\mu_1(A) = \mu_2(A)$ for all $A \in \mathcal{C}^{\cap f}$ (cf. Gaenssler-Stute (1977), Satz 1.4.10).

We will show below that for any net (μ_α) in $M_a(S)$ and any $\mu_i \in \mathcal{M}_b(S)$, $\mu_\alpha \xrightarrow[b]{} \mu_i$, $i=1,2$, implies $\mu_1 = \mu_2$.

For this we need the following auxiliary result:

(29) For any $A\subset S$, any $\varepsilon>0$, and any separable $S_o\subset S$, there exists an $f_\varepsilon\in U_b^b(S)$ such that $0\leq f\leq 1$,
$\text{rest}_{\complement(A\cap S_o^c)^\varepsilon} f_\varepsilon \equiv 0$ and $\text{rest}_{A\cap S_o^c} f_\varepsilon \equiv 1$.

<u>Proof.</u> It follows from Lemma 11 (ii) that

$$f_\varepsilon(x) := \max\left[\left(1 - \frac{d(x,A\cap S_o^c)}{\varepsilon}\right),0\right],\ x\in S,$$

has the stated properties. □

<u>LEMMA 13.</u> Let $\mu_i\in M_b(S)$ be separable, $i=1,2$, and suppose that

(+) $\int f d\mu_1 = \int f d\mu_2$ for all $f\in U_b^b(S)$;

then $\mu_1 = \mu_2$.

<u>Proof.</u> Let S_i be the separable subsets of S for which $\mu_i(S_i^c) = \mu_i(S)$, $i=1,2$; put $S_o := S_1^c\cup S_2^c$ to get a separable subset of S for which $\mu_i(S_o^c) = \mu_i(S)$, $i=1,2$. Now, given an arbitrary $A\in C^{\cap f}$ and $n\in\mathbb{N}$, choose $f_n \equiv f_{1/n}$ according to (29) to get a sequence $(f_n)\subset U_b^b(S)$ for which

$\lim_{n\to\infty} f_n = 1_{A\cap S_c^o}$; from this, by Lebesgue's theorem and (+)

it follows that

$$\mu_1(A) = \mu_1(A\cap S_o^c) = \mu_2(A\cap S_o^c) = \mu_2(A). \quad \square$$

Lemma 13, together with the equivalence of (g') and (h') in (28) implies the result announced above (cf. Definition 4 (i)):

<u>Lemma 14.</u> For any net (μ_α) in $M_a(S)$ with $\mu_\alpha \xrightarrow[b]{} \mu_i$, $i=1,2$, we have $\mu_1 = \mu_2$.

<u>WEAK CONVERGENCE AND MAPPINGS (Continuous Mapping Theorems):</u>

Let $S = (S,d)$ and $S' = (S',d')$ be two metric spaces and suppose again that $\mathcal{A}$ is a σ-algebra of subsets of S such that $\mathcal{B}_b(S) \subset \mathcal{A} \subset \mathcal{B}(S)$; let $g: S \to S'$ be $\mathcal{A},\mathcal{B}_b(S')$-measurable and let $\mu_\alpha\in M_a(S)$ and $\mu\in M_b(S)$, respectively, μ separable. Then μ_α and μ induce measures ν_α and ν on $\mathcal{B}_b(S')$, defined by

$\nu_\alpha(B') := \mu_\alpha(g^{-1}(B'))$ and $\nu(B') := \tilde{\mu}(g^{-1}(B'))$ for $B' \in \mathcal{B}_b(S')$, where $g^{-1}(B') = \{x \in S: g(x) \in B'\}$ and where $\tilde{\mu}$ is again the unique Borel extension of μ (cf. (24)).

We are interested in conditions on g under which $\mu_\alpha \xrightarrow[b]{} \mu$ implies $\nu_\alpha \equiv \mu_\alpha \circ g^{-1} \xrightarrow[b]{} \nu \equiv \tilde{\mu} \circ g^{-1}$. It can be shown by examples that measurability of g alone is not sufficient for preserving weak convergence. As we will see, some continuity assumptions on g will be needed. The corresponding theorems are then usually called <u>CONTINUOUS MAPPING THEOREMS</u>.

<u>THEOREM 3.</u>

Let $S = (S,d)$ and $S' = (S',d')$ be metric spaces, let A be a σ-algebra of subsets of S such that $\mathcal{B}_b(S) \subset A \subset \mathcal{B}(S)$, and let $g: S \to S'$ be $A,\mathcal{B}_b(S')$-measurable and continuous. Let (μ_α) be a net in $M_a(S)$ and let $\mu \in M_b(S)$ be separable such that $\mu_\alpha \xrightarrow[b]{} \mu$. Then $\nu_\alpha \equiv \mu_\alpha \circ g^{-1} \xrightarrow[b]{} \nu \equiv \tilde{\mu} \circ g^{-1}$.

Theorem 3 is a special case of the following result where the continuity assumption on g is weakened:

<u>THEOREM 4.</u> Let $S = (S,d)$ and $S' = (S',d')$ be metric spaces, let A be a σ-algebra of subsets of S such that $\mathcal{B}_b(S) \subset A \subset \mathcal{B}(S)$, and let (μ_α) be a net in $M_a(S)$ and $\mu \in M_b(S)$ be separable such that $\mu_\alpha \xrightarrow[b]{} \mu$; let $g: S \to S'$ be $A,\mathcal{B}_b(S')$-measurable such that $\tilde{\mu}(D(g)) = 0$. Then $\nu_\alpha \equiv \mu_\alpha \circ g^{-1} \xrightarrow[b]{} \nu \equiv \tilde{\mu} \circ g^{-1}$.
(Note that $D(g) \in \mathcal{B}(S)$; cf. P. Billingsley (1968), p. 225-226.)

<u>Proof.</u> Note that $\nu_\alpha \in M_b(S')$ and $\nu \in M_b(S')$, whence $\nu_\alpha \xrightarrow[b]{} \nu$ iff (i) ν is separable and (ii) $\lim_\alpha \int_{S'} f d\nu_\alpha = \int_{S'} f d\nu$ for all $f \in C_b^b(S')$ where (ii) is equivalent to any of the conditions (a)-(h') in (28) (with S replaced by S' and A replaced by $A' = \mathcal{B}_b(S')$).

1.) ν is separable:

since μ is separable, there exists a separable $S_o \subset S$ such that $\mu(S_o^c) = \mu(S)$.

Let $T_o \subset S_o$ be countable and dense in S_o (as well as in S_o^c) and let $T_o' := g(T_o)$; we will show that $S_o' := g(S_o^c \setminus D(g)) \cup T_o'$ is a separable subset of S' with $\nu((S_o')^c) = \nu(S')$.

For this we will show that T_o' (being countable) is dense in S_o': in fact, let (w.l.o.g.) $y \in g(S_o^c \setminus D(g))$, i.e., $y = g(x)$ for some $x \in S_o^c \setminus D(g)$. Since T_o is dense in S_o^c there exists a sequence $(x_n)_{n\in\mathbb{N}} \subset T_o$ such that $x_n \to x$ and therefore, since $x \notin D(g)$, we have $g(x_n) \to g(x) = y$, where $g(x_n) \in T_o'$. Next, since $g^{-1}((S_o')^c) \supset g^{-1}(g(S_o^c \setminus D(g))) \supset S_o^c \setminus D(g)$ and since $\tilde{\mu}(D(g)) = 0$, we have

$$\nu((S_o')^c) = \tilde{\mu}(g^{-1}((S_o')^c)) \geq \tilde{\mu}(S_o^c \setminus D(g)) = \tilde{\mu}(S_o^c) - \tilde{\mu}(S_o^c \cap D(g))$$

$$= \tilde{\mu}(S_o^c) = \mu(S_o^c) = \mu(S) = \tilde{\mu}(S) = \tilde{\mu}(g^{-1}(S')) = \nu(S').$$

2.) It remains to show (ii) $\lim_\alpha \int_{S'} f d\nu_\alpha = \int_{S'} f d\nu$ for all $f \in C_b^b(S')$.

For this, given any $f \in C_b^b(S')$, we have that $f \circ g: S \to \mathbb{R}$ is a bounded function belonging to $\mathcal{F}_a(S)$ which is $\tilde{\mu}$-a.e. continuous, and therefore it follows from (28) (cf. (e')) that

$$\lim_\alpha \int_{S'} f d\nu_\alpha = \lim_\alpha \int_S (f \circ g) d\mu_\alpha = \int_S (f \circ g) d\tilde{\mu} = \int_{S'} f d\nu, \text{ which proves (ii). } \square$$

The following lemma is in some sense an inverse result:

<u>LEMMA 15.</u> Let $S = (S,d)$ be a metric space, (μ_α) be a net in $M_a(S)$ and let $\mu \in M_b(S)$ be separable such that $\mu_\alpha \circ f^{-1} \xrightarrow[b]{} \tilde{\mu} \circ f^{-1}$ for all $f \in C_a^b(S)$. Then $\mu_\alpha \xrightarrow[b]{} \mu$.

<u>Proof.</u> Note that in the present case $S' = \mathbb{R}$ (a separable metric space), whence $\nu_\alpha \equiv \mu_\alpha \circ f^{-1}$ and $\nu \equiv \tilde{\mu} \circ f^{-1}$ are separable Borel measures on $\mathcal{B} = \mathcal{B}(\mathbb{R})$. Now, for any $f \in C_a^b(S)$ and any $g \in C_b^b(\mathbb{R}) = C^b(\mathbb{R})$ we have

$$\lim_\alpha \int_S (g \circ f) d\mu_\alpha = \lim_\alpha \int_{\mathbb{R}} g d\nu_\alpha = \int_{\mathbb{R}} g d\nu = \int_S (g \circ f) d\tilde{\mu}.$$

Furthermore, for any $f \in C_a^b(S)$ there exists a $c>0$ such that $|f| \leq c$, whence for

$$g(t) := \begin{cases} -c, & \text{if } t<-c \\ t, & \text{if } |t| \leq c, t \in \mathbb{R}, \\ c, & \text{if } t>c \end{cases}$$

we have $g \in C^b(\mathbb{R})$ and $g \circ f = f$. Therefore it follows that $\lim_\alpha \int f d\mu_\alpha = \int f d\tilde{\mu}$ for all $f \in C_a^b(S)$ implying the assertion since μ is, by assumption, separable. □

For the next mapping theorem we need the following auxiliary lemma, the proof of which is left to the reader.

LEMMA 16. Let $S = (S,d)$ and $S' = (S',d')$ be metric spaces; given g_n, $g: S \to S'$, $n \in \mathbb{N}$, let

$E \equiv E((g_n),g) := \{x \in S: \exists (x_n)_{n\in\mathbb{N}} \subset S \text{ s.t. } x_n \to x \text{ but } g_n(x_n) \not\to g(x)\}$.

Then $x \notin E$ iff for every $\varepsilon>0$ there exists a $k \in \mathbb{N}$ and a $\delta>0$ such that $n \geq k$ and $d(x,y) < \delta$ together imply $d'(g(x),g_n(y)) < \varepsilon$.

THEOREM 5. Let $S = (S,d)$ and $S' = (S',d')$ be metric spaces, A be a σ-algebra of subsets of S such that $\mathcal{B}_b(S) \subset A \subset \mathcal{B}(S)$, and let $(\mu_n)_{n\in\mathbb{N}}$ be a sequence in $M_a(S)$ and $\mu \in M_b(S)$ be separable such that $\mu_n \underset{b}{\rightarrow} \mu$; let g_n, $g: S \to S'$ be $A,\mathcal{B}_b(S')$-measurable, $n \in \mathbb{N}$, such that

$\tilde{\mu}^*(E) = \inf\{\tilde{\mu}(B): B \supset E, B \in A\} = 0$. Then $\nu_n \equiv \mu_n \circ g_n^{-1} \underset{b}{\rightarrow} \nu \equiv \tilde{\mu} \circ g^{-1}$.

Proof. (cf. P. Billingsley (1968), Proof of Th. 5.5).

1.) ν is separable: this is shown as in the proof of Theorem 4, replacing $g(T_o)$ there by $T_o' := \bigcup_{n\in\mathbb{N}} g_n(T_o)$.

2.) We are going to show

$$(+)\quad \lim_{n\to\infty} \nu_n(S') = \nu(S')$$

and

$$(++)\quad \liminf_{n\to\infty} \nu_n(G) \geq \nu(G) \text{ for all } G \in \mathcal{G}(S') \cap \mathcal{B}_b(S').$$

(Note that (+) together with (++) imply the assertion according to (28) with S replaced by S' and A replaced by $A' = \mathcal{B}_b(S')$.)

ad (+): $\mu_n \underset{b}{\rightarrow} \mu$ implies (cf. (28)) $\mu_n(S) \to \mu(S)$ and therefore

$\nu_n(S') = \mu_n(g_n^{-1}(S')) = \mu_n(S) \to \mu(S) = \tilde{\mu}(S) = \tilde{\mu}(g^{-1}(S')) = \nu(S')$.

ad (++): Given an arbitrary $G \in \mathcal{G}(S') \cap \mathcal{B}_b(S')$, we have

(a) $g^{-1}(G) \subset E \cup \bigcup_{k\in\mathbb{N}} T_k^o$, where $T_k := \bigcap_{n\geq k} g_n^{-1}(G) \in \mathcal{A}$,

and

(b) $\nu(G) = \tilde{\mu}(g^{-1}(G)) \leq \mu(\bigcup_{k\in\mathbb{N}} T_k^o)$.

<u>ad (a):</u> It suffices to show that $x \in \complement E$ and $g(x) \in G$ together imply $x \in T_k^o$ for some k. Now, since $G \in \mathcal{G}(S')$ we have that for some $\varepsilon>0$ $B_{d'}(g(x),\varepsilon) \subset G$; on the other hand, by Lemma 16 $x \in \complement E$ implies that there exists a $k \in \mathbb{N}$ and a $\delta>0$ such that $d'(g(x),g_n(y)) < \varepsilon$ whenever $n\geq k$ and $d(x,y) < \delta$; therefore $g_n(y) \in G$ for all $n\geq k$ and all $y \in S$ with $d(x,y) < \delta$ implying $B_d(x,\delta) \subset g_n^{-1}(G)$ for all $n\geq k$, whence $B_d(x,\delta) \subset T_k$, and therefore $x \in T_k^o$.

<u>ad (b):</u> $\tilde{\mu}(g^{-1}(G)) \underset{(a)}{\leq} \tilde{\mu}^*(E \cup \bigcup_{k\in\mathbb{N}} T_k^o) \leq \tilde{\mu}^*(E) + \tilde{\mu}^*(\bigcup_{k\in\mathbb{N}} T_k^o)$

$= \tilde{\mu}^*(\bigcup_{k\in\mathbb{N}} T_k^o)$; note that for $A \in \mathcal{B}(S)$, $\tilde{\mu}^*(A) \geq \tilde{\mu}(A)$ by (23); we will show that even $\tilde{\mu}^* = \tilde{\mu}$ on $\mathcal{B}(S)$ which proves (b).

For this, let $A \in \mathcal{B}(S)$; it suffices to show that $\tilde{\mu}^*(A) \leq \tilde{\mu}(A)$.

Now, $\tilde{\mu}(A) = \tilde{\mu}(S_o^c \cap A) = \tilde{\mu}(S_o^c \cap A')$ for some $A' \in \mathcal{B}_b(S)$ (noticing that for separable S_o^c one has $S_o^c \cap A \in \mathcal{B}(S_o^c) = \mathcal{B}_b(S_o^c) = S_o^c \cap \mathcal{B}_b(S)$), and therefore $\tilde{\mu}(S_o^c \cap A') = \mu(A' \cup \complement S_o^c) \geq \tilde{\mu}^*(A)$, since $A \subset A' \cup \complement S_o^c \in \mathcal{B}_b(S) \subset \mathcal{A}$.

Now, since $T_k^o \subset T_{k+1}^o$ and therefore $\tilde{\mu}(T_k^o) \uparrow \tilde{\mu}(\bigcup_{k\in\mathbb{N}} T_k^o)$, for every $\varepsilon>0$, there exists a $k_o \in \mathbb{N}$ such that

$$\tilde{\mu}(\bigcup_{k\in\mathbb{N}} T_k^o) \leq \tilde{\mu}(T_k^o) + \varepsilon \text{ for all } k \geq k_o,$$

and therefore, by (b), we obtain

$$\nu(G) \leq \tilde{\mu}(T_k^o) + \varepsilon \text{ for all } k \geq k_o.$$

But $\mu_n \xrightarrow[b]{} \mu$ implies (cf. (28)) that for every $k\in\mathbb{N}$

$$\tilde{\mu}(T_k^o) \leq \liminf_{n\to\infty} (\mu_n)_*(T_k^o),$$

and therefore, noticing that $T_k^o \subset g_n^{-1}(G)$ for sufficiently large n, we obtain

$$\tilde{\mu}(T_k^o) \leq \liminf_{n\to\infty} \mu_n(g_n^{-1}(G)) = \liminf_{n\to\infty} \nu_n(G),$$

whence $\nu(G) \leq \liminf_{n\to\infty} \nu_n(G) + \varepsilon$ for every $\varepsilon>0$, which implies (++). □

WEAK CONVERGENCE CRITERIA AND COMPACTNESS:

As before, let $S = (S,d)$ be a (possibly non-separable) metric space, let $M_a^1(S)$ be the space of all p-measures on a σ-algebra $\mathcal{A}$ with $\mathcal{B}_b(S) \subset \mathcal{A} \subset \mathcal{B}(S)$ and let $M_b^1(S)$ be the space of all p-measures on $\mathcal{B}_b(S)$.

DEFINITION 5. Let $(\mu_\alpha)_{\alpha\in A}$ be a net in $M_a^1(S)$; then $(\mu_\alpha)_{\alpha\in A}$ is called δ-tight iff

(30) $$\sup_{K\in\mathcal{K}(S)} \inf_{\delta>0} \liminf_{\alpha\in A} \mu_\alpha(K^\delta) = 1.$$

(Note that $K^\delta \in \mathcal{B}_b(S) \subset \mathcal{A}$ according to Lemma 11 (ii).)

The following two results were proved by M.J. Wichura (1968), Th. 1.3 and Th. 1.4; in view of (27) b) they can be restated as follows (where in Theorem 7 the assumption of (S,d) being topologically complete cannot be dispensed with, in general).

THEOREM 6 (Wichura). Let $(\mu_\alpha)_{\alpha\in A} \subset M_a^1(S)$ be δ-tight.
Then there exists a subnet $(\mu_{\alpha'})_{\alpha'\in A'}$ of $(\mu_\alpha)_{\alpha\in A}$ and a separable $\mu\in M_b^1(S)$ such that $\mu_{\alpha'} \xrightarrow[b]{} \mu$.

THEOREM 7 (Wichura). Let $S = (S,d)$ be a topologically complete metric space and (μ_α) be a net in $M_a^1(S)$; then there exists a separable $\mu\in M_b^1(S)$ with $\mu_\alpha \xrightarrow[b]{} \mu$ iff

(a) $\liminf_\alpha \int f d\mu_\alpha = \limsup_\alpha \int f d\mu_\alpha$ for all $f \in U_b^b(S)$,

and (b) (μ_α) is δ-tight.

We are going to prove here instead the following versions of Theorem 6 and 7 (cf. Remark (31) below):

THEOREM 6*. Let $(\mu_\alpha)_{\alpha\in A}$ be a net in $M_a^1(S)$ fulfilling the following two conditions:

(b_1) For every $(f_n)_{n\in\mathbb{N}} \subset U_b^b(S)$ with $f_n \downarrow 0$ one has

$$\limsup_\alpha \int f_n d\mu_\alpha \to 0 \text{ as } n\to\infty.$$

(b_2) There exists a separable $S_o \subset S$ such that

$$\liminf_\alpha \int f d\mu_\alpha \geq 1 \text{ for all } f \in U_b^b(S) \text{ with } f \geq 1_{S_o^c} .$$

Then there exists a subnet $(\mu_{\alpha'})_{\alpha'\in A'}$ of $(\mu_\alpha)_{\alpha\in A}$ and a separable $\mu \in M_b^1(S)$ with $\mu(S_o^c) = 1$ such that $\mu_\alpha \xrightarrow[b]{} \mu$.

THEOREM 7*. Let $S = (S,d)$ be an arbitrary metric space and (μ_α) be a net in $M_a^1(S)$; then there exists a separable $\mu \in M_b^1(S)$ with $\mu_\alpha \xrightarrow[b]{} \mu$ iff the following conditions are fulfilled:
(a) as in Theorem 7 and (b_i), i=1,2, as in Theorem 6*, where in this connection the separable S_o with $\mu(S_o^c) = 1$ and the separable S_o occurring in (b_2) coincide.

Proof of Theorem 6*. Let $\mu_\alpha(f) := \int f d\mu_\alpha$ for $f \in U_b^b(S)$ and consider the net

$$\alpha \mapsto (\mu_\alpha(f))_{f\in U_b^b(S)} \in \prod_{f\in U_b^b(S)} [-\|f\|,\|f\|]$$

where $\|f\| := \sup_{x\in S} |f(x)|$. Since the product space $\prod_{f\in U_D^b(S)} [-\|f\|,\|f\|]$ is compact in the product topology (Tychonov's theorem), there exists a convergent subnet, say $\alpha' \mapsto (\mu_{\alpha'}(f))_{f\in U_b^b(S)}$, $\alpha'\in A'$. Therefore $\lim_{\alpha'\in A'} \mu_{\alpha'}(f)$ exists for each $f \in U_b^b(S)$.

Let $\mu(f) := \lim_{\alpha'\in A'} \mu_{\alpha'}(f)$ for $f \in U_b^b(S)$;

then $\mu: U_b^b(S) \longrightarrow \mathbb{R}$ is positive, linear, and normed.

We are going to show that μ is also σ-smooth on $U_b^b(S)$:

for this, let $(f_n)_{n\in\mathbb{N}} \subset U_b^b(S)$ with $f_n \downarrow 0$; then it follows by (b_1) that

$$\mu(f_n) = \lim_{\alpha'} \mu_{\alpha'}(f_n) = \limsup_{\alpha'} \int f_n d\mu_{\alpha'}$$

$$\leq \limsup_{\alpha} \int f_n d\mu_\alpha \to 0 \text{ as } n\to\infty.$$

Therefore, according to the Daniell-Stone representation theorem, there exists one and only one $\mu \in \mathcal{M}_b^1(S)$ such that

$$\mu(f) = \int f d\mu \text{ for all } f \in U_b^b(S).$$

Hence, in view of (28) (cf. the equivalence of (g') and (h')) it follows that $\mu_{\alpha'} \xrightarrow[b]{} \mu$, if we finally show that $\mu(S_o^c) = 1$ (i.e. μ separable).
For this we use (b_2) according to which

$$(+) \quad \liminf_{\alpha} \int f d\mu_\alpha \geq 1 \text{ for all } f \in U_b^b(S) \text{ with } f \geq 1_{S_o^c};$$

taking

$$f_n(x) := \max\,[1 - nd(x,S_o^c),0],\ x\in S,$$

we obtain a sequence $(f_n)_{n\in\mathbb{N}} \subset U_b^b(S)$ with $0 \leq f_n \leq 1$ and $1_{S_o^c} \leq f_n \leq 1_{(S_o^c)^{1/n}}$, whence by the σ-smoothness of μ

(note that $S_o^c, (S_o^c)^{1/n} \in \mathcal{B}_b(S)$ by Lemma 11 (ii)),

$$\mu(S_o^c) = \inf_{n\in\mathbb{N}} \mu((S_o^c)^{1/n}) \geq \inf_n \int f_n d\mu = \inf_n \lim_{\alpha'} \int f_n d\mu_{\alpha'}$$

$$\geq \inf_n \liminf_{\alpha} \int f_n d\mu_\alpha \underset{(+)}{\geq} 1, \text{ whence } \mu(S_o^c) = 1. \quad \square$$

<u>Proof of Theorem 7*.</u> <u>Only if-part:</u> Suppose $\mu_\alpha \xrightarrow[b]{} \mu$; then (a) is a consequence of (28) (cf. the equivalent statements (g') and (h')).

<u>ad (b_1):</u> Let $(f_n)_{n\in\mathbb{N}} \subset U_b^b(S)$ with $f_n \downarrow 0$; then (cf. again the equivalence of (g') and (h') in (28)) $\limsup_{\alpha} \int f_n d\mu_\alpha = \lim_{\alpha} \int f_n d\mu_\alpha = \int f_n d\mu \to 0$ as $n\to\infty$ according to the σ-smoothness of μ on $U_b^b(S)$.

<u>ad (b_2):</u> Since, by assumption, μ is separable, there exists a separable $S_o \subset S$

such that $\mu(S_o^c) = \mu(S)$; therefore, for any $f \in U_b^b(S)$ with $f \geq 1_{S_o^c}$ one has

$$\liminf_\alpha \int f d\mu_\alpha = \lim_\alpha \int f d\mu_\alpha = \int f d\mu \geq \mu(S_o^c) = \mu(S) = 1.$$

<u>If-part:</u> It suffices to show that there exists a $\mu \in M_b^1(S)$ with $\mu(S_o^c) = 1$ such that for any subnet $(\mu_{\alpha'})$ of (μ_α) there exists a further subnet $(\mu_{\alpha''})$ such that $\mu_{\alpha''} \xrightarrow[b]{} \mu$.

For this, let $(\mu_{\alpha'})_{\alpha' \in A'}$ be an arbitrary subnet of $(\mu_\alpha)_{\alpha \in A}$; then it is easy to show that $(\mu_{\alpha'})_{\alpha' \in A'}$ fulfills (b_1) and (b_2) and therefore, by Theorem 6*, there exists a subnet $(\mu_{\alpha''})_{\alpha'' \in A''}$ of $(\mu_{\alpha'})_{\alpha' \in A'}$ and a $\mu_{A',A''} \in M_b^1(S)$ with $\mu_{A',A''}(S_o^c) = 1$, such that $\mu_{\alpha''} \xrightarrow[b]{} \mu_{A',A''}$.

We are going to show that $\mu_{A',A''}$ in fact does not depend on A' or A", whence for μ being the common value of all the $\mu_{A',A''}$ we get $\mu_\alpha \xrightarrow[b]{} \mu$, which will conclude the proof.

For this, given any $f \in U_b^b(S)$, we have by (a)

$$\liminf_{\alpha \in A} \int f d\mu_\alpha \leq \liminf_{\alpha'' \in A''} \int f d\mu_{\alpha''} = \int f d\mu_{A',A''}$$

$$= \limsup_{\alpha'' \in A''} \int f d\mu_{\alpha''} \leq \limsup_{\alpha \in A} \int f d\mu_\alpha = \liminf_{\alpha \in A} \int f d\mu_\alpha,$$

whence $\int f d\mu_{A',A''} = \int f d\mu_{\tilde{A}',\tilde{A}''}$, for all $f \in U_b^b(S)$

and any other subnet $(\mu_{\tilde{\alpha}''})_{\tilde{\alpha}'' \in \tilde{A}''}$ of $(\mu_{\tilde{\alpha}'})_{\tilde{\alpha}' \in \tilde{A}'}$

which is a subnet of $(\mu_\alpha)_{\alpha \in A}$, with $\mu_{\tilde{\alpha}''} \xrightarrow[b]{} \mu_{\tilde{A}',\tilde{A}''}$;

therefore Lemma 13 implies the assertion. □

<u>(31) REMARK.</u> Any δ-tight net $(\mu_\alpha) \subset M_a^1(S)$ fulfills (b_i), i=1,2, but not vice versa (look at $\mu_\alpha \equiv \mu$ with a separable $\mu \in M_b^1(S)$ which is not tight).

<u>Proof.</u> <u>ad (b_1):</u> Let $(f_n)_{n \in \mathbb{N}} \subset U_b^b(S)$ with $f_n \downarrow 0$ and assume w.l.o.g. $\sup_n f_n \leq 1$; then for every $n \in \mathbb{N}$, every $\delta > 0$, and every $K \in \mathcal{K}(S)$ we have

$$\limsup_\alpha \int f_n d\mu_\alpha = \limsup_\alpha \left(\int_{K^\delta} f_n d\mu_\alpha + \int_{\complement K^\delta} f_n d\mu_\alpha \right)$$

$$\leq \limsup_\alpha \int_{K^\delta} f_n d\mu_\alpha + \limsup_\alpha \int_{\complement K^\delta} f_n d\mu_\alpha$$

$$\leq \text{(since } f_n \leq 1) \sup_{x\in K^\delta} f_n(x) + \limsup_\alpha \mu_\alpha(\complement K^\delta) \leq \sup_{x\in K^\delta} f_n(x) + \sup_{\delta>0} \limsup_\alpha \mu_\alpha(\complement K^\delta).$$

Now, given any $\varepsilon>0$, there exists by assumption (cf. (30) and look at complements) a $K_\varepsilon \in K(S)$ such that $\sup_{\delta>0} \limsup_\alpha \mu_\alpha(\complement K_\varepsilon^\delta) \leq \varepsilon/3$.

Therefore, for any $\varepsilon>0$ there exists a $K_\varepsilon \in K(S)$ such that for all $n \in \mathbb{N}$ and $\delta>0$

$$\limsup_\alpha \int f_n d\mu_\alpha \leq \sup \{f_n(x): x \in K_\varepsilon^\delta\} + \varepsilon/3.$$

Furthermore, it is easy to show that for any $\varepsilon>0$ and $n \in \mathbb{N}$ there exists a $\delta(\varepsilon,n)$ such that

$$\sup \{f_n(x): x \in K_\varepsilon^{\delta(\varepsilon,n)}\} \leq \sup \{f_n(x): x \in K_\varepsilon\} + \varepsilon/3.$$

We thus obtain that for any $\varepsilon>0$ there exists a $K_\varepsilon \in K(S)$ such that for every $n \in \mathbb{N}$

$$\limsup_\alpha \int f_n d\mu_\alpha \leq \sup \{f_n(x): x \in K_\varepsilon\} + \varepsilon/3 + \varepsilon/3.$$

But, since K_ε is compact, $\sup \{f_n(x): x \in K_\varepsilon\} \to 0$ as $n\to\infty$, whence $\limsup_\alpha \int f_n d\mu_\alpha \leq \varepsilon$ for sufficiently large n, which implies (b_1).

<u>ad (b_2):</u> δ-tightness of (μ_α) implies that for every $n \in \mathbb{N}$ there exists a $K_n \in K(S)$ such that $\inf_{\delta>0} \liminf_\alpha \mu_\alpha(K_n^\delta) \geq 1 - \frac{1}{n}$.

Put $S_o := \bigcup_{n\in\mathbb{N}} K_n$ to obtain a separable $S_o \subset S$; then, given any $f \in U_b^b(S)$ with $f \geq 1_{S_o^c}$, we must show that

$$(+) \quad \liminf_\alpha \int f d\mu_\alpha \geq 1.$$

Since $f \geq 1_{K_n}$ for each n, it follows (by continuity of f) that for every $n \in \mathbb{N}$ and every $\varepsilon>0$ there exists a $\delta_o = \delta_o(\varepsilon,n) > 0$ such that $\inf \{f(x): x \in K_n^{\delta_o}\} \geq 1 - \varepsilon$, whence $\int f d\mu_\alpha \geq (1-\varepsilon)\, \mu_\alpha(K_n^{\delta_o})$. Therefore, for every $\varepsilon>0$ and every $n \in \mathbb{N}$ we have $\liminf_\alpha \int f d\mu_\alpha \geq (1-\varepsilon) \liminf_\alpha \mu_\alpha(K_n^{\delta_o})$

$\geqq (1-\varepsilon) \inf_\delta \liminf_\alpha \mu_\alpha(K_n^\delta) \geqq (1-\varepsilon)(1-\frac{1}{n})$, which implies (b_2). □

(32) Remark. The proof of Theorem 7^* shows that any net $(\mu_\alpha)_{\alpha\in A} \subset M_a^1(S)$ which fulfills (b_i), i=1,2, is a compact net in $M_a^1(S)$ (i.e. for any subnet $(\mu_{\alpha'})_{\alpha'\in A'}$ of $(\mu_\alpha)_{\alpha\in A}$ there exists a further subnet $(\mu_{\alpha''})_{\alpha''\in A''}$ of $(\mu_{\alpha'})_{\alpha'\in A'}$ and a separable $\mu \in M_b^1(S)$ such that $\mu_{\alpha''} \xrightarrow[b]{} \mu$).

The following lemma prepares for the next theorem (cf. M.J. Wichura (1968), Theorem 1.2 (a)).

LEMMA 17. Let (μ_α) be a net in $M_a(S)$ and $\mu \in M_b(S)$ be separable, i.e., $\mu(S_o^c) = \mu(S)$ for some separable $S_o \subset S$; let $\mathcal{C} \subset \mathcal{A}$ be such that

(33) for each $x \in S_o^c$ $\{C \in \mathcal{C}: x \in C^o\}$ is a neighborhood base at x,

and let $\mathcal{C}^{\cap f}$ denote the class of all finite intersections of members of $\mathcal{C}$. Suppose that

$$(+) \quad \lim_\alpha \mu_\alpha(C) = \tilde{\mu}(C) \text{ for all } C \in \mathcal{C}^{\cap f}.$$

Then

$$\liminf_\alpha \mu_\alpha(G) \geqq \tilde{\mu}(G) \text{ for all } G \in \mathcal{G}(S) \cap \mathcal{A}.$$

(Here again $\tilde{\mu}$ denotes the unique Borel extension of μ and $\mathcal{A}$ is a σ-algebra of subsets of S with $\mathcal{B}_b(S) \subset \mathcal{A} \subset \mathcal{B}(S)$.)

Proof. Given any $G \in \mathcal{G}(S) \cap \mathcal{A}$, it follows by (33) that for every $x \in G \cap S_o^c$ there exists a $C_x \in \mathcal{C}$ such that $x \in C_x^o \subset G_x \subset G$, whence $G \cap S_o^c \subset \bigcup_{x\in G\cap S_o^c} C_x^o$, which means that $\{C_x^o \cap S_o^c : x \in G \cap S_o^c\}$ is an open covering of $G \cap S_o^c$ in the separable subspace (S_o^c, d) of (S,d). Therefore (cf. Billingsley (1968), p. 216) there exists a countable subcovering of $G \cap S_o^c$, i.e.,

$$G \cap S_o^c \subset \bigcup_{n\in\mathbb{N}} (C_{x_n}^o \cap S_o^c) \text{ with } x_n \in G \cap S_o^c,\ n \in \mathbb{N}.$$

Put $C_n := C_{x_n}$, $n \in \mathbb{N}$; then $\bigcup_{n\in\mathbb{N}} C_n \subset \bigcup_{x\in G\cap S_o^c} C_x \subset G$, whence

$$\tilde{\mu}(G) \geq \tilde{\mu}(\bigcup_n C_n) = \tilde{\mu}(\bigcup_n (C_n \cap S_o^c)) \geq \tilde{\mu}(G \cap S_o^c) = \tilde{\mu}(G),$$

i.e., $\tilde{\mu}(G) = \tilde{\mu}(\bigcup_n C_n)$.

Put $C_1' := C_1$ and $C_n' := C_n \setminus \bigcup_{i=1}^{n-1} C_i$, $n \geq 2$, to get pairwise disjoint sets $C_n' \in \mathcal{A}$ with $\bigcup_{n\in\mathbb{N}} C_n' = \bigcup_{n\in\mathbb{N}} C_n$, for which one can easily show (using the assumption (+)) that

$$\lim_\alpha \mu_\alpha(C_n') = \tilde{\mu}(C_n') \text{ for all } n \in \mathbb{N}.$$

Therefore, for every $n \in \mathbb{N}$ we have

$$(++) \qquad \lim_\alpha \mu_\alpha(\bigcup_{i=1}^n C_i') = \lim_\alpha \sum_{i=1}^n \mu_\alpha(C_i') = \sum_{i=1}^n \tilde{\mu}(C_i') = \tilde{\mu}(\bigcup_{i=1}^n C_i').$$

Since $\tilde{\mu}(G) = \tilde{\mu}(\bigcup_{n\in\mathbb{N}} C_n) = \tilde{\mu}(\bigcup_{n\in\mathbb{N}} C_n')$, there exists for each $\varepsilon>0$, an $n = n(\varepsilon) \in \mathbb{N}$ such that $\tilde{\mu}(\bigcup_{i=1}^n C_i') \geq \tilde{\mu}(G) - \varepsilon$, and therefore (note also that $G \supset \bigcup_{i\in\mathbb{N}} C_i'$)

$$\liminf_\alpha \mu_\alpha(G) \geq \liminf_\alpha \mu_\alpha(\bigcup_{i=1}^n C_i') \underset{(++)}{=} \tilde{\mu}(\bigcup_{i=1}^n C_i') \geq \tilde{\mu}(G) - \varepsilon,$$

which proves the assertion. □

<u>THEOREM 8.</u> Let (μ_α) be a net in $M_a^1(S)$ and $\mu \in M_b^1(S)$ be separable (i.e., $\mu(S_o^c) = \mu(S) = 1$ for some separable $S_o \subset S$).

Suppose that $\mathcal{C} \subset \{B \in \mathcal{B}_b(S) : \tilde{\mu}(\partial B) = 0\}$ fulfills (33).

Then the following two assertions are equivalent:

(i) $\lim_\alpha \mu_\alpha(C) = \mu(C)$ for all $C \in \mathcal{C}^{\cap f}$

(ii) $\mu_\alpha \xrightarrow[b]{} \mu$.

<u>Proof.</u> <u>(i) ⇒ (ii):</u> Follows immediately from Lemma 17 and (28) (cf. the equivalence of (a') and (g') there); note that $\lim_\alpha \mu_\alpha(S) = \mu(S)$ is trivially

fulfilled for p-measures μ_α and μ.

(ii) ⇒ (i): Again (28) (cf. the equivalence of (g') and (f')) yields

$\lim_\alpha \mu_\alpha(B) = \mu(B)$ for all $B \in \{B \in \mathcal{B}_b(S): \tilde{\mu}(\partial B) = 0\} =: \mathcal{R}_{\tilde{\mu}} = \mathcal{R}_{\tilde{\mu}}^{\cap f} \supset C^{\cap f}$. □

We will consider next a Cramér-type result which is useful in applications.

For this, let again $S = (S,d)$ be a (possibly non-separable) metric space, $\mathcal{A}$ be a σ-algebra of subsets of S such that $\mathcal{B}_b(S) \subset \mathcal{A} \subset \mathcal{B}(S)$, and let $(\xi_n)_{n\in\mathbb{N}}$ be a sequence of random elements in $(S,\mathcal{A})$ and ξ be a random element in $(S,\mathcal{B}_b(S))$, being all defined on a common p-space $(\Omega,\mathcal{F},\mathbb{P})$. Then

(34) ξ_n is said to converge in law to ξ (denoted by $\xi_n \xrightarrow{\mathcal{L}_b} \xi$) iff $\mathcal{L}\{\xi_n\} \xrightarrow[b]{} \mathcal{L}\{\xi\}$ (in the sense of our Definition 4).

Now, let $(\eta_n)_{n\in\mathbb{N}}$ be another sequence of random elements in $(S,\mathcal{A})$ defined on the same p-space $(\Omega,\mathcal{F},\mathbb{P})$, and let

$$d(\xi_n,\eta_n)(\omega) := d(\xi_n(\omega),\eta_n(\omega)), \ \omega \in \Omega.$$

Note that for non-separable S, $d(\xi_n,\eta_n)$ need not be a random variable.

THEOREM 9a. Suppose that in the setting just decribed

$$\lim_{n\to\infty} \mathbb{P}^*(d(\xi_n,\eta_n) > \delta) = 0 \text{ for every } \delta > 0,$$

where $\mathbb{P}^*$ denotes the outer p-measure pertaining to $\mathbb{P}$.

Then $\xi_n \xrightarrow{\mathcal{L}_b} \xi$ iff $\eta_n \xrightarrow{\mathcal{L}_b} \xi$.

Proof. By symmetry, it suffices to show that

$$\xi_n \xrightarrow{\mathcal{L}_b} \xi \quad \text{implies} \quad \eta_n \xrightarrow{\mathcal{L}_b} \xi.$$

So, assume $\xi_n \xrightarrow{\mathcal{L}_b} \xi$ and let $f \in U_b^b(S)$ be arbitrary but fixed; then according to (28) (cf. (h')) it suffices to show that

$$(+)\quad \lim_{n\to\infty} |\,\mathbb{E}(f(\xi_n)) - \mathbb{E}(f(\eta_n))| = 0.$$

(Note that $f(\xi_n)$ and $f(\eta_n)$, as well as $f(\xi)$, are random variables.)

ad (+): Given an arbitrary $\varepsilon>0$ there exists (by uniform continuity of f) a $\delta = \delta(\varepsilon) > 0$ such that $|f(x) - f(y)| \leqq \varepsilon$ whenever $d(x,y) \leqq \delta$; also $\|f\| = \sup_{x\in S} |f(x)| < \infty$.

Therefore,

$$|\,\mathbb{E}(f(\xi_n)) - \mathbb{E}(f(\eta_n))| \leqq \int |f(\xi_n) - f(\eta_n)|\, d\mathbb{P}$$

$$= \int^* |f(\xi_n) - f(\eta_n)|\, d\mathbb{P} \leqq \int^* 1_{\{d(\xi_n,\eta_n)>\delta\}}\, |f(\xi_n) - f(\eta_n)|\, d\mathbb{P}$$

$$+ \int^* 1_{\{d(\xi_n,\eta_n)\leqq\delta\}}\, |f(\xi_n) - f(\eta_n)|\, d\mathbb{P}$$

$$\leqq 2\, \|f\|\, \mathbb{P}^*(d(\xi_n,\eta_n) > \delta) + \varepsilon \to \varepsilon \text{ as } n \to \infty,$$

whence $\limsup_{n\to\infty} |\,\mathbb{E}(f(\xi_n)) - \mathbb{E}(f(\eta_n))| \leqq \varepsilon$ for every $\varepsilon > 0$,

which implies (+). □

The following version of Theorem 9a is useful as well.

THEOREM 9a*. Let $(\xi_n)_{n\in\mathbb{N}}$ and $(\eta_n)_{n\in\mathbb{N}}$ be sequences of random elements in $(S,\mathcal{A})$, defined on a common p-space $(\Omega,\mathcal{F},\mathbb{P})$ such that

(a) $\quad \lim_{n\to\infty} \mathbb{P}^*(d(\xi_n,\eta_n) > \delta) = 0$ for every $\delta > 0$.

Let $S' = (S',d')$ be another metric space and

$H: S \to S'$ be $\mathcal{A},\mathcal{B}_b(S')$-measurable,

and such that

(b) $\quad d'(H(x),H(y)) \leqq L\cdot d(x,y)$ for all $x,y \in S$

and some constant $0 < L < \infty$.

Then, for any random element ζ in $(S',\mathcal{B}_b(S'))$,

$$H(\xi_n) \xrightarrow{\mathcal{L}_b} \zeta \text{ iff } H(\eta_n) \xrightarrow{\mathcal{L}_b} \zeta.$$

Proof. $H(\xi_n)$ and $H(\eta_n)$ are random elements in $(S',\mathcal{B}_b(S'))$ for which by (a) and (b)

$$\mathbb{P}^*(d'(H(\xi_n), H(\eta_n)) > \delta) \leq \mathbb{P}^*(d(\xi_n,\eta_n) > \delta/L) \to 0$$

for every $\delta>0$, whence the assertion follows from Theorem 9a. □

REMARK. Instead of (b) it suffices to assume only that H is uniformly continuous.

THEOREM 9b. Let $(\xi_n)_{n\in\mathbb{N}}$ be a sequence of random elements in (S,A) and let ξ be a random element in $(S,\mathcal{B}_b(S))$ being all defined on some common p-space $(\Omega,F,\mathbb{P})$. Suppose that ξ is $\mathbb{P}$-a.s. constant; then $\xi_n \xrightarrow{L_b} \xi$ implies

$$\lim_{n\to\infty} \mathbb{P}^*(d(\xi_n,\xi) > \delta) = 0 \text{ for every } \delta > 0.$$

Proof. We show first

$$(+) \qquad \lim_{n\to\infty} \mathbb{E}(|f\circ\xi_n - f\circ\xi|) = 0 \text{ for all } f \in U_b^b(S).$$

In fact, for each $f \in U_b^b(S)$ we have (cf. Theorem 3) that $f\circ\xi_n \xrightarrow{L_b} f\circ\xi$, $f\circ\xi_n$ and $f\circ\xi$ being real random variables such that $f\circ\xi$ is $\mathbb{P}$-a.s. constant, whence (by classical probability theory) $f\circ\xi_n \overset{\mathbb{P}}{\to} f\circ\xi$ (where $\overset{\mathbb{P}}{\to}$ denotes convergence in probability). Since f is bounded, $\{f\circ\xi_n : n\in\mathbb{N}\}$ is uniformly integrable and therefore $f\circ\xi_n \xrightarrow{L^1} f\circ\xi$ which proves (+).

We are going to show that (+) implies

$$\lim_{n\to\infty} \mathbb{P}^*(d(\xi_n,\xi) > \delta) = 0 \text{ for every } \delta > 0.$$

For this, let $\delta>0$ be arbitrary; since $L\{\xi\}(S_o^c) = 1$ for some separable $S_o \subset S$ there exists a countable and dense subset $\{x_i : i\in\mathbb{N}\}$ of S_o^c and we have

$$(*) \qquad \mathbb{P}(\xi \in S_o^c) = 1.$$

Then, for each $i\in\mathbb{N}$, there exists an $f_i \in U_b^b(S)$ such that $0\leq f_i\leq 1$ and

$$f_i(x) = \begin{cases} 0 \text{ if } x\in B^o(x_i,\delta/4) \\ 1 \text{ if } x\in \complement B^o(x_i,\delta/2), \end{cases}$$

where $B^o(x_i,r)$ denotes the open ball with center x_i and radius r.

In fact, take

$$f_i(x) := 1 - \max\left[\left(1 - \frac{d(x, B^o(x_i,\delta/4)\cap S_o^c)}{\delta/4}\right), 0\right]$$

to get such a function.

Now, let $A_1 := \{\xi \in B^o(x_1,\delta/4)\}$ and for $i \geq 2$ let

$$A_i := \{\xi \in B^o(x_i,\delta/4),\ \xi \in \complement B^o(x_1,\delta/4), \ldots, \xi \in \complement B^o(x_{i-1},\delta/4)\};$$

then $A_i \in F$, the A_i's being pairwise disjoint and such that $\mathbb{P}(\bigcup_{i\in\mathbb{N}} A_i) = 1$ according to (*). Therefore

$$\mathbb{P}^*(d(\xi_n,\xi) > \delta) \leq \sum_{i\in\mathbb{N}} \mathbb{P}^*(\{d(\xi_n,\xi) > \delta\} \cap A_i)$$

$$\leq \sum_{i\in\mathbb{N}} \mathbb{P}^*(\{d(\xi_n,x_i) > \tfrac{3}{4}\delta\} \cap A_i) \leq \sum_{i\in\mathbb{N}} \int^* 1_{A_i} |f_i \circ \xi_n - f_i \circ \xi| \, d\mathbb{P}$$

$$= \sum_{i\in\mathbb{N}} \int_{A_i} |f_i \circ \xi_n - f_i \circ \xi| d\mathbb{P},$$

where the last inequality follows from the fact that for all $\omega \in \{d(\xi_n,x_i) > \frac{3}{4}\delta\} \cap A_i$ one has $f_i(\xi_n(\omega)) = 1$ and $f_i(\xi(\omega)) = 0$ by construction of the f_i's .

If we put $g_n(i) := \int_{A_i} |f_i \circ \xi_n - f_i \circ \xi| d\mathbb{P}$ and $g(i) := \mathbb{P}(A_i)$ for each $i \in \mathbb{N}$, we obtain functions g_n and g on $\mathbb{N}$ for which

$0 \leq g_n \leq g$ and $\sum_{i\in\mathbb{N}} g(i) = \sum_{i\in\mathbb{N}} \mathbb{P}(A_i) = \mathbb{P}(\bigcup_{i\in\mathbb{N}} A_i) = 1,$

i.e., the g_n's are integrable functions on $\mathbb{N}$ (integrable w.r.t. the counting measure on $\mathbb{N}$) being dominated by an integrable function g; since, by assumption (+),

$$\lim_{n\to\infty} g_n(i) = 0 \quad \text{for all } i \in \mathbb{N},$$

it follows from Lebesgue's dominated convergence theorem that

$$\limsup_{n\to\infty} \mathbb{P}^*(d(\xi_n,\xi) > \delta) \leq \lim_{n\to\infty} \sum_{i\in\mathbb{N}} g_n(i) = 0. \quad \square$$

Finally, concerning the speed of convergence we have the following result:

THEOREM 10. Let ξ_n, $n \in \mathbb{N}$, and η be random elements in $(S,\mathcal{A})$ defined on a common p-space $(\Omega,\mathcal{F},\mathbb{P})$ such that for some sequence $a_n \downarrow 0$

(a') $$\mathbb{P}^*(d(\xi_n,\eta) > a_n) = \mathcal{O}(a_n).$$

Let $H: S \to \mathbb{R}$ be $\mathcal{A},\mathcal{B}$-measurable and such that

(b') $$|H(x) - H(y)| \leq L \cdot d(x,y) \quad \text{for all } x,y \in S$$

and some constant $0 < L < \infty$.

Assume further that $\mathcal{L}\{H(\eta)\}$ is absolutely continuous w.r.t. Lebesgue measure λ such that

(c') $$||h|| = \sup_{t\in\mathbb{R}} |h(t)| =: M < \infty \quad \text{for} \quad h \in \frac{d\mathcal{L}\{H(\eta)\}}{d\lambda}.$$

Then

$$\sup_{t\in\mathbb{R}} |\mathbb{P}(H(\xi_n) \leq t) - \mathbb{P}(H(\eta) \leq t)| = \mathcal{O}(a_n).$$

Proof. Let $t \in \mathbb{R}$ be arbitrary but fixed; then

$$\mathbb{P}(H(\xi_n) \leq t) - \mathbb{P}(H(\eta) \leq t)$$

$$\underset{(a')}{\leq} \mathbb{P}^*(H(\xi_n) \leq t,\ d(\xi_n,\eta) \leq a_n) + \mathcal{O}(a_n) - \mathbb{P}(H(\eta) \leq t)$$

$$\underset{(b')}{\leq} \mathbb{P}(H(\xi_n) \leq t,\ |H(\xi_n) - H(\eta)| \leq L\cdot a_n) + \mathcal{O}(a_n) - \mathbb{P}(H(\eta) \leq t)$$

$$\leq \mathbb{P}(H(\eta) \leq t + L\cdot a_n) + \mathcal{O}(a_n) - \mathbb{P}(H(\eta) \leq t)$$

$$\underset{(c')}{\leq} M \cdot L \cdot a_n + \mathcal{O}(a_n) = \mathcal{O}(a_n).$$

In the same way one obtains that

$$\mathbb{P}(H(\xi_n) > t) - \mathbb{P}(H(\eta) > t) = \mathcal{O}(a_n),$$

whence also

$$\mathbb{P}(H(\eta) \leq t) - \mathbb{P}(H(\xi_n) \leq t) = \mathcal{O}(a_n),$$

so that in summary

$$\sup_{t\in\mathbb{R}} |\mathbb{P}(H(\xi_n) \leq t) - \mathbb{P}(H(\eta) \leq t)| = \mathcal{O}(a_n). \quad \square$$

SOME REMARKS ON PRODUCT SPACES:

Let $S' = (S',d')$ and $S'' = (S'',d'')$ be two (possibly non-separable) metric spaces.

Let $S := S' \times S''$ be the Cartesian product of S' and S'' and let $d := \max(d',d'')$, i.e.,

$$d((x',x''),(y',y'')) := \max(d'(x',y'),d''(x'',y''))$$

for $(x',x'') \in S$ and $(y',y'') \in S$.

Then $S = (S,d)$ is again a (possibly non-separable) metric space.

<u>REMARK.</u> (1) $\mathcal{B}_b(S) \subset \mathcal{B}_b(S') \otimes \mathcal{B}_b(S'')$

and (2) $\mathcal{B}(S') \otimes \mathcal{B}(S'') \subset \mathcal{B}(S)$,

the inclusions being strict in general as can be shown by examples.

Let A' and A'' be σ-algebras of subsets of S' and S'', respectively, such that

$$\mathcal{B}_b(S') \subset A' \subset \mathcal{B}(S') \quad \text{and} \quad \mathcal{B}_b(S'') \subset A'' \subset \mathcal{B}(S'').$$

Then

$$\mathcal{B}_b(S) \underset{(1)}{\subset} \mathcal{B}_b(S') \otimes \mathcal{B}_b(S'') \subset A' \otimes A'' \subset \mathcal{B}(S') \otimes \mathcal{B}(S'') \underset{(2)}{\subset} \mathcal{B}(S),$$

i.e., putting e.g., $A := \mathcal{B}_b(S') \otimes \mathcal{B}_b(S'')$ ... (a)

or $A := A' \otimes A''$ ... (a'),

we have again

$\mathcal{B}_b(S) \subset A \subset \mathcal{B}(S)$ for the product space $S = S' \times S''$.

Now, let ξ_n, $n \in \mathbb{N}$, be random elements in (S',A'),

ξ be a random element in $(S',\mathcal{B}_b(S'))$,

η_n, $n \in \mathbb{N}$, be random elements in (S'',A''),

and let η be a random element in $(S'',\mathcal{B}_b(S''))$;

suppose that all these random elements are defined on a common p-space $(\Omega,\mathcal{F},\mathbb{P})$.

Then (ξ_n,η_n), $n \in \mathbb{N}$, are random elements in (S,A) (for both choices of A as in (a) or (a')) and

$$(\xi,\eta) \text{ is a random element in } (S,\mathcal{B}_b(S') \otimes \mathcal{B}_b(S''))$$

as well as in $(S,\mathcal{B}_b(S))$ (cf. (1) in the above remark).

Thus, considering (ξ,η) as a random element in $(S,\mathcal{B}_b(S))$,

$$(\xi_n,\eta_n) \xrightarrow{L_b} (\xi,\eta)$$

is again defined in the sense of (34), i.e., as

$$L\{(\xi_n,\eta_n)\}\ (\in M_a(S)) \underset{b}{\rightarrow} L\{(\xi,\eta)\}\ (\in M_b(S)).$$

Supplementing the results contained in Theorems 9a and 9b we can prove within the setting just described the following Theorems 9c and 9d:

THEOREM 9c. Suppose that η equals $\mathbb{P}$-a.s. some constant c;

then $\xi_n \xrightarrow{L_b} \xi$ and $\eta_n \xrightarrow{L_b} \eta$ together imply $(\xi_n,\eta_n) \xrightarrow{L_b} (\xi,\eta)$.

Proof. According to Theorem 9b,

$\eta_n \xrightarrow{L_b} \eta$ and $\eta = c$ $\mathbb{P}$-a.s. imply $\lim_{n\to\infty} \mathbb{P}^*(d''(\eta_n,\eta) > \delta) = 0$ for every $\delta>0$.

Since $d((\xi_n,\eta_n),(\xi_n,\eta)) = \max(d'(\xi_n,\xi_n),\ d''(\eta_n,\eta)) = d''(\eta_n,\eta)$,

we thus have

$$\lim_{n\to\infty} \mathbb{P}^*(d((\xi_n,\eta_n),(\xi,\eta)) > \delta) = 0 \text{ for every } \delta>0.$$

Therefore, by Theorem 9a, the assertion of the present theorem will follow if we show

$$(+) \qquad (\xi_n,\eta) \xrightarrow{L_b} (\xi,\eta).$$

ad (+): 1.) $L\{(\xi,\eta)\}$ is separable:

since $L\{\xi\}$ is separable, there exists a separable $S'_o \subset S'$ such that $L\{\xi\}(S'^c_o) = 1$. Take $S_o := S'^c_o \times \{c\}$ to get a separable and closed subset $S_o = S^c_o$ of S for which

$$L\{(\xi,\eta)\}(S_o) = \mathbb{P}((\xi,\eta)\in S_o) = \mathbb{P}((\xi,\eta)\in S'^c_o \times \{c\})$$
$$= \mathbb{P}((\xi,c)\in S'^c_o \times \{c\}) = \mathbb{P}(\xi \in S'^c_o) = L\{\xi\}(S'^c_o) = 1.$$

2.) According to the Portmanteau theorem (cf. (h') there) it remains to show that

$$\int_S f\,d\mu_n \longrightarrow \int_S f\,d\mu \quad \text{for all } f \in U^b_b(S),$$

where $\mu_n := L\{(\xi_n,\eta)\}$ and $\mu := L\{(\xi,\eta)\}$.

Now, given any $f: S = S' \times S'' \to \mathbb{R}$ being bounded, d-uniformly continuous and $\mathcal{B}_b(S)$-measurable, it follows from (1) in the remark made at the beginning that f is also $\mathcal{B}_b(S') \otimes \mathcal{B}_b(S'')$-measurable,

whence

$$f': S' \to \mathbb{R}, \text{ defined by } f'(x') := f(x',c),\ x' \in S',$$

is $\mathcal{B}_b(S')$-measurable, and thus $f' \in U_b^b(S')$.

But now, with $\mu_n' := L\{\xi_n\}$ and $\mu' := L\{\xi\}$, we obtain from $\xi_n \xrightarrow{L_b} \xi$ (using again the Portmanteau theorem):

$$\int_S f\, d\mu_n = \int_\Omega f\circ(\xi_n,\eta_n)d\mathbb{P} = \int_\Omega f\circ(\xi_n,c)d\mathbb{P} = \int_\Omega f'\circ\xi_n\, d\mathbb{P}$$

$$= \int_{S'} f'd\mu_n' \longrightarrow \int_{S'} f'd\mu' = \int_\Omega f'\circ\xi\, d\mathbb{P} = \int_\Omega f\circ(\xi,c)\, d\mathbb{P}$$

$$= \int_\Omega f\circ(\xi,\eta)d\mathbb{P} = \int_S f\, d\mu. \quad \square$$

For sequences of independent random elements one gets

THEOREM 9d. Suppose that ξ_n and η_n are independent for each $n \in \mathbb{N}$ and suppose also that ξ and η are independent. Then the following two statements are equivalent:

(i) $\xi_n \xrightarrow{L_b} \xi$ and $\eta_n \xrightarrow{L_b} \eta$

(ii) $(\xi_n,\eta_n) \xrightarrow{L_b} (\xi,\eta)$.

Proof. (i) ⇒ (ii): 1.) $L\{(\xi,\eta)\}$ is separable:

since both, $L\{\xi\}$ and $L\{\eta\}$ are separable, there exist $S_o' \subset S'$ and $S_o'' \subset S''$ such that (S_o',d') and (S_o'',d'') are separable and

$L\{\xi\}(S_o'^c) = L\{\eta\}(S_o''^c) = 1.$

Put $S_o := S_o'^c \times S_o''^c$ to get a separable and closed subspace of $S = (S,d)$ $(S = S' \times S'',\ d = \max(d',d''))$ for which

$L\{(\xi,\eta)\}(S_o^c) = (L\{\xi\} \times L\{\eta\})(S_o'^c \times S_o''^c) = L\{\xi\}(S_o'^c) \cdot L\{\eta\}(S_o''^c) = 1.$

2.) According to the Portmanteau theorem (cf. (a') there) it remains to show

(+) $\liminf_{n\to\infty} L\{(\xi_n,\eta_n)\}(G) \geq \widetilde{L\{(\xi,\eta)\}}(G)$ for all $G \in G(S) \cap A$

(where $A = A' \otimes A''$). For this, let $\mu' := L\{\xi\}$ and $\mu'' := L\{\eta\}$ and let

$$C := \{A' \times A'' : A' \in A', \ \widetilde{\mu'}(\partial A') = 0, \ A'' \in A'', \ \widetilde{\mu''}(\partial A'') = 0\};$$

then C is closed under finite intersections, i.e. $C = C^{\cap f}$, and (33) holds which means that

for each $x \in S_o^c$ $\{C \in C: x \in C^o\}$ is a neighborhood base at x.

Furthermore, by assumption and the Portmanteau theorem (cf. (f') there), we have for $\mu'_n = L\{\xi_n\}$ and $\mu''_n = L\{\eta_n\}$

$$\lim_{n\to\infty} (\mu'_n \times \mu''_n)(A' \times A'') = \lim_{n\to\infty} \mu'_n(A')\cdot\mu''_n(A'') = \widetilde{\mu'}(A')\cdot\widetilde{\mu''}(A'')$$

$$= (\widetilde{\mu'} \times \widetilde{\mu''})(A' \times A'') = \widetilde{\mu' \times \mu''}(A' \times A'') \quad \text{for all} \quad A' \times A'' \in C = C^{\cap f},$$

whence (+) follows from Lemma 17.

<u>(ii) ⇒ (i):</u> 1.) Both $L\{\xi\}$ and $L\{\eta\}$ are separable:

since $L\{(\xi,\eta)\}$ is separable there exists a separable $S_o \subset S = S' \times S''$ such that $L\{(\xi,\eta)\}(S_o^c) = 1$. Put

$$S'_o := \{x \in S' : \exists y \in S'' \text{ such that } (x,y) \in S_o\}$$

to get a separable $S'_o \subset S'$ for which $S_o^c \subset \pi'^{-1}(S_o'^c)$, whence

$$L\{\xi\}(S_o'^c) = (L\{\xi\} \times L\{\eta\})(\pi'^{-1}(S_o'^c)) = L\{(\xi,\eta)\}(\pi'^{-1}(S_o'^c))$$

$$\geq L\{(\xi,\eta)\}(S_o^c) = 1, \text{ i.e., } L\{\xi\}(S_o'^c) = 1;$$

here π' denotes the projection of $S = S' \times S''$ onto S'.

In the same way one shows that $L\{\eta\}$ is separable.

2.) According to the Portmanteau theorem (cf. (a') there) it remains to show that for $\mu'_n = L\{\xi_n\}$ and $\mu' = L\{\xi\}$

(+) $\liminf_{n\to\infty} \mu'_n(G') \geq \widetilde{\mu'}(G')$ for all $G' \in G(S') \cap A'$

and that for $\mu''_n = L\{\eta_n\}$ and $\mu'' = L\{\eta\}$

(++) $\liminf_{n\to\infty} \mu''_n(G'') \geq \widetilde{\mu''}(G'')$ for all $G'' \in \mathcal{G}(S'') \cap \mathcal{A}''$.

We will show (+); the proof of (++) runs analogously.

ad (+): Let $G' \in \mathcal{G}(S') \cap \mathcal{A}'$ be arbitrary but fixed; then

$$\pi'^{-1}(G') = G' \times S'' \in \mathcal{A} \cap \mathcal{G}(S) \quad (\mathcal{A} = \mathcal{A}' \otimes \mathcal{A}'')$$

and $\mu'_n(G') = (\mu'_n \times \mu''_n)(\pi'^{-1}(G')) = (\mu'_n \times \mu''_n)(G' \times S'')$ for each $n \in \mathbb{N}$.

By assumption and the Portmanteau theorem (cf. (a') there) we therefore obtain

$$\liminf_{n\to\infty} \mu'_n(G') = \liminf_{n\to\infty} (\mu'_n \times \mu''_n)(G' \times S'')$$

$$\geq (\widetilde{\mu' \times \mu''})(G' \times S'') = \widetilde{\mu'}(G') \cdot \widetilde{\mu''}(S'') = \widetilde{\mu'}(G'). \quad \square$$

Remark. Using the continuous mapping theorem (Theorem 3) one easily gets an alternative proof of "(ii) ⇒ (i)" in Theorem 9d, even without imposing the independence assumptions.

SEQUENTIAL COMPACTNESS:

We have shown before (cf. (32)) that any net $(\mu_\alpha) \subset M_a^1(S)$ which fulfills (b_i), i=1,2, is a compact net in $M_a^1(S)$. At this point we ask the question whether the same is true for sequences instead of nets, i.e., whether for any sequence $(\mu_n)_{n\in\mathbb{N}} \subset M_a^1(S)$ fulfilling (b_i), i=1,2, there exists a subsequence $(\mu_{n_k})_{k\in\mathbb{N}}$ and a separable $\mu \in M_b^1(S)$ such that $\mu_{n_k} \xrightarrow[b]{} \mu$ (as $k\to\infty$).

(Note that a subnet of a sequence need not be a sequence!)

If (b_i), i=1,2, is replaced by the (stronger) assumption of $(\mu_n)_{n\in\mathbb{N}}$ being δ-tight (cf. (31)), then it follows that the answer is affirmative; in fact, as shown by Dudley (1966), Theorem 1, the following is true:

(35) For any δ-tight sequence $(\mu_n)_{n\in\mathbb{N}} \subset M_a^1(S)$ there exists a subsequence $(\mu_{n_k})_{k\in\mathbb{N}}$ of $(\mu_n)_{n\in\mathbb{N}}$ and a Borel p-measure $\tilde{\mu}$ (on $\mathcal{B}(S)$) such that

(36) $\lim_{k\to\infty} \int^* f d\mu_{n_k} = \lim_{k\to\infty} \int_* f d\mu_{n_k} = \int f d\tilde{\mu}$ for all $f \in C^b(S)$.

Based on this result we obtain in a first step the following theorem:

THEOREM 11. Let $(\mu_n)_{n\in\mathbb{N}} \subset M_a^1(S)$ be δ-tight; then there exists a subsequence $(\mu_{n_k})_{k\in\mathbb{N}}$ of $(\mu_n)_{n\in\mathbb{N}}$ and a separable $\mu \in M_b^1(S)$ such that $\mu_{n_k} \xrightarrow[b]{} \mu$.

Proof. Apply (35) to get a subsequence $(\mu_{n_k})_{k\in\mathbb{N}}$ of $(\mu_n)_{n\in\mathbb{N}}$ and a Borel p-measure $\tilde{\mu}$ for which (36) holds true. Then it can be shown as in the "(h') ⇒ (b)" part of the proof of (28) that (36) implies

$$(+) \qquad \limsup_{k\to\infty} \mu_{n_k}^*(F) \leq \tilde{\mu}(F) \quad \text{for all} \quad F \in \mathcal{F}(S).$$

(In fact, given an arbitrary $F \in \mathcal{F}(S)$, there exists for every $n\in\mathbb{N}$ an $\varepsilon_n > 0$ such that $\tilde{\mu}(F^{\varepsilon_n}) \leq \tilde{\mu}(F) + \frac{1}{n}$; taking then

$$f_n(x) := \begin{cases} d(x, \complement F^{\varepsilon_n})/\varepsilon_n & \text{if } \complement F^{\varepsilon_n} \neq \emptyset, \\ 1 \text{ if } \complement F^{\varepsilon_n} = \emptyset, \end{cases} \qquad x \in S,$$

and $g_n := \min(f_n, 1)$, we obtain a sequence of functions g_n having the following properties for every $n\in\mathbb{N}$:

① $g_n \in C^b(S)$, ② $\operatorname{rest}_{\complement F^{\varepsilon_n}} g_n \equiv 0$ and ③ $\operatorname{rest}_F g_n \equiv 1$.

Therefore, for every $n\in\mathbb{N}$ we obtain

$$\limsup_{k\to\infty} \mu_{n_k}^*(F) = \limsup_{k\to\infty} \int^* 1_F \, d\mu_{n_k} \underset{③}{\leq} \limsup_{k\to\infty} \int^* g_n \, d\mu_{n_k}$$

$$\underset{(36),①}{=} \int g_n \, d\tilde{\mu} \underset{②}{=} \int_{F^{\varepsilon_n}} g_n \, d\tilde{\mu} \leq \tilde{\mu}(F^{\varepsilon_n}) \leq \tilde{\mu}(F) + \frac{1}{n}, \text{ which implies (+).)}$$

Now, we are going to show that (due to the δ-tightness of (μ_n))

$$(++) \qquad \tilde{\mu} \text{ is necessarily tight,}$$

whence $\mu := \operatorname{rest}_{\mathcal{B}_b(S)} \tilde{\mu}$ is also tight and therefore separable (cf. (25)) and thus (noticing also (24)) we can apply (28) (cf. the equivalent statements (g) and (g')) to obtain the result, i.e., $\mu_{n_k} \xrightarrow[b]{} \mu$.

ad (++): Since $(\mu_n)_{n\in\mathbb{N}}$ is δ-tight, it follows that for every $n\in\mathbb{N}$ there exists a $K_n \in K(S)$ such that

$$(+++) \quad \liminf_{k\to\infty} \mu_{n_k}(K_n^{1/2m}) \geq 1 - \frac{1}{n} \quad \text{for all } m \in \mathbb{N}.$$

W.l.o.g. we may assume $K_n \uparrow$ and therefore

$$\tilde{\mu}(\bigcup_{n\in\mathbb{N}} K_n) = \lim_{n\to\infty} \tilde{\mu}(K_n) = \lim_{n\to\infty} (\lim_{m\to\infty} \tilde{\mu}(K_n^{1/m}))$$

$$\geq \lim_{n\to\infty} (\limsup_{m\to\infty} \tilde{\mu}((K_n^{1/2m})^c)) \underset{(+)}{\geq} \lim_n \limsup_m \limsup_{k\to\infty} \mu_{n_k}^*((K_n^{1/2m})^c)$$

$$\geq \lim_n \limsup_m \liminf_k \mu_{n_k}(K_n^{1/2m}) \underset{(+++)}{\geq} 1. \quad \square$$

The proof of Theorem 11 also shows that the following result holds true:

<u>THEOREM 11*.</u> If $S_o = (S_o, d)$ is a separable subspace of S and if $(\mu_n)_{n\in\mathbb{N}} \subset M_a^1(S)$ is <u>δ-tight w.r.t. S_o</u> (i.e., if $\sup_{K\in K(S_o)} \inf_{\delta>0} \liminf_{n\to\infty} \mu_n(K^\delta) = 1$), then there exists a subsequence $(\mu_{n_k})_{k\in\mathbb{N}}$ of $(\mu_n)_{n\in\mathbb{N}}$ and a $\mu \in M_b^1(S)$ with $\mu(S_o^c) = 1$ such that $\mu_{n_k} \xrightarrow[b]{} \mu$.

As to our question raised at the beginning, it was shown by J. Schattauer (1982) that the assertion of Theorem 11 even holds if the assumption of δ-tightness of $(\mu_n)_{n\in\mathbb{N}}$ is replaced by the (weaker) conditions (b_i), i=1,2:

<u>THEOREM 11a).</u> Let $(\mu_n)_{n\in\mathbb{N}}$ be a sequence in $M_a^1(S)$ fulfilling the following two conditions:

(b_1) For every sequence $(f_m)_{m\in\mathbb{N}} \subset U_b^b(S)$ with $f_m \downarrow 0$ one has
$\limsup_n \int f_m d\mu_n \to 0$ as $m \to \infty$.

(b_2) There exists a separable $S_o \subset S$ such that
$\liminf_n \int f\mu_n \geq 1$ for all $f \in U_b^b(S)$ with $f \geq 1_{S_o^c}$.

Then there exists a subsequence $(\mu_{n_k})_{k\in\mathbb{N}}$ of $(\mu_n)_{n\in\mathbb{N}}$ and a $\mu \in M_b^1(S)$ with $\mu(S_o^c) = 1$ such that $\mu_{n_k} \xrightarrow[b]{} \mu$ (as $k \to \infty$).

For the proof of this theorem we need an auxiliary result which is based on the following

DEFINITION. Let $S = (S,d)$ be a metric space and $A_i \subset S$, $i=1,2$; A_1 and A_2 are said to be d-strictly separated if either $A_1^{\delta_1} \cap A_2 = \emptyset$ for some $\delta_1 > 0$ or $A_1 \cap A_2^{\delta_2} = \emptyset$ for some $\delta_2 > 0$,

where $A_i^{\delta_i} := \{x \in S: d(x,A_i) < \delta_i\}$, $i=1,2$.

PROPOSITION (cf. E. Hewitt (1947), Theorem 1).

Let $S = (S,d)$ be a metric space, and let G be a subset of $U^b(S)$ such that for every d-strictly separated pair $F_1,F_2 \in F(S)$ there exists a function $g \in G$ such that $\sup_{x\in F_1} g(x) < \inf_{x\in F_2} g(x)$ (or $\sup_{x\in F_2} g(x) < \inf_{x\in F_1} g(x)$). Then G is an "analytic generator" of $U^b(S)$, i.e., for every $f \in U^b(S)$ and every positive real number ε there exist functions $f_1,\ldots,f_k \in G$ and a polynomial $P(z_1,\ldots,z_k) \equiv$

$$\sum_{\ell_1=0}^{L_1} \cdots \sum_{\ell_k=0}^{L_k} \alpha_{\ell_1\ldots\ell_k} z_1^{\ell_1} \cdots z_k^{\ell_k} \quad \text{(with real coefficients } \alpha_{\ell_1\ldots\ell_k})$$

such that

$$\|f - P(f_1,\ldots,f_k)\| := \sup_{x\in S} |f(x) - P(f_1,\ldots,f_k)(x)| < \varepsilon.$$

Proof of the proposition. This follows along the same lines as in Hewitt (1947) noticing that the functions $\psi,\varphi,h,h_1,\ldots,h_n$ and

φ, $\frac{3}{2}(\varphi - h_1)$, $(\frac{3}{2})^i(\varphi - h_1 - \frac{2}{3} h_2 - \ldots - (\frac{2}{3})^{i-1} h_i)$, $2 \leqq i \leqq n$, respectively,

occurring there are uniformly continuous which implies that the sets

$$F_1^f := \{x \in S: f(x) \leqq -\tfrac{1}{3}\} \quad\text{and}\quad F_2^f := \{x \in S: f(x) \geqq \tfrac{1}{3}\},$$

for $f \in \{\varphi, (\frac{3}{2})^i(\varphi - h_1 - \frac{2}{3} h_2 - \ldots - (\frac{2}{3})^{i-1} h_i),\ 1 \leqq i \leqq n\}$,

are d-strictly separated:

In fact, $f \in U^b(S)$ implies that for $\varepsilon = \frac{1}{6}$ there exists a $\delta>0$ such that $|f(x) - f(y)| < \frac{1}{6}$ whenever $d(x,y) < \delta$; thus given any $x \in (F_1^f)^\delta$, we have $d(x,x_o) < \delta$ for some $x_o \in F_1^f$ and therefore $|f(x) - f(x_o)| < \frac{1}{6}$ and $f(x_o) \leqq -\frac{1}{3}$ (since $x_o \in F_1^f$) which implies $f(x) \leqq -\frac{1}{6}$ for all $x \in (F_1^f)^\delta$; since $f(x) \geqq \frac{1}{3}$ for all $x \in F_2^f$, we thus have $(F_1^f)^\delta \cap F_2^f = \emptyset$. □

Proof of Theorem 11a). According to (b_2), let $T \subset S_o$ be countable and dense in S_o (as well as in S_o^c), say $T = \{x_1, x_2, \ldots\}$, and let

$G_1 := \{\min(d(\cdot, x_n), 1): n \in \mathbb{N}\}$,

$G_2 := \{f: S \to \mathbb{R}: f = \min_{1 \leq i \leq n} g_i,\ g_i \in G_1,\ i=1,\ldots,n,\ n \in \mathbb{N}\}$, and

$G_3 := \{f: S \to \mathbb{R}: f = g_1^{\ell_1} \cdots g_k^{\ell_k}$ for some $g_i \in G_2$, $\ell_1, \ldots, \ell_k \in \mathbb{N} \cup \{0\}$, $k \in \mathbb{N}\}$;

then $G_1 \subset G_2 \subset G_3$ with G_3 being a countable class of functions in $U_b^b(S)$ (cf. Lemma 11 (ii)).

Therefore, by the diagonal method, there exists a subsequence $(\mu_{n_k})_{k \in \mathbb{N}}$ of $(\mu_n)_{n \in \mathbb{N}}$ such that

(i) $\lim_{k \to \infty} \int f d\mu_{n_k}$ exists for all $f \in G_3$.

Let $G_4 := \{f: S \to \mathbb{R}: f = \min(d(\cdot, F^\varepsilon \cap S_o^c), 1)$ for some $F \in F(S_o^c)$, $\varepsilon > 0\}$;

then (cf. Lemma 11 (ii)) $G_4 \subset U_b^b(S)$, and

(ii) For any $f \in G_4$ there exists a sequence $(f_n)_{n \in \mathbb{N}} \subset G_2$ such that $f_n \downarrow f$ as $n \to \infty$.

ad (ii): Let $f \in G_4$, i.e., $f = \min(d(\cdot, F^\varepsilon \cap S_o^c), 1)$, $F \in F(S_o^c)$, $\varepsilon > 0$.

It is easy to show that $T \cap F^\varepsilon$ is countable and dense in $F^\varepsilon \cap S_o^c$; let $T \cap F^\varepsilon = \{z_1, z_2, \ldots\}$; then $d(\cdot, F^\varepsilon \cap S_o^c) = \inf_n d(\cdot, z_n)$, and therefore

$$g_n := \inf_{1 \leq i \leq n} d(\cdot, z_i) \downarrow \inf_i d(\cdot, z_i), \text{ i.e., } f_n := \min(g_n, 1) \downarrow f,$$

where $f_n = \min_{1 \leq i \leq n} (\min(d(\cdot, z_i), 1)) \in G_2$ for each n which proves (ii).

Now, let $G_5 := \{f: S \to \mathbb{R}: f = g_1^{\ell_1} \cdots g_k^{\ell_k}$ for some $g_i \in G_4$, $\ell_1, \ldots, \ell_k \in \mathbb{N} \cup \{0\}$, $k \in \mathbb{N}\}$;

then, since $G_4 \subset U_b^b(S)$, we have also

(iii) $G_5 \subset U_b^b(S)$.

On the other hand, it follows from (ii) that

(iv) For any $f \in G_5$ there exists a sequence $(f_n)_{n\in\mathbb{N}} \subset G_3$ such that

$f_n \downarrow f$ as $n \to \infty$.

Furthermore,

(v) $\lim_{k\to\infty} \int f d\mu_{n_k}$ exists for all $f \in G_5$.

<u>ad (v):</u> Let $f \in G_5$; then, by (iv), there exists a sequence $(f_m)_{m\in\mathbb{N}} \subset G_3$ such that $f_m \downarrow f$ as $m \to \infty$. Since $f_m - f \downarrow 0$ and $f_m - f \in U_b^b(S)$, we obtain by (b_1) that $\limsup_{n\to\infty} \int (f_m - f)d\mu_n \to 0$ as $m \to \infty$, and therefore also

$\limsup_{k\to\infty} \int (f_m - f)d\mu_{n_k} \to 0$ as $m \to \infty$. Since

$$\limsup_k \int (f_m - f)d\mu_{n_k} \geq \limsup_k \int f_m d\mu_{n_k} - \limsup_k \int f d\mu_{n_k} \geq 0,$$

it follows that $\limsup_k \int f_m d\mu_{n_k} - \limsup_k \int f d\mu_{n_k} \to 0$ as $m \to \infty$,

and therefore we obtain by (i)

ⓐ $$\lim_{m\to\infty} \lim_{k\to\infty} \int f_m d\mu_{n_k} = \limsup_{k\to\infty} \int f d\mu_{n_k}.$$

On the other hand, since $\liminf_k \int (f - f_m)d\mu_{n_k} = -\limsup_k \int (f_m - f)d\mu_{n_k}$,

we have $\liminf_k \int (f - f_m)d\mu_{n_k} \to 0$ as $m \to \infty$. Since

$$\liminf_k \int (f - f_m)d\mu_{n_k} \leq \liminf_k \int f d\mu_{n_k} - \liminf_k \int f_m d\mu_{n_k} \leq 0,$$

we thus obtain in the same way as before, using (i), that

$\lim_{m\to\infty} \lim_{k\to\infty} \int f_m d\mu_{n_k} = \liminf_{k\to\infty} \int f d\mu_{n_k}$, whence together with ⓐ the assertion in (v) follows.

Finally, let $G_6 := \{f: S \to \mathbb{R}: f = P(g_1,\ldots,g_k)$ for some $g_i \in G_4$, $1 \leq i \leq k$, $k \in \mathbb{N}\}$;

then, by (iii), $G_6 \subset U_b^b(S)$, and it can be easily shown that (v) implies

(vi) $\lim_{k\to\infty} \int f d\mu_{n_k}$ exists for all $f \in G_6$.

Now, let $U^b(S_o^c) := \{f: S_o^c \to \mathbb{R}: f$ bounded and uniformly (d-)continuous$\}$ and consider $G_4' := \{\text{rest}_{S_o^c} f: f \in G_4\} \subset U^b(S_o^c)$.

Let $F_1, F_2 \in \mathcal{F}(S_o^c)$ be a d-strictly separated pair of closed subsets in the metric space $S_o^c = (S_o^c, d)$, i.e., (w.l.o.g.) there exists a $\delta>0$ such that $(F_1^\delta \cap S_o^c) \cap F_2 = \emptyset$.

Put $f := \min(d(\cdot, F_1^{\delta/2} \cap S_o^c), 1)$; then $f \in \mathcal{G}_4$ and $g := \text{rest}_{S_o^c} f \in \mathcal{G}_4'$; we will show that

(b) $$\sup_{x\in F_1} g(x) < \inf_{x\in F_2} g(x).$$

ad (b): $x \in F_1$ implies $d(x, F_1^{\delta/2} \cap S_o^c) = 0$ since $F_1 \subset S_o^c$, and therefore $f(x) = 0$ for all $x \in F_1$ whence $\sup_{x\in F_1} g(x) = 0$.

On the other hand, $x \in F_2$ together with $(F_1^\delta \cap S_o^c) \cap F_2 = \emptyset$ implies $d(x, F_1) \geqq \delta$ and therefore $d(x, F_1^{\delta/2}) \geqq \delta/2$; thus $d(x, F_1^{\delta/2} \cap S_o^c) \geqq \delta/2$ for all $x \in F_2$, i.e.,

$$\inf_{x\in F_2} g(x) \geqq \min(\delta/2, 1) \text{ which proves (b).}$$

Therefore, by our proposition, $\mathcal{G}_4'$ is an analytic generator of $U^b(S_o^c)$, i.e., for every $h \in U^b(S_o^c)$ there exists a sequence $(g_n)_{n\in\mathbb{N}}$ such that $g_n = P_n(g_{n1}, g_{n2}, \ldots, g_{nk_n})$ with $g_{ni} \in \mathcal{G}_4'$, $1 \leqq i \leqq k_n$, and $\sup_{x\in S_c^o} |h(x) - g_n(x)| \to 0$ as $n \to \infty$.

Since $g_{ni} \in \mathcal{G}_4'$, $g_{ni} = \text{rest}_{S_o^c} f_{ni}$ for some $f_{ni} \in \mathcal{G}_4$, whence $f_n := P_n(f_{n1}, f_{n2}, \ldots, f_{nk_n}) \in \mathcal{G}_6$ with $\text{rest}_{S_o^c} f_n = g_n$ for each $n \in \mathbb{N}$.

We thus obtain that

(vii) For any $f \in U_b^b(S)$ there exists a sequence $(f_n)_{n\in\mathbb{N}} \subset \mathcal{G}_6$ such that

$$\sup_{x\in S_o^c} |f(x) - f_n(x)| \to 0 \text{ as } n \to \infty.$$

Furthermore, we will show that

(viii) $\lim_{k\to\infty} \int f d\mu_{n_k}$ exists for all $f \in U_b^b(S)$.

ad (viii): Let $f \in U_b^b(S)$; then, by (vii), there exists a sequence $(f_n)_{n\in\mathbb{N}} \subset \mathcal{G}_6$ such that $\sup_{x\in S_o^c} |f(x) - f_n(x)| \to 0$ as $n \to \infty$; therefore, given an arbitrary but fixed $m \in \mathbb{N}$ there exists an $n_o = n_o(m) \in \mathbb{N}$ such that $\sup_{x \in S_o^c} |f(x) - f_{n_o}(x)| < \frac{1}{m}$. Since f and f_{n_o} are uniformly continuous, there exists a $\delta_m > 0$ such that $|f(x) - f(y)| < \frac{1}{m}$ and $|f_{n_o}(x) - f_{n_o}(y)| < \frac{1}{m}$ whenever $d(x,y) < \delta_m$. Now, let $\tilde{S} := (S_o^c)^{\delta_m}$; then, for any $x \in \tilde{S}$ there exists a $y \in S_o^c$ such that $d(x,y) < \delta_m$, and therefore

$$|f_{n_o}(x) - f(x)| \leq |f_{n_o}(x) - f_{n_o}(y)| + |f_{n_o}(y) - f(y)| + |f(y) - f(x)| < \frac{3}{m}$$

for all $x \in \tilde{S}$, whence $f(x) \leq f_{n_o}(x) + \frac{3}{m}$ and $f(x) \geq f_{n_o}(x) - \frac{3}{m}$ for all $x \in \tilde{S}$.

Since $\tilde{S} \in \mathcal{B}_b(S)$ (cf. Lemma 11 (ii)), it follows that

Ⓒ $\int f d\mu_{n_k} \leq \int_{\tilde{S}} (f_{n_o} + \frac{3}{m}) d\mu_{n_k} + \int_{\complement\tilde{S}} f d\mu_{n_k}$ for all $k \in \mathbb{N}$, and

Ⓓ $\int f d\mu_{n_k} \geq \int_{\tilde{S}} (f_{n_o} - \frac{3}{m}) d\mu_{n_k} + \int_{\complement\tilde{S}} f d\mu_{n_k}$ for all $k \in \mathbb{N}$.

Furthermore, it follows from (b_2) that

Ⓔ $\limsup_k \mu_{n_k}(\complement\tilde{S}) = 0.$

<u>ad Ⓔ:</u> $1_{\complement\tilde{S}} = 1_{\complement(S_o^c)^{\delta_m}} \leq \min\left(\frac{d(\cdot, S_o^c)}{\delta_m}, 1\right) =: f^o \in U_b^b(S)$, whence

$\limsup_k \mu_{n_k}(\complement\tilde{S}) \leq \limsup_k \int f^o d\mu_{n_k} = \limsup_k \left(1 - \int (1 - f^o) d\mu_{n_k}\right)$

$= 1 - \liminf_k \int (1 - f^o) d\mu_{n_k} \leq 0$, since $1 - f^o \geq 1_{S_o^c}$ and thus

$\liminf_k \int (1 - f^o) d\mu_{n_k} \geq 1$ by (b_2). This proves Ⓔ.

Next, it can be easily shown that Ⓔ implies

Ⓕ $\lim_{k\to\infty} \int_{\complement\tilde{S}} f d\mu_{n_k} = 0$ for all $f \in U_b^b(S)$.

But then, it follows from Ⓒ, Ⓓ and Ⓕ that

$$\limsup_k \int f d\mu_{n_k} \leq \limsup_k \int_{\tilde{S}} f_{n_o} d\mu_{n_k} + \frac{3}{m}, \text{ and}$$

$$\liminf_k \int f d\mu_{n_k} \geq \liminf_k \int_{\tilde{S}} f_{n_o} d\mu_{n_k} - \frac{3}{m}.$$

Furthermore, ⓕ together with (vi) imply easily that

$$\limsup_k \int_{\tilde{S}} f_{n_o} d\mu_{n_k} = \liminf_k \int_{\tilde{S}} f_{n_o} d\mu_{n_k} = \lim_{k\to\infty} \int_{\tilde{S}} f_{n_o} d\mu_{n_k}$$

and therefore $\limsup_k \int f d\mu_{n_k} - \liminf_k \int f d\mu_{n_k} \leq \frac{6}{m}$

which implies the assertion in (viii) since we started with an arbitrary m.

But now, putting $\mu(f) := \lim_{k\to\infty} \int f d\mu_{n_k}$ for $f \in U_b^b(S)$,

the assertion of Theorem 11 a) follows as in the proof of Theorem 6* applying the Daniell-Stone representation theorem (cf. H. Bauer (1978), 3. Auflage, S. 188) noticing that $\mathcal{B}_b(S)$ coincides with the smallest σ-algebra with respect to which all $f \in U_b^b(S)$ are measurable.

This concludes the proof of Theorem 11 a). □

SKOROKHOD-DUDLEY-WICHURA REPRESENTATION THEOREM:

Let again S = (S,d) be a (possibly non-separable) metric space and suppose that $\mathcal{A}$ is a σ-algebra of subsets of S such that $\mathcal{B}_b(S) \subset \mathcal{A} \subset \mathcal{B}(S)$; let $(\xi_n)_{n\in\mathbb{N}}$ be a sequence of random elements in $(S,\mathcal{A})$ and ξ be a random element in $(S,\mathcal{B}_b(S))$ such that $\xi_n \xrightarrow{\mathcal{L}_b} \xi$ (cf. (34)).

Then the Skorokhod-Dudley-Wichura Representation Theorem states:

THEOREM 12. $\xi_n \xrightarrow{\mathcal{L}_b} \xi$ implies that there exists a sequence $\hat{\xi}_n$, $n \in \mathbb{N}$, of random elements in $(S,\mathcal{A})$ and a random element $\hat{\xi}$ in $(S,\mathcal{B}_b(S))$ being all defined on an appropriate p-space $(\hat{\Omega},\hat{\mathcal{F}},\hat{\mathbb{P}})$ such that $\mathcal{L}\{\hat{\xi}_n\} = \mathcal{L}\{\xi_n\}$ (on $\mathcal{A}$) for all $n \in \mathbb{N}$, $\mathcal{L}\{\hat{\xi}\} = \mathcal{L}\{\xi\}$ (on $\mathcal{B}_b(S)$) and $\hat{\xi}_n \to \hat{\xi}$ $\hat{\mathbb{P}}$-almost surely as $n \to \infty$ (i.e., there exists an $\hat{\Omega}_o \subset \hat{\Omega}$ with $\hat{\Omega}_o \in \hat{\mathcal{F}}$ and $\hat{\mathbb{P}}(\hat{\Omega}_o) = 1$ such that for all $\hat{\omega} \in \hat{\Omega}_o$ $\lim_{n\to\infty} d(\hat{\xi}_n(\hat{\omega}), \hat{\xi}(\hat{\omega})) = 0$).

For complete and separable metric spaces this result was proved by A.V. Skorokhod (1956); it was generalized to arbitrary separable metric spaces by R.M. Dudley (1968), and in its present form (for arbitrary metric spaces) it was first proved by M.J. Wichura (1970); cf. also R.M. Dudley (1976), Lectures 19 and 24.

Our proof will be based on the one given by Dudley (1976). For this, we need the following proposition.

Proposition. Let $S = (S,d)$ be a metric space, $\mu \in M_b^1(S)$ be separable, i.e., $\mu(S_o^c) = 1$ for some separable $S_o^c \subset S$; then, given any $\varepsilon>0$, there exists a sequence $(A_n)_{n\in\mathbb{N}}$ of pairwise disjoint subsets A_n of S having the following properties:

(i) $S_o^c \subset \bigcup_{n\in\mathbb{N}} A_n$

(ii) $\tilde{\mu}(\partial A_n) = 0$ for all $n \in \mathbb{N}$ (where $\tilde{\mu}$ denotes the unique Borel extension of μ (cf. (24)))

(iii) $\operatorname{diam}(A_n) := \sup_{x,y\in A_n} d(x,y) < \varepsilon$ for all $n \in \mathbb{N}$, and

(iv) $A_n \in \mathcal{B}_b(S)$ for all $n \in \mathbb{N}$.

Proof. Let $\{x_1,x_2,\ldots\}$ be dense in S_o^c. For each $n \in \mathbb{N}$, the open ball $B(x_n,\delta)$ is a $\tilde{\mu}$-continuity set (i.e., $\tilde{\mu}(\partial B(x_n,\delta)) = 0$) except for at most countably many values of δ; hence, given any $\varepsilon>0$, for each $n \in \mathbb{N}$ there exists an ε_n such that $\varepsilon/4 < \varepsilon_n < \varepsilon/2$ and $\tilde{\mu}(\partial B(x_n,\varepsilon_n)) = 0$. Now, let $A_1 := B(x_1,\varepsilon_1)$, and recursively for $n>1$ $A_n := B(x_n,\varepsilon_n) \setminus \bigcup_{j<n} B(x_j,\varepsilon_j)$. Then (i) - (iv) are fulfilled:

In fact, (iii) and (iv) follow at once by construction, (ii) holds since the class of all $\tilde{\mu}$-continuity sets forms an algebra containing each $B(x_n,\varepsilon_n)$; finally, given any $x \in S_o^c$ there exists an x_k such that $d(x,x_k) < \varepsilon/4$ whence $x \in B(x_k,\varepsilon/4) \subset B(x_k,\varepsilon_k) \subset \bigcup_{n=1}^{k} A_n$, implying (i). □

Proof of Theorem 12. Let us start by giving a description of the basic steps along which the proof will go, postponing some details to its end. For this, let $P := \mathcal{L}\{\xi\}$ on $\mathcal{B}_b(S)$ with $P(S_o^c) = 1$ for some separable $S_o \subset S$, and let

$P_n := L\{\xi_n\}$ on A, $n \in \mathbb{N}$.

STEP 1. For each $k \in \mathbb{N}$, by the proposition take a sequence $(A_{kj})_{j\in\mathbb{N}}$ of disjoint $\tilde{P}$-continuity sets $A_{kj} \in \mathcal{B}_b(S)$ such that $\operatorname{diam}(A_{kj}) < \frac{1}{k}$ for all $j \in \mathbb{N}$. Since $\bigcup_{j\in\mathbb{N}} A_{kj} \supset S_o^c$ and $P(S_o^c) = 1$, there exists a $J_k < \infty$ such that

(a) $\sum_{1\leq j\leq J_k} P(A_{kj}) > 1 - 2^{-k}$ (where w.l.o.g. we may assume

$P(A_{kj}) > 0$ for all $1 \leq j \leq J_k$).

Applying (28) (cf. (f') there) we obtain

(b) For each $k \in \mathbb{N}$ there exists an $n_k \in \mathbb{N}$ such that for

$1 \leq j \leq J_k$ $|P_n(A_{kj}) - P(A_{kj})| < 2^{-k} \min_{1\leq j\leq J_k} P(A_{kj})$ for

all $n \geq n_k$.

We may assume w.l.o.g. $1 < n_1 < n_2 < \ldots$.

STEP 2. For each $n \in \mathbb{N}$ let $S_n := S$, $I_n := I := [0,1]$, $T_n := S_n \times I_n$, $\mathcal{B}_n := A \otimes \mathcal{B}(I_n)$ (with $\mathcal{B}(I_n) := I_n \cap \mathcal{B}$), and $Q_n := P_n \times \lambda$, λ being Lebesgue measure on $\mathcal{B}(I_n)$; furthermore, let $T_o := S \times I$, $\mathcal{B}_o := \mathcal{B}_b(S) \otimes \mathcal{B}(I)$ and $Q_o := P \times \lambda$.

For each $k \in \mathbb{N}$, $1 \leq j \leq J_k$ and $n \geq n_k$ let

$$f(n,k,j) := \begin{cases} \dfrac{P(A_{kj})}{P_n(A_{kj})}, & \text{if } P_n(A_{kj}) > P(A_{kj}) \ (> 0) \\ 1 \text{ otherwise,} & \end{cases}$$

$$g(n,k,j) := \begin{cases} \dfrac{P_n(A_{kj})}{P(A_{kj})}, & \text{if } P_n(A_{kj}) < P(A_{kj}), \\ 1 \text{ otherwise,} & \end{cases}$$

$B_{nkj} := A_{kj} \times [0,f(n,k,j)]$, considered as a subset of T_n, and

$C_{nkj} := A_{kj} \times [0,g(n,k,j)]$, considered as a subset of T_o, i.e.,

$B_{nkj} \in \mathcal{B}_n$ and $C_{nkj} \in \mathcal{B}_o$; then, by the definition of f and g, we have

(c) $Q_n(B_{nkj}) = Q_o(C_{nkj}) = \min(P_n(A_{kj}), P(A_{kj}))$; furthermore, it follows from (b) that

(d) $\min(g(n,k,j), f(n,k,j)) \geq 1 - 2^{-k}$.

Let $B_{nko} := T_n \setminus \bigcup_{1\leq j\leq J_k} B_{nkj}$ and $C_{nko} := T_o \setminus \bigcup_{1\leq j\leq J_k} C_{nkj}$,

For $k = 0$ let $J_o := 0$, $B_{noo} := T_n$ and $C_{noo} := T_o$.

Let $n_o := 1$ and for each $n \in \mathbb{N}$, let $k(n) \in \mathbb{N} \cup \{0\}$ be the unique k such that $n_k \leq n < n_{k+1}$; then T_n is the disjoint union of sets $D_{nj} := B_{nk(n)j}$, i.e.,

(e) $T_n = \sum_{0\leq j\leq J_{k(n)}} D_{nj}$; likewise $T_o = \sum_{0\leq j\leq J_{k(n)}} E_{nj}$ with

$E_{nj} := C_{nk(n)j}$.

It follows from (c) and (d) that

(f) $Q_n(D_{nj}) = Q_o(E_{nj}) > 0$ if $j \geq 1$.

STEP 3. For each $n \in \mathbb{N}$, given any $x \in T_o$, let $j = j(n,x)$ be the j such that $x \in E_{nj}$ (cf. (e)). Let

$$A := \{x \in T_o : Q_o(E_{nj(n,x)}) > 0 \quad \forall n \in \mathbb{N}\}.$$

Then $\complement A = \bigcup_{n\in\mathbb{N}} \{x \in T_o : Q_o(E_{nj(n,x)}) = 0\} \overset{(f)}{=} \bigcup_{\{n\in\mathbb{N}, Q_o(E_{no})=0\}} E_{no} \in \mathcal{B}_o$

and $Q_o(\complement A) = 0$, whence

(g) $A \in \mathcal{B}_o$ and $Q_o(A) = 1$.

Therefore, $\tilde{Q}_o(A \cap B) := Q_o(B)$, $B \in \mathcal{B}_o$, is a well defined p-measure on $A \cap \mathcal{B}_o$.

For $x \in A$ and any $B \in \mathcal{B}_n$ let

$$P_{nx}(B) := Q_n(B \cap D_{nj(n,x)})/Q_o(E_{nj(n,x)}).$$

It follows from (f) that

(h) the P_{nx}, $x \in A$, are p-measures on $\mathcal{B}_n$, belonging to a finite set $\{P_{nj}\}$, where $P_{nj} := P_{nx}$ if $x \in A \cap E_{nj} \in A \cap \mathcal{B}_o$, $0 \leq j \leq J_{k(n)}$.

For $x \in A$ let

$\mu_x := \times_{n\in\mathbb{N}} P_{nx}$ be the product measure of the P_{nx} on the product σ-algebra $\mathcal{B} := \bigotimes_{n\in\mathbb{N}} \mathcal{B}_n$ in the product space $T := \times_{n\in\mathbb{N}} T_n$.

Let $\hat{\mu}$: $A \times \mathcal{B} \to [0,1]$ be defined by $\hat{\mu}(x,B) := \mu_x(B)$ for $x \in A$ and $B \in \mathcal{B}$; then $\hat{\mu}$ is a "transition probability (or Markov kernel) from $(A, A \cap \mathcal{B}_o)$ into $(T,\mathcal{B})$", i.e.,

(i) (1) For each $x \in A$ $\hat{\mu}(x,\cdot)$ is a p-measure on $\mathcal{B}$, and

(2) For each $B \in \mathcal{B}$ $\hat{\mu}(\cdot,B)$: $A \to I = [0,1]$ is $A \cap \mathcal{B}_o$ $\mathcal{B}(I)$-measurable.

Of course, (1) holds true here and (2) will be shown later.

Therefore (cf. Gaenssler-Stute (1977), Satz 1.8.10)

$\hat{\mathbb{P}} := \tilde{Q}_o \times \hat{\mu}$ defines a p-measure on

$\hat{F} := (A \cap \mathcal{B}_o) \otimes \mathcal{B}$ in

$\hat{\Omega} := A \times T$, where (cf. Gaenssler-Stute (1977), 1.8.7 and 1.8.9)

(j) $$\hat{\mathbb{P}}(C) = \int_A \int_T 1_C(x,y)\hat{\mu}(x,dy)\tilde{Q}_o(dx) = \int_A \hat{\mu}(x,C_x)\tilde{Q}_o(dx)$$

for $C \in \hat{F}$; note that $C_x := \{y \in T: (x,y) \in C\} \in \mathcal{B}$.

<u>STEP 4.</u> $(\hat{\Omega},\hat{F},\hat{\mathbb{P}})$ as obtained before being the desired p-space, let, for $n \in \mathbb{N}$, $\hat{\xi}_n$: $\hat{\Omega} \to S$ be the natural projection of $\hat{\Omega} = A \times [\times_{n\in\mathbb{N}} (S_n \times I_n)]$ onto $S_n = S$; then the $\hat{\xi}_n$'s are random elements in (S,A) and

(k) $$L\{\hat{\xi}_n\} = L\{\xi_n\} \text{ (on } A\text{) for all } n \in \mathbb{N}.$$

In fact, for any $A' \in A$, $L\{\hat{\xi}_n\}(A') = \hat{\mathbb{P}}(\hat{\xi}_n^{-1}(A'))$

$$\underset{(j)}{=} \int_A \mu_x(T_1 \times \ldots \times T_{n-1} \times (A' \times I_n) \times T_{n+1} \times \ldots)\tilde{Q}_o(dx)$$

$$= \int_A P_{nx}(A' \times I_n)\tilde{Q}_o(dx) \underset{(h)}{=} \sum_{0\le j\le J_{k(n)}} P_{nj}(A' \times I_n)\tilde{Q}_o(A \cap E_{nj})$$

$$= \sum_j P_{nj}(A' \times I_n)Q_o(E_{nj}) = \sum_j Q_n((A' \times I_n) \cap D_{nj}) \underset{(e)}{=} Q_n(A' \times I_n)$$

$$= P_n(A') = L\{\xi_n\}(A').$$

Next, let $\hat{\xi} := \Pi_S^{T_o} \circ i(A) \circ \Pi_A^{\hat{\Omega}} : \hat{\Omega} \to S$, where $\Pi_A^{\hat{\Omega}}$ is the natural projection of $\hat{\Omega} = A \times T$ onto A, i(A) is the injection of A into T_o, and $\Pi_S^{T_o}$ is the natural projection of $T_o = S \times I$ onto S; then $\hat{\xi}$ is a random element in $(S, \mathcal{B}_b(S))$ and

(ℓ) $$L\{\hat{\xi}\} = L\{\xi\} \quad (\text{on } \mathcal{B}_b(S)).$$

In fact, for any $B \in \mathcal{B}_b(S)$, $L\{\hat{\xi}\}(B) = \hat{\mathbb{P}}(\hat{\xi}^{-1}(B))$

$$= \hat{\mathbb{P}}((\Pi_A^{\hat{\Omega}})^{-1} \circ (i(A))^{-1} \circ (\Pi_S^{T_o})^{-1}(B)) = \hat{\mathbb{P}}((\Pi_A^{\hat{\Omega}})^{-1} \circ (i(A))^{-1}(B \times I))$$

$$= \hat{\mathbb{P}}((\Pi_A^{\hat{\Omega}})^{-1}(A \cap (B \times I))) = \hat{\mathbb{P}}([A \cap (B \times I)] \times T) \underset{(j)}{=} \int_{A \cap (B \times I)} \mu_x(T) \tilde{Q}_o(dx)$$

$$= \tilde{Q}_o(A \cap (B \times I)) = Q_o(B \times I) = P(B) = L\{\xi\}(B).$$

Now, let $\hat{\Omega}_o := \liminf_{n\to\infty} \hat{\Omega}_{o,n}$, where

$$\hat{\Omega}_{o,n} := \sum_{1 \le j \le J_{k(n)}} ([A \cap E_{nj}] \times T_1 \times \ldots \times T_{n-1} \times D_{nj} \times T_{n+1} \times \ldots) \in \hat{F};$$

then $\hat{\Omega}_o \in \hat{F}$ and

(m) $$\lim_{n\to\infty} d(\hat{\xi}_n(\hat{\omega}), \hat{\xi}(\hat{\omega})) = 0 \quad \text{for all } \hat{\omega} \in \hat{\Omega}_o.$$

In fact, for any $\hat{\omega} \in \hat{\Omega}_o$ there exists an $n_o \in \mathbb{N}$ such that for all $n \ge n_o$ there exists a $j(n)$, $1 \le j(n) \le J_{k(n)}$, such that

$\hat{\xi}_n(\hat{\omega}) \in A_{k(n)j(n)}$ and $\hat{\xi}(\hat{\omega}) \in A_{k(n)j(n)}$ (note that $\Pi_A^{\hat{\Omega}}(\hat{\omega}) \in A \cap E_{nj(n)}$ implies $i(A)(\Pi_A^{\hat{\Omega}}(\hat{\omega})) \in E_{nj(n)}$ whence $\Pi_S^{T_o}(i(A)(\Pi_A^{\hat{\Omega}}(\hat{\omega}))) \in A_{k(n)j(n)}$);

cf. the definition of the sets D_{nj} and E_{nj}, respectively.

Therefore, for all $n \ge n_o$, $d(\hat{\xi}_n(\hat{\omega}), \hat{\xi}(\hat{\omega})) \le \text{diam}(A_{k(n)j(n)}) \le \frac{1}{k(n)} \to 0$ as $n \to \infty$ (since $k(n) \to \infty$ as $n \to \infty$).

Next we will show that $\hat{\mathbb{P}}(\hat{\Omega}_o) = 1$. For this we will prove later that

(n) $$Q_o(\limsup_{n\to\infty} E_{no}) = 0.$$

Now,

$$\complement\hat{\Omega}_{o,n} = \sum_{1 \le j \le J_{k(n)}} ([A \cap E_{nj}] \times T_1 \times \ldots \times T_{n-1} \times \complement D_{nj} \times T_{n+1} \times \ldots)$$

$$+ ([A \cap E_{no}] \times T_1 \times \ldots \times T_n \times \ldots)$$

$$= \hat{\Omega}_{1,n} + \hat{\Omega}_{2,n}, \text{ say,}$$

where $\hat{\mathbb{P}}(\hat{\Omega}_{1,n}) = \sum_j \int_{A \cap E_{nj}} P_{nx}(\complement D_{nj}) \tilde{Q}_o(dx) = \sum_j P_{nj}(\complement D_{nj}) \tilde{Q}_o(A \cap E_{nj})$

$= \sum_j \dfrac{Q_n((\complement D_{nj}) \cap D_{nj})}{Q_o(E_{nj})} Q_o(E_{nj}) = 0$ for all $n \in \mathbb{N}$, and therefore

$$\hat{\mathbb{P}}(\limsup_{n\to\infty} \complement\hat{\Omega}_{o,n}) = \hat{\mathbb{P}}(\limsup_{n\to\infty} \hat{\Omega}_{2,n}) = \hat{\mathbb{P}}([A \cap \limsup_{n\to\infty} E_{no}] \times T)$$

$$= \tilde{Q}_o(A \cap \limsup_{n\to\infty} E_{no}) = Q_o(\limsup_{n\to\infty} E_{no}) = 0 \text{ by (n).}$$

It follows that $\hat{\mathbb{P}}(\hat{\Omega}_o) = \hat{\mathbb{P}}(\liminf_{n\to\infty} \hat{\Omega}_{o,n}) = 1 - \hat{\mathbb{P}}(\limsup_{n\to\infty} \complement\hat{\Omega}_{o,n}) = 1.$

It remains to show (i) (2) and (n):

<u>ad (i) (2):</u> We have to show that

(+) $\mathcal{D} := \{B \in \mathcal{B}: \hat{\mu}(\cdot,B): A \to I = [0,1], \text{ is } A \cap \mathcal{B}_o, \mathcal{B}(I)\text{-measurable}\} = \mathcal{B}$.

If $B = T_1 \times \ldots \times T_{n-1} \times B_n \times T_{n+1} \times \ldots$ for some $B_n \in \mathcal{B}_n$, then for each $t \in I$

$\{x \in A: \hat{\mu}(x,B) \leq t\} = \{x \in A: \mu_x(B) \leq t\} = \{x \in A: P_{nx}(B_n) \leq t\} \underset{(h)}{=}$

$\bigcup_{\{j: P_{nj}(B_n) \leq t\}} A \cap E_{nj} \in A \cap \mathcal{B}_o$, whence $B \in \mathcal{D}$ for all these sets.

From this and the product form of μ_x it follows that the class $\mathcal{C}$ of finite intersections of sets B just considered is also contained in $\mathcal{D}$. Since $\mathcal{C}$ is a $\cap$-closed generator of $\mathcal{B}$, we get (+) as in Gaenssler-Stute (1977), 1.8.5.

<u>ad (n):</u> It follows from (a) that $\sum_k P(S \setminus \bigcup_{1\leq j\leq J_k} A_{kj}) \leq \sum_k 2^{-k} < \infty$,

whence, by the Borel-Cantelli lemma

$$P(\limsup_{k\to\infty}(S \setminus \bigcup_{1\leq j\leq J_k} A_{kj})) = 0, \text{ i.e., } P(\liminf_{k\to\infty} \bigcup_{1\leq j\leq J_k} A_{kj}) = 1$$

and thus

$$P(\liminf_{n\to\infty} \bigcup_{1\leq j\leq J_{k(n)}} A_{k(n)j}) = 1 \text{ as } k(n) \to \infty \text{ for } n \to \infty.$$

Furthermore,

$$\lambda(\liminf_{n\to\infty} [0, \min_{1\leq j\leq J_{k(n)}} g(n,k(n),j)]) = 1, \quad \text{since for any} \quad t \in I = [0,1]$$

with $t < 1$, $\min_{1\leq j\leq J_{k(n)}} g(n,k(n),j) \underset{(d)}{\geq} 1 - 2^{-k(n)} > t$ for all large enough n.

Since $\liminf_{n\to\infty} \bigcup_{1\leq j\leq J_{k(n)}} E_{nj} \supset (\liminf_{n\to\infty} \bigcup_{1\leq j\leq J_{k(n)}} A_{k(n)j}) \times$

$$\times (\liminf_{n\to\infty} [0, \min_{1\leq j\leq J_{k(n)}} g(n,k(n),j)]),$$

we thus obtain $Q_o(\liminf_{n\to\infty} \bigcup_{1\leq j\leq J_{k(n)}} E_{nj}) = 1$ which implies (n) since

$$\complement(\bigcup_{1\leq j\leq J_{k(n)}} E_{nj}) = E_{no}.$$

This concludes the proof of Theorem 12. □

Following a suggestion of Ron Pyke, let us demonstrate at this place the usefulness of the representation theorem for proving the following version of Theorem 5 (cf. Lemma 16 for the definition of the set E).

THEOREM 5'. Let $S = (S,d)$ and $S' = (S',d')$ be metric spaces, and $\mathcal{A}$ a σ-algebra of subsets of S such that $\mathcal{B}_b(S) \subset \mathcal{A} \subset \mathcal{B}(S)$. For $n \in \mathbb{N}$ let $g_n: S \to S'$ be $\mathcal{A},\mathcal{B}_b(S')$-measurable and let $g: S \to S'$ be $\mathcal{B}_b(S)$, $\mathcal{B}_b(S')$-measurable.
Let $(\xi_n)_{n\in\mathbb{N}}$ be a sequence of random elements in $(S,\mathcal{A})$ and ξ be a random element in $(S,\mathcal{B}_b(S))$ such that $\xi_n \xrightarrow{\mathcal{L}_b} \xi$ and $\widetilde{\mathcal{L}\{\xi\}}^*(E) = 0$. Then

$$g_n(\xi_n) \equiv g_n \circ \xi_n \xrightarrow{\mathcal{L}_b} g(\xi) \equiv g \circ \xi.$$

(Note that $g_n(\xi_n)$ and $g(\xi)$ are random elements in $(S',\mathcal{B}_b(S'))$.)

Proof. As in the proof of Theorem 4 it is shown that
$\mathcal{L}\{g(\xi)\} = \mathcal{L}\{\xi\} \circ g^{-1}$ ($= \widetilde{\mathcal{L}\{\xi\}} \circ g^{-1}$) is separable. Now according to Theorem 12, there exists a p-space $(\hat{\Omega},\hat{F},\hat{\mathbb{P}})$ and on it random elements $\hat{\xi}_n$ in $(S,\mathcal{A})$ and a random element $\hat{\xi}$ in $(S,\mathcal{B}_b(S))$ such that

$L\{\hat{\xi}_n\} = L\{\xi_n\}$ (on A) for all $n \in \mathbb{N}$, $L\{\hat{\xi}\} = L\{\xi\}$ (on $\mathcal{B}_b(S)$),

and

$\hat{\xi}_n(\hat{\omega}) \to \hat{\xi}(\hat{\omega})$ (as $n \to \infty$) for all $\hat{\omega} \in \hat{\Omega}_o$, where $\hat{\Omega}_o \in \hat{F}$ with $\hat{\mathbb{P}}(\hat{\Omega}_o) = 1$.

Let $\hat{\Omega}_1 := \{\hat{\xi} \in \mathbf{C}E\}$ and $\hat{\Omega}_2 := \hat{\Omega}_o \cap \hat{\Omega}_1$; then for all $\hat{\omega} \in \hat{\Omega}_2$,

$g_n(\hat{\xi}_n(\hat{\omega})) \to g(\hat{\xi}(\hat{\omega}))$ (as $n \to \infty$). Since $\hat{\mathbb{P}}(\hat{\Omega}_o) = 1$ and $\hat{\mathbb{P}}_*(\hat{\Omega}_1) = 1$

(note that $\widetilde{L\{\hat{\xi}\}}_* (\mathbf{C}E) = \widetilde{L\{\xi\}}_* (\mathbf{C}E) = 1$) we have $\hat{\mathbb{P}}_*(\hat{\Omega}_2) = 1$, whence there exists $\hat{\Omega}_3 \in \hat{F}$ such that $\hat{\Omega}_3 \subset \hat{\Omega}_2$ and $\hat{\mathbb{P}}(\hat{\Omega}_3) = 1$. It follows that for $\hat{\omega} \in \hat{\Omega}_3$ and each $f \in U_b^b(S')$

$$f \circ g_n \circ \hat{\xi}_n(\hat{\omega}) \to f \circ g \circ \hat{\xi}(\hat{\omega}) \quad (\text{as } n \to \infty)$$

whence, by Lebesgue's theorem,

$\hat{\mathbb{E}}(f \circ g_n \circ \hat{\xi}_n) \to \hat{\mathbb{E}}(f \circ g \circ \hat{\xi})$, i.e., $\int f dL\{g_n(\hat{\xi}_n)\} \to \int f dL\{g(\hat{\xi})\}$ (as $n \to \infty$).

Since $L\{g_n(\hat{\xi}_n)\} = L\{\hat{\xi}_n\} \circ g_n^{-1} = L\{\xi_n\} \circ g_n^{-1} = L\{g_n(\xi_n)\}$

and $L\{g(\hat{\xi})\} = L\{\hat{\xi}\} \circ g^{-1} = L\{\xi\} \circ g^{-1} = L\{g(\xi)\}$, the assertion follows by (28) (cf. (h') there). □

Next, we want to make some specific remarks concerning the special case $S = D[0,1]$ reviewing at the same time some of the key results from Billingsley's (1968) book (cf. Appendix A in G. Shorack (1979)).

THE SPACE D[0,1]:

Let $D \equiv D[0,1]$ be the space of all right continuous functions on the unit interval $[0,1]$ that have left hand limits at all points $t \in (0,1]$. Cf. P. Billingsley (1968), Lemma 1, p. 110, and its consequences concerning specific properties of functions $x \in D$; among others, $\sup_{t\in[0,1]} |x(t)| < \infty$ for all $x \in D$. If not stated otherwise, the space D will be equipped with the supremum metric ρ, i.e.

$$\rho(x,y) := \sup_{t\in[0,1]} |x(t) - y(t)| \quad \text{for } x,y \in D.$$

(By the way, (D,ρ) is a linear topological space whereas (D,s), with s being the Skorokhod metric, is not (cf. P. Billingsley (1968), p. 123, 3.)). Note that $(S,d) = (D,\rho)$ is a non-separable metric space (in fact, look at $x_s := 1_{[s,1]}$, $s \in (0,1)$, to obtain an uncountable set of functions in D for which $\rho(x_s,x_{s'}) = 1$ for $s \neq s'$).

Also, as pointed out by D.M. Chibisov (1965), (cf. P. Billingsley (1968), Section 18), the empirical df U_n (based on independent random variables (on some p-space $(\Omega,\mathcal{F},\mathbb{P})$) being uniformly distributed on $[0,1]$) cannot be considered as a random element in $(D,\mathcal{B}(D,\rho))$ (i.e. $U_n: \Omega \to D$ is not $\mathcal{F},\mathcal{B}(D,\rho)$-measurable), where $\mathcal{B}(D,\rho)$ denotes the Borel σ-algebra in (D,ρ). But, considering instead the smaller σ-algebra $\mathcal{B}_b(D) \equiv \mathcal{B}_b(D,\rho)$ generated by the open (ρ-) balls we have

(37) $\mathcal{B}_b(D) = \sigma(\{\pi_t: t \in [0,1]\})$,

where $\sigma(\{\pi_t: t \in [0,1]\})$ denotes the σ-algebra generated by the coordinate projections $\pi_t \equiv \pi_t(D)$ from D onto $\mathbb{R}$, defined by $\pi_t(x) := x(t)$ for $x \in D$.

(Note that (37) implies that U_n is $\mathcal{F},\mathcal{B}_b(D)$-measurable since $\mathcal{F}$, $\sigma(\{\pi_t: t \in [0,1]\})$-measurability of U_n is equivalent with $\mathcal{F},\mathcal{B}$-measurability of $\pi_t(U_n) = U_n(t)$ for each fixed $t \in [0,1]$ where the latter is satisfied since $U_n(t)$ is a random variable.)

Proof of (37). Let $T := \mathbb{Q} \cap [0,1]$ be the set of rational numbers in $[0,1]$; then, by the right continuity of each $x \in D$ one has

(a) $\rho(x_1,x_2) = \sup_{t\in T} |x_1(t) - x_2(t)|$ for every $x_1,x_2 \in D$.

Therefore, for any $x_o \in D$ and any $r > 0$

$$\{x \in D: \rho(x,x_o) \leq r\} = \bigcap_{t\in T} \{x \in D: |x(t) - x_o(t)| \leq r\}$$

$$= \bigcap_{t\in T} \pi_t^{-1}([x_o(t) - r, x_o(t) + r]) \in \sigma(\{\pi_t: t \in [0,1]\});$$ thus

$\mathcal{B}_b(D) \subset \sigma(\{\pi_t: t \in [0,1]\})$; (note that $\{x \in D: \rho(x,x_o) < r\}$

$$= \bigcup_{m\in\mathbb{N}} \{x \in D: \rho(x,x_o) \leq r - \tfrac{1}{m}\}).$$

To verify the other inclusion it suffices to show that for every fixed $t \in [0,1]$ and $r \in \mathbb{R}$ one has

(b) $$\{x \in D: \pi_t(x) < r\} \in \mathcal{B}_b(D).$$

For this we define, given the fixed t and r, for any $n, k \in \mathbb{N}$ and $s \in [0,1]$

$$x_n^k(s) := \begin{cases} 0, \text{ if } s < t \\ r - \frac{1}{k} - n, \text{ if } s \in [t, t + \frac{1}{k}) \cap [0,1] \\ 0, \text{ if } s \in [t + \frac{1}{k}, \infty) \cap [0,1]. \end{cases}$$

Then $x_n^k \in D$ and it follows that

(c) $$\{x \in D: \pi_t(x) < r\} = \bigcup_{n\in\mathbb{N}} \bigcup_{k\in\mathbb{N}} \{x \in D: \rho(x, x_n^k) \leqq n\},$$

which proves (b).

As to (c), let $x_o \in \bigcup_{n\in\mathbb{N}} \bigcup_{k\in\mathbb{N}} \{x \in D: \rho(x,x_n^k) \leqq n\}$; then

$\rho(x_o, x_n^k) \leqq n$ for some n and k, whence

$$n \geqq |x_o(t) - x_n^k(t)| = |x_o(t) - r + \frac{1}{k} + n|$$

$$\geqq x_o(t) - r + \frac{1}{k} + n, \text{ and therefore}$$

$$x_o(t) \leqq r - \frac{1}{k} < r, \text{ i.e. } \pi_t(x_o) < r.$$

On the other hand, if $x_o(t) < r$, $x_o \in D$, choose $n_o \in \mathbb{N}$ such that

$\sup_{t\in[0,1]} |x_o(t)| \leqq \min(n_o, n_o - r)$; then it can be easily shown that

$$x_o \in \bigcup_{k\in\mathbb{N}} \{x \in D: \rho(x, x_{n_o}^k) \leqq n_o\},$$

which proves (c). □

<u>(38) REMARK.</u> Comparing (37) with the known result that the Borel σ-algebra $\mathcal{B}(D,s)$ in (D,s), equipped with the Skorokhod metric s (cf. P. Billingsley (1968), Chapter 3), coincides also with $\sigma(\{\pi_t: t \in [0,1]\})$, we obtain that

$$\mathcal{B}(D,s) = \mathcal{B}_b(D,\rho).$$

It is also known, that for any sequence $(x_n)_{n\in\mathbb{N}} \subset D$ and $x \in D$, $\lim_{n\to\infty} \rho(x_n,x) = 0$ always implies $\lim_{n\to\infty} s(x_n,x) = 0$;

on the other hand, if $\lim_{n\to\infty} s(x_n,x) = 0$ for some continuous x, then

$\lim_{n\to\infty} \rho(x_n,x) = 0$ (hence the Skorokhod topology relativized to the space of all continuous functions on [0,1] coincides with the uniform topology there).

Let $C \equiv C[0,1]$ be the space of all continuous functions on [0,1] and consider again the supremum metric ρ on C.

Then $(S_o,d) = (C,\rho)$ is a separable metric space being here a closed subspace of (D,ρ), i.e., we have $S_o^c = S_o$ in the present situation. (Note that $x \in C$ is even uniformly continuous.)

Therefore, denoting by $\mathcal{B}(C,\rho)$ the Borel σ-algebra in (C,ρ) we have (cf. Lemma 11)

$$C \cap \mathcal{B}(D,\rho) = \mathcal{B}(C,\rho) = \mathcal{B}_b(C,\rho) \subset C \cap \mathcal{B}_b(D,\rho) \subset C \cap \mathcal{B}(D,\rho),$$

$$\text{and} \quad C \in \mathcal{B}_b(D,\rho), \text{ i.e.,}$$

(39) $$\mathcal{B}(C,\rho) = \mathcal{B}_b(C,\rho) = C \cap \mathcal{B}_b(D,\rho) \quad \text{and} \quad C \in \mathcal{B}_b(D,\rho).$$

In what follows let ξ_n, $n \in \mathbb{N}$, and ξ be random elements in $(D,\mathcal{B}_b(D,\rho))$ which are all defined on a common p-space $(\Omega,F,\mathbb{P})$. Following (34) we write

$\xi_n \xrightarrow{L_b} \xi$ iff $L\{\xi_n\} \underset{b}{\rightarrow} L\{\xi\}$ in which case (by our definition of $\underset{b}{\rightarrow}$ - convergence) $L\{\xi\}$ is assumed to be separable.

On the other hand, in view of (38), $L\{\xi_n\}$ and $L\{\xi\}$ may also be considered as Borel measures on $\mathcal{B}(D,s)$, whence the usual concept of weak convergence of Borel measures can also be used, which means that

$\xi_n \xrightarrow{L} \xi$ iff, by definition, $L\{\xi_n\}$ on $\mathcal{B}(D,s)$ converges weakly to $L\{\xi\}$ on $\mathcal{B}(D,s)$ in the sense of Billingsley (1968).

<u>LEMMA 18.</u> If $\xi_n \xrightarrow{L_b} \xi$, then $\xi_n \xrightarrow{L} \xi$; on the other hand, if $\xi_n \xrightarrow{L} \xi$ and $L\{\xi\}(C) = 1$, then $\xi_n \xrightarrow{L_b} \xi$.

<u>Proof.</u> Note first that (D,s) is a separable metric space whence we can use (28) with $\mathcal{B}_b(D,s) = A = \mathcal{B}(D,s)$, which gives us

(+) $\xi_n \xrightarrow{L} \xi \Leftrightarrow \lim_{n\to\infty} \mathbb{E}(f(\xi_n)) = \mathbb{E}(f(\xi))$ for all bounded

$\mathcal{B}(D,s)$, $\mathcal{B}$-measurable functions $f\colon D \to \mathbb{R}$

which are $L\{\xi\}$-a.e. continuous.

1.) Consider an $f\colon D \to \mathbb{R}$; then:

if f is s-continuous, it is also ρ-continuous and (cf. (38)) $\mathcal{B}_b(D,\rho)$, $\mathcal{B}$-measurable. Therefore

$\xi_n \xrightarrow{L_b} \xi$ implies that $\lim_{n\to\infty} \mathbb{E}(f(\xi_n)) = \mathbb{E}(f(\xi))$ for all bounded s-continuous $f\colon D \to \mathbb{R}$, whence $\xi_n \xrightarrow{L} \xi$.

2.) $\xi_n \xrightarrow{L} \xi$ implies, according to (+), that $\lim_{n\to\infty} \mathbb{E}(f(\xi_n)) = \mathbb{E}(f(\xi))$ for all bounded $\mathcal{B}(D,s)$, $\mathcal{B}$-measurable $f\colon D \to \mathbb{R}$ which are $L\{\xi\}$-a.e. continuous. Since $L\{\xi\}(C) = 1$ implies (cf. (38)) that any ρ-continuous f is also $L\{\xi\}$-a.e. s-continuous, we obtain, using again that $\mathcal{B}(D,s) = \mathcal{B}_b(D,\rho)$, that $\lim_{n\to\infty} \mathbb{E}(f(\xi_n)) = \mathbb{E}(f(\xi))$ for all bounded, ρ-continuous, and $\mathcal{B}_b(D,\rho)$, $\mathcal{B}$-measurable $f\colon D \to \mathbb{R}$; furthermore, since $C = (C,\rho)$ is a closed separable subspace of (D,ρ) with $L\{\xi\}(C) = 1$, we finally obtain (cf. (28)(h')) that $\xi_n \xrightarrow{L_b} \xi$. □

Now we are going on in reviewing here some of the key results of Billingsley's (1968) book. The following lemma is well known (cf. Yu.V. Prohorov (1956)):

<u>LEMMA 19.</u> Let $F\colon [0,1] \to \mathbb{R}$ be a continuous function and $a>1$, $b>0$ be constants such that for some random element ξ in

$$(\mathbb{R}^{[0,1]}, \mathcal{B}_{[0,1]}) \quad (\mathcal{B}_{[0,1]} := \bigotimes_{t\in[0,1]} \mathcal{B}_t \text{ with } \mathcal{B}_t \equiv \mathcal{B})$$

(40) $\mathbb{E}(|\xi(t) - \xi(s)|^b) \leq |F(t) - F(s)|^a$ for all $0 \leq s \leq t \leq 1$;

then there exists a random element $\hat{\xi}$ in $(D,\mathcal{B}_b(D,\rho))$ such that $L\{\hat{\xi}\}|\mathcal{B}_{[0,1]} = L\{\xi\}$ and $(L\{\hat{\xi}\}|\mathcal{B}_b(D,\rho))(C) = 1$. (Note that $D \cap \mathcal{B}_{[0,1]} = \mathcal{B}_b(D,\rho)$ (cf. (37)) and

$C \in \mathcal{B}_b(D,\rho)$ (cf. (39)).)

In what follows we shall write $\xi_n \xrightarrow[\text{f.d.}]{L} \xi$, if the finite dimensional distributions (fidis) of ξ_n converge weakly to the corresponding fidis of ξ. (Recall that, given a r.e. ξ in $(D,\mathcal{B}_b(D,\rho))$, the fidis of ξ (or $L\{\xi\}$, respectively) are defined as the image measures that $\pi_{t_1,\ldots,t_k}(D)\colon D \to \mathbb{R}^k$ induce on $\mathbb{B}_k$ from $L\{\xi\}$ on $\mathcal{B}_b(D,\rho)$ $(= \sigma(\{\pi_t(D)\colon t \in [0,1]\}))$ for each fixed $t_1,\ldots,t_k \in [0,1]$, $k \geq 1$, where $\pi_{t_1,\ldots,t_k}(D)(x) := (x(t_1),\ldots,x(t_k))$ for $x \in D$; note that $\pi_{t_1,\ldots,t_k}$ is $\mathcal{B}_b(D,\rho)$, $\mathbb{B}_k$-measurable.)

DEFINITION 6. Let $(\xi_n)_{n\in\mathbb{N}}$ be a sequence of random elements in $(D,\mathcal{B}_b(D,\rho)) = (D,\mathcal{B}(D,s))$;

(i) (ξ_n) is said to be relatively L-sequentially compact, iff for any subsequence $(L\{\xi_{n'}\})$ of $(L\{\xi_n\})$ there exists a further subsequence $(L\{\xi_{n''}\})$ of $(L\{\xi_{n'}\})$ and a p-measure μ on $\mathcal{B}(D,s)$ such that $L\{\xi_{n''}\}$ converges weakly to μ in the sense of Billingsley (1968).

(ii) (ξ_n) is said to be relatively L_b-sequentially compact, iff for any subsequence $(L\{\xi_{n'}\})$ of $(L\{\xi_n\})$ there exists a further subsequence $(L\{\xi_{n''}\})$ of $(L\{\xi_{n'}\})$ and a separable p-measure μ on $\mathcal{B}_b(D,\rho)$ (in (D,ρ)!) such that $L\{\xi_{n''}\} \xrightarrow[b]{} \mu$.

The following theorem is well known (cf. P. Billingsley (1968), Th. 15.1).

THEOREM 13. Let (ξ_n) be relatively L-sequentially compact and suppose that $\xi_n \xrightarrow[\text{f.d.}]{L} \xi$; then $\xi_n \xrightarrow{L} \xi$.

The next theorem gives sufficient conditions for (ξ_n) to be relatively L-sequentially compact.

For this, given any $x \in D$ and $B \in [0,1] \cap \mathbb{B}$, let

$$\|x\| := \sup_{t\in[0,1]} |x(t)|,$$

and

$$w_x(B) := \sup_{s,t \in B} |x(t) - x(s)|.$$

THEOREM 14. Let $(\xi_n)_{n \in \mathbb{N}}$ be a sequence of random elements in $(D, \mathcal{B}_b(D, \rho))$, all defined on a common p-space $(\Omega, \mathcal{F}, \mathbb{P})$, and satisfying the following set of conditions (A)-(D):

(A):
$$\limsup_{n \to \infty} \mathbb{P}(\|\xi_n\| > m) \to 0 \text{ as } m \to \infty.$$

(B): For every $\varepsilon > 0$, $\limsup_{n \to \infty} \mathbb{P}(w_{\xi_n}([0,\delta)) \geq \varepsilon) \to 0$ as $\delta \to 0$

and $\limsup_{n \to \infty} \mathbb{P}(w_{\xi_n}([\delta,1)) \geq \varepsilon) \to 0$ as $\delta \to 1$.

(C): There exist constants $a > 1$, $b > 0$ and, for every $n \in \mathbb{N}$ there exist monotone increasing functions $F_n: [0,1] \to \mathbb{R}$ such that for every $\varepsilon > 0$ and any $0 \leq r \leq s \leq t \leq 1$

$$\mathbb{P}(|\xi_n(s) - \xi_n(r)| \geq \varepsilon, |\xi_n(t) - \xi_n(s)| \geq \varepsilon) \leq \varepsilon^{-b}(F_n(t) - F_n(r))^a.$$

(D): There exists a monotone increasing and continuous function $F: [0,1] \to \mathbb{R}$ such that for the F_n's occurring in (C) and any $0 \leq s \leq t \leq 1$

$$\limsup_{n \to \infty} (F_n(t) - F_n(s)) \leq F(t) - F(s).$$

Then (ξ_n) is relatively L-sequentially compact.

(41) REMARK. Given any $x \in D$ and $\delta > 0$, let

$$w_x''(\delta) := \sup_{\substack{0 \leq r \leq s \leq t \leq 1 \\ t-r \leq \delta}} \min \{|x(s) - x(r)|, |x(t) - x(s)|\}.$$

Then (C) and (D) together imply

(C''): For every $\varepsilon > 0$, $\limsup_{n \to \infty} \mathbb{P}(w_{\xi_n}''(\delta) \geq \varepsilon) \to 0$ as $\delta \to 0$.

As to Theorem 14, it is shown in Billingsley (1968), Theorem 15.3 that (A), (B) and (C'') together imply the assertion of Theorem 14.

So we will prove here only the statement made in (41).

For notational convenience we shall write $\xi_n(s,t]$ instead of $\xi_n(t) - \xi_n(s)$

for $0 \leq s \leq t \leq 1$.

a) Given an arbitrary $\varepsilon>0$, $t \in [0,1)$ and $\delta \leq 1-t$, it follows from Theorem 12.5 in Billingsley (1968) together with (C) that for every $n \in \mathbb{N}$ and every $m \in \mathbb{N}$

$$\mathbb{P}\Big(\bigcup_{0\leq i\leq j\leq k\leq 2^m} \{\min [|\xi_n(t + \tfrac{i}{2^m}\delta, t + \tfrac{j}{2^m}\delta]|, |\xi_n(t + \tfrac{j}{2^m}\delta, t + \tfrac{k}{2^m}\delta]|] \geq \varepsilon\}\Big)$$

$\leq K(a,b)\cdot\varepsilon^{-b}(F_n(t+\delta) - F_n(t))^a$, where $K(a,b)$ is a constant depending only on a and b.

Therefore, due to the right-continuity of the sample paths of ξ_n, putting

$$w''_x([t,t+\delta]) := \sup_{t\leq r\leq s\leq t'\leq t+\delta} \min\{|x(r,s]|, |x(s,t']|\}$$

for $x \in D$, $\delta>0$ and $t \leq 1-\delta$,

it follows that $\mathbb{P}(w''_{\xi_n}([t,t+\delta]) \geq \varepsilon)$

$$\leq K(a,b)\cdot\varepsilon^{-b}(F_n(t+\delta) - F_n(t))^a.$$

b) Let, for any $\delta>0$, $m = m(\delta) := [\frac{1}{2\delta}]$ (where $[x]$ stands for the integer part of x); then, for every $n \in \mathbb{N}$,

$$\mathbb{P}(w''_{\xi_n}(\delta) \geq \varepsilon) \leq \sum_{i=0}^{m-1} \mathbb{P}(w''_{\xi_n}([\tfrac{i}{m}, \tfrac{i+1}{m}]) \geq \varepsilon) + \sum_{i=0}^{m-2} \mathbb{P}(w''_{\xi_n}([\tfrac{2i+1}{2m}, \tfrac{2i+3}{2m}]) \geq \varepsilon)$$

$$\underset{a)}{\leq} K(a,b)\cdot\varepsilon^{-b}\Big[\sum_{i=0}^{m-1}(F_n(\tfrac{i+1}{m}) - F_n(\tfrac{i}{m}))^a + \sum_{i=0}^{m-2}(F_n(\tfrac{2i+3}{2m}) - F_n(\tfrac{2i+1}{2m}))^a\Big],$$

which implies by (D) that

$$\limsup_{n\to\infty} \mathbb{P}(w''_{\xi_n}(\delta) \geq \varepsilon) \leq K(a,b)\cdot\varepsilon^{-b}\cdot 2(w_F(\tfrac{1}{m}))^{a-1}\cdot(F(1) - F(0)),$$

where $w_F(\frac{1}{m}) := \sup\{F(t) - F(s): s \leq t,\ t-s \leq \frac{1}{m}\}$

$= w_F(\frac{1}{m(\delta)}) \to 0$ as $\delta \to 0$ (since F is uniformly continuous).

This proves (C''). □

(42) <u>REMARK.</u> Let us consider in Theorem 14 instead of (B) and (C) the following conditions (B') and (C'), respectively:

(B'): For every $\varepsilon>0$, $\limsup_{n\to\infty} \mathbb{P}(|\xi_n(\delta) - \xi_n(0)| \geq \varepsilon) \to 0$ as $\delta \to 0$

and $\limsup_{n\to\infty} \mathbb{P}(|\xi_n(1) - \xi_n(\delta)| \geq \varepsilon) \to 0$ as $\delta \to 1$;

(C'): There exist constants $a_i, b_i > 0$, $i=1,2$, such that $a_1 + a_2 > 1$ and, for every $n \in \mathbb{N}$ there exist monotone increasing functions $F_n:[0,1] \to \mathbb{R}$ such that for any $0 \leq r \leq s \leq t \leq 1$

$$\mathbb{E}(|\xi_n(s) - \xi_n(r)|^{b_1} \cdot |\xi_n(t) - \xi_n(s)|^{b_2}) \leq (F_n(s) - F_n(r))^{a_1} \cdot (F_n(t) - F_n(s))^{a_2};$$

then (C") together with (B') imply (B), and (C') implies (C).

<u>THEOREM 15.</u> Let ξ_n, $n \in \mathbb{N}$, and ξ be random elements in $(D, \mathcal{B}_b(D,\rho))$, all defined on a common p-space $(\Omega, \mathcal{F}, \mathbb{P})$, and suppose that (C) (or (C')) and (D) together with the following conditions (E) and (F) are fulfilled:

(E): $\xi_n \xrightarrow[f.d.]{L} \xi$;

(F): $L\{\xi\}(\{x \in D: x(1) \neq x(1-0)\}) = 0$;

then $\xi_n \xrightarrow{L} \xi$.

<u>Proof.</u> As remarked in (42), (C') implies (C) which together with (D) implies (C") according to (41). But (E) together with (F) and (C") imply the assertion according to Theorem 15.4 in Billingsley (1968) (cf. also Gaenssler-Stute (1977), Satz 8.5.6.). □

In view of Lemma 18 we thus obtain the following L_b-convergence theorem:

<u>THEOREM 16.</u> Let ξ_n, $n \in \mathbb{N}$, and ξ be random elements in $(D, \mathcal{B}_b(D,\rho))$, all defined on a common p-space $(\Omega, \mathcal{F}, \mathbb{P})$, and suppose that $L\{\xi\}(C) = 1$.
Then (C) (or (C')) together with (D) and (E) imply $\xi_n \xrightarrow{L_b} \xi$.

The following result is used in G. Shorack's (1979) paper concerning ξ_n's of a special nature.

THEOREM 17. Let, for every $n \in \mathbb{N}$, $T_n := \{t_o^n, t_1^n, \dots, t_{m_n}^n\}$ be such that $0 = t_o^n \leq t_1^n \leq \dots \leq t_{m_n}^n = 1$. Let $(\xi_n)_{n\in\mathbb{N}}$ be a sequence of random elements in $(D, \mathcal{B}_b(D,\rho))$ such that for all n and $i \leq m_n$ ξ_n is constant on $[t_{i-1}^n, t_i^n)$, i.e.,

$$\omega_{\xi_n}([t_{i-1}^n, t_i^n)) = 0 \quad \text{a.s.}$$

Furthermore, assume that the following conditions (i) - (iii) are fulfilled:

(i) $\max_{i \leq m_n} (t_i^n - t_{i-1}^n) \to 0$ as $n \to \infty$;

(ii) There exists a sequence $(F_n)_{n\in\mathbb{N}}$ of monotone increasing functions F_n: $[0,1] \to \mathbb{R}$ such that for some $a>1$ and $b>0$

$$\mathbb{P}(|\xi_n(s) - \xi_n(r)| \geq \varepsilon,\ |\xi_n(t) - \xi_n(s)| \geq \varepsilon) \leq \varepsilon^{-b}(F_n(t) - F_n(r))^a$$

for every $\varepsilon>0$ and any set $\{r,s,t\} \subset T_n$ with $r \leq s \leq t$;

(iii) There exists a monotone increasing and continuous function F: $[0,1] \to \mathbb{R}$ such that for the F_n's occurring in (ii)

either ⓐ $F_n(t) - F_n(s) \leq F(t) - F(s)$ for every n and any $0 \leq s \leq t \leq 1$

or ⓑ $F_n(t) \to F(t)$ as $n \to \infty$ for every $t \in [0,1]$.

Then $(\xi_n)_{n\in\mathbb{N}}$ satisfies Ⓒ and Ⓓ.

Proof. Let, for each $n \in \mathbb{N}$, φ_n: $[0,1] \to T_n$ be defined by

$$\varphi_n(t) := \max\{r \leq t\colon r \in T_n\},\ t \in [0,1].$$

Then, according to (i), $\lim_{n\to\infty} \varphi_n(t) = t$ for every $t \in [0,1]$.

Now, put $F_n' := F_n \circ \varphi_n$, $n \in \mathbb{N}$, to get a sequence of monotone increasing functions on $[0,1]$; we are going to show that Ⓒ and Ⓓ are satisfied with F_n' (instead of F_n there):

As to Ⓒ, by the assumed nature of the ξ_n's, we have for any $0 \leq t_1 \leq t_2 \leq 1$

$$\xi_n(t_2) - \xi_n(t_1) = \xi_n(\varphi_n(t_2)) - \xi_n(\varphi_n(t_1)),$$

which implies by (ii) that for every $\varepsilon>0$ and any $0 \leq r \leq s \leq t \leq 1$

$$\mathbb{P}(|\xi_n(s) - \xi_n(r)| \geq \varepsilon,\ |\xi_n(t) - \xi_n(s)| \geq \varepsilon) \leq \varepsilon^{-b}(F_n'(t) - F_n'(r))^a,$$

which proves Ⓒ.

As to Ⓓ, we have to show that for any $0 \leq s \leq t \leq 1$

$$(+) \quad \limsup_{n\to\infty} (F'_n(t) - F'_n(s)) \leq F(t) - F(s).$$

But this follows easily from (iii); in fact, (iii) ⓐ implies that for any $0 \leq s \leq t \leq 1$ $\quad F'_n(t) - F'_n(s) = F_n(\varphi_n(t)) - F_n(\varphi_n(s))$

$\leq F(\varphi_n(t)) - F(\varphi_n(s)) \to F(t) - F(s)$ as $n \to \infty$, which implies (+).

On the other hand, (iii) ⓑ implies by the Polya-Cantelli theorem that

$$\sup_{t\in[0,1]} |F_n(t) - F(t)| \to 0 \text{ as } n \to \infty \text{ and therefore,}$$

for any $t \in [0,1]$, $|F'_n(t) - F(t)| \leq |F(t) - F(\varphi_n(t))|$

$+ |F(\varphi_n(t)) - F_n(\varphi_n(t))| \to 0$ as $n \to \infty$, which implies (+). □

This concludes our short review of some of the key results in Billingsley's (1968) book to be used in Section 4 when proving functional central limit theorems for weighted empirical processes along the lines of Shorack's (1979) paper; concerning the L_b-statements there (cf. Theorem 18 and 19 in Section 4) it is possible to modify the above mentioned criteria in Billingsley's book in such a way that they allow for proofs working totally within the theory of L_b-convergence (cf. Remark (73)(b) in Section 4) as it will be the case for the following example concerning Donsker's functional central limit theorem for the uniform empirical process $\alpha_n \equiv (\alpha_n(t))_{t\in[0,1]}$, defined by

$$\alpha_n(t) := n^{1/2}(U_n(t) - t), \; t \in [0,1],$$

where U_n is the empirical distribution function based on independent random variables having uniform distribution on [0,1].

According to (37), α_n can be considered as a random element in $(D,\mathcal{B}_b(D,\rho))$ as well as in $(D,\mathcal{B}(D,s))$ (cf. (38)) and it follows from the multidimensional Central Limit Theorem that

(43) $\alpha_n \xrightarrow[f.d.]{L} B^o$,

where $B^o \equiv (B^o(t))_{t\in[0,1]}$ is the Brownian bridge.

As to B^o, having all its sample paths in the separable and closed subspace $C = (C,\rho)$ of $D = (D,\rho)$, it follows from (39) that $L\{B^o\}$, being originally defined on $\mathcal{B}(C,\rho)$, may be considered as well on $\mathcal{B}_b(D,\rho)$ having the additional property that $L\{B^o\}(C) = 1$. Therefore, B^o may be considered as a random element in $(D,\mathcal{B}_b(D,\rho))$, too, with $L\{B^o\}$ being concentrated on C, whence by Lemma 18 one has

(44) (i) $\alpha_n \xrightarrow{L} B^o$ iff (ii) $\alpha_n \xrightarrow{L_b} B^o$.

It was conjectured by J.L. Doob (1949) and shown by M.D. Donsker (1952) that (44)(i) holds true. There are various ways of proving this result which is known as <u>Donsker's functional central limit theorem for the uniform empirical process:</u>

One may e.g. use Theorem 15 by showing that the hypotheses Ⓒ and Ⓓ are fulfilled (cf. Gaenssler-Stute (1977), Lemma 10.2.2) or one may apply Theorem 15.5 in Billingsley's (1968) book; as to the latter one has to show that

(45) For each positive ε and η there exist a δ, $0 < \delta < 1$, and an integer n_o such that for all $n \geq n_o$

$$\mathbb{P}(w_{\alpha_n}(\delta) > \varepsilon) < \eta,$$

where $w_x(\delta) := \sup_{\substack{|t-s|<\delta \\ t,s\in[0,1]}} |x(t) - x(s)|$ for $x \in D$.

(By the way, it follows from Theorem 15.5 in Billingsley (1968) together with Lemma 18 that (45) is a sufficient condition for $(\alpha_n)_{n\in\mathbb{N}}$ to be relatively L_b-sequentially compact.)

As to (45), this can be shown either by using Donker's invariance principle for partial sum processes (in case of independent exponential random variables) (cf. L. Breiman (1968), problem 9, p. 296) or by more direct computations using the structural properties of empirical measures as presented in Section 1 (cf. W. Stute (1982)) yielding at the same time an independent proof of (44)(ii) <u>within the theory of $\mathcal{L}_b$-convergence in (D,ρ)</u>: in fact, it can be shown (cf. Proposition B_2 in Section 4) that (45) implies δ-tightness of $(\mathcal{L}\{\alpha_n\})_{n\in\mathbb{N}}$ w.r.t. $S_o = C[0,1]$, and therefore Theorem 11^* together with an application of Theorem 3 yields (44)(ii) in view of (43). This also indicates the way to prove Functional Central Limit Theorems for more general empirical processes (empirical $\mathcal{C}$-processes indexed by classes $\mathcal{C}$ of sets) in the setting of $\mathcal{L}_b$-convergence of random elements in appropriately chosen metric spaces.

Before doing this in the next section we want to supplement the present one by some remarks on random change of time (cf. Billingsley (1968), Chapter 3,17.).

RANDOM CHANGE OF TIME:

Following Billingsley (1968) we will briefly indicate here that so-called random change of time arguments are valid also within the context of $\mathcal{L}_b$-convergence (even with simplified proofs not relying on Skorokhod's topology); in this connection the reader should remind our remarks on product spaces.

For this, let D_o consist of those elements φ of $D \equiv D[0,1]$ that are increasing and satisfy $0 \leqq \varphi(t) \leqq 1$ for all t. Such a φ represents a transformation of the time interval $[0,1]$.
We topologize D_o by relativizing the uniform topology of D.
Then (37) implies that $D_o \in \mathcal{B}_b(D)$ and therefore

$$\mathcal{B}_b(D_o) \subset A_o := D_o \cap \mathcal{B}_b(D) = \{B \subset D_o : B \in \mathcal{B}_b(D)\} \subset \mathcal{B}(D_o).$$

For $x \in D$ and $\varphi \in D_o$, let

$$x \circ \varphi : [0,1] \to \mathbb{R}$$

be defined by $(x \circ \varphi)(t) := x(\varphi(t))$, $t \in [0,1]$. Then $x \circ \varphi$ lies in D and, if

$$\psi : D \times D_o \to D$$

is defined by $\psi(x,\varphi) := x \circ \varphi$, then ψ is $\mathcal{B}_b(D) \otimes \mathcal{A}_o$, $\mathcal{B}_b(D)$-measurable, i.e. one has

$$(+) \quad \psi^{-1}(\mathcal{B}_b(D)) \subset \mathcal{A} := \mathcal{B}_b(D) \otimes \mathcal{A}_o$$

where $\mathcal{A}$ is a σ-algebra in the product space $S = D \times D_o$ (being equipped with the maximum metric d (cf. our remarks on product spaces)) such that

$$\mathcal{B}_b(S) \subset \mathcal{A} \subset \mathcal{B}(S).$$

<u>ad (+):</u> cf. Billingsley (1968) p. 232 for a proof being based on the fact that $\mathcal{B}_b(D) = \sigma(\{\pi_t : t \in [0,1]\})$ by (37). □

Now, let ξ_n, $n \in \mathbb{N}$, and ξ be random elements in $(D,\mathcal{B}_b(D))$ and, in addition, let η_n, $n \in \mathbb{N}$, and η be random elements in $(D_o,\mathcal{A}_o)$ all defined on a common p-space $(\Omega,\mathcal{F},\mathbb{P})$.

Then (ξ_n,η_n), $n \in \mathbb{N}$, and (ξ,η) are random elements in

$$(S,\mathcal{A}) = (D \times D_o, \mathcal{B}_b(D) \otimes \mathcal{A}_o)$$

and so, by (+),

$\xi_n \circ \eta_n = \psi(\xi_n,\eta_n)$, $n \in \mathbb{N}$, and $\xi \circ \eta = \psi(\xi,\eta)$ are random elements in $(D,\mathcal{B}_b(D))$ resulting from subjecting ξ_n and ξ to the random change of time represented by η_n and η, respectively.

Concerning a "$(\xi_n,\eta_n) \xrightarrow{\mathcal{L}_b} (\xi,\eta)$"-statement, (ξ,η) may be considered as a random element in $(S,\mathcal{B}_b(S))$, since $\mathcal{B}_b(S) \subset \mathcal{A}$, thus being in accordance with our definition of $\mathcal{L}_b$-convergence.

When asking for conditions under which

$$(++) \qquad (\xi_n,\eta_n) \xrightarrow{\mathcal{L}_b} (\xi,\eta) \text{ implies } \xi_n \circ \eta_n \xrightarrow{\mathcal{L}_b} \xi \circ \eta$$

we know from the continuous mapping theorem (Theorem 4) that (++) holds if ψ is $\mathcal{A},\mathcal{B}_b(D)$-measurable and $\widetilde{\mathcal{L}\{(\xi,\eta)\}}$-a.e. d-continuous.

Now, the required measurability of ψ is guaranteed by (+) and it follows as in Billingsley (1968), p. 145, that ψ is also $\widetilde{\mathcal{L}\{(\xi,\eta)\}}$-a.e. d-continuous if $\mathcal{L}\{\xi\}(C) = \mathcal{L}\{\eta\}(C) = 1$ for $C \equiv C[0,1]$; in fact, if $\mathcal{L}\{\xi\}$ and $\mathcal{L}\{\eta\}$ concentrate on C, then $L\{(\xi,\eta)\}(C \times (C \cap D_o)) = 1$, and it is easy to show that ψ is d-continuous on $C \times (C \cap D_o)$.

It remains of course the question of when

$$(\xi_n,\eta_n) \xrightarrow{L_b} (\xi,\eta)$$

holds and here Theorem 9c can be used leading to the following result on stability of L_b-convergence in $D \equiv D[0,1]$ under random change of time:

<u>THEOREM.</u> Suppose that ξ_n, $n \in \mathbb{N}$, and ξ are random elements in $(D,\mathcal{B}_b(D))$ such that $\xi_n \xrightarrow{L_b} \xi$ and $L\{\xi\}(C) = 1$. Let η_n, $n \in \mathbb{N}$, and η be random elements in (D_o,A_o) such that $\eta_n \xrightarrow{L_b} \eta$ and η equals $\mathbb{P}$-a.s. some function belonging to $C \equiv C[0,1]$*).

Then $\xi_n \circ \eta_n$, $n \in \mathbb{N}$, and $\xi \circ \eta$ are random elements in $(D,\mathcal{B}_b(D))$ for which $\xi_n \circ \eta_n \xrightarrow{L_b} \xi \circ \eta$.

---

*) This last assumption may be omitted by considering instead the set $C \times \{c\}$ as separable support of $L\{(\xi,\eta)\}$ if $\eta = c$ $\mathbb{P}$-a.s.

4. Functional Central Limit Theorems.

In the last section we have already mentioned Donsker's functional central limit theorem for the uniform empirical process $\alpha_n \equiv (\alpha_n(t))_{t\in[0,1]}$, where $\alpha_n(t) = n^{1/2}(U_n(t) - t)$, $U_n(t)$ being the empirical df based on independent random variables η_i having uniform distribution on the sample space $X = [0,1]$ with its Borel σ-algebra $\mathcal{B} = [0,1] \cap \mathbb{B}$.

In the setting of an empirical $\mathcal{C}$-process $\beta_n \equiv (\beta_n(C))_{C\in\mathcal{C}}$ the uniform empirical process α_n is a very special case taking $\mathcal{C} = \{[0,t]: t \in [0,1]\}$ and identifying $\alpha_n(t)$ with $\beta_n(C) = n^{1/2}(\mu_n(C) - \mu(C))$ for $C = [0,t]$, μ_n being the empirical measure based on $\eta_1,\ldots,\eta_n$ and μ being the uniform distribution on $[0,1]$; note that $\mu_n(C) = U_n(t)$ and $\mu(C) = t$ for $C = [0,t]$.

The present section is concerned with some extensions of Donsker's functional central limit theorem in its form (44)(ii) to more general situations.

FUNCTIONAL CENTRAL LIMIT THEOREMS FOR EMPIRICAL $\mathcal{C}$-PROCESSES:

Let $X = (X,\mathcal{B})$ be an arbitrary measurable space considered as a sample space for a given sequence $\xi_1,\xi_2,\ldots$ of i.i.d. random elements in $(X,\mathcal{B})$, the ξ_i's being defined on some common p-space $(\Omega,\mathcal{F},\mathbb{P})$ with law μ on $\mathcal{B}$. If not stated otherwise we will consider the canonical model

$$(\Omega,\mathcal{F},\mathbb{P}) = (X^{\mathbb{N}}, \mathcal{B}_{\mathbb{N}}, \times_{\mathbb{N}} \mu)$$

with the ξ_i's being the coordinate projections of $X^{\mathbb{N}}$ onto X.

Let $\mu_n(B) = \frac{1}{n} \sum_{i=1}^{n} 1_B(\xi_i)$, $B \in \mathcal{B}$, be the empirical measure based on $\xi_1,\ldots,\xi_n$.

Now, given some subclass $\mathcal{C}$ of $\mathcal{B}$, consider the empirical $\mathcal{C}$-process $\beta_n \equiv (\beta_n(C))_{C\in\mathcal{C}}$, defined by

$$\beta_n(C) := n^{1/2}(\mu_n(C) - \mu(C)),\ C \in \mathcal{C},$$

as a stochastic process (on $(\Omega,\mathcal{F},\mathbb{P})$) indexed by $\mathcal{C}$.

As mentioned in Section 1, its covariance structure is given by

$$\mathrm{cov}(\beta_n(C_1),\beta_n(C_2)) = \mu(C_1 \cap C_2) - \mu(C_1)\mu(C_2),\quad C_1,C_2 \in \mathcal{C}.$$

So, the analogue of (44)(ii) would be the statement that (in the sense of (34))

(46) $\beta_n \xrightarrow{\mathcal{L}_b} \mathbb{G}_\mu$, $\mathbb{G}_\mu \equiv (G_\mu(C))_{C\in\mathcal{C}}$ being a mean-zero Gaussian process with $\mathrm{cov}(G_\mu(C_1),G_\mu(C_2)) = \mu(C_1 \cap C_2) - \mu(C_1)\mu(C_2)$, $C_1,C_2 \in \mathcal{C}$.

But this amounts at first to make a proper choice for a metric space $S = (S,d)$ together with a suitable separable subspace S_o serving as sample spaces for β_n and its limiting process $\mathbb{G}_\mu$, respectively.

Following Dudley (1978) we propose to choose $S_o \equiv \mathcal{U}^b(\mathcal{C},d_\mu) :=$ $\{\varphi\colon \mathcal{C} \to \mathbb{R}\colon \varphi$ bounded and uniformly d_μ-continuous$\}$, where d_μ is the pseudo-metric defined on $\mathcal{C}$ by

$$d_\mu(C_1,C_2) := \mu(C_1 \,\Delta\, C_2),\quad C_1,C_2 \in \mathcal{C},$$

($C_1 \,\Delta\, C_2$ denoting the symmetric difference between C_1 and C_2).

Note that, concerning the $\mu(C)$-part of $\beta_n(C)$, $C \to \mu(C)$ is a function belonging to S_o (since $|\mu(C_1) - \mu(C_2)| \leq d_\mu(C_1,C_2)$).

In order to cope also with the $\mu_n(C)$-part of $\beta_n(C)$ (and the factor $n^{1/2}$), let

$$S \equiv D_o(\mathcal{C},\mu) := \{\varphi = \varphi_1 + \varphi_2\colon \varphi_1 \in S_o \text{ and } \varphi_2 = \sum_{i=1}^{k} a_i\varepsilon_{x_i} \text{ for some } a_i \in \mathbb{R},\ x_i \in X,\ 1 \leq i \leq k,\ k \in \mathbb{N}\}.$$

Note that S is a linear space containing S_o as a linear subspace; also $\beta_n(\cdot,\omega) \in S$ for all $\omega \in \Omega$.

Finally, let S (and its subspace S_o) be metrized by the metric $d := \rho$, where ρ is the supremum-metric, i.e.,

$$\rho(\varphi',\varphi'') := \sup_{C\in\mathcal{C}} |\varphi'(C) - \varphi''(C)| \quad \text{for } \varphi',\varphi'' \in S.$$

Note that the closure $D(\mathcal{C},\mu)$ of $D_o(\mathcal{C},\mu)$ in the Banach space $\ell^\infty(\mathcal{C}) = (\ell^\infty(\mathcal{C}),\rho)$ of all bounded real-valued functions on $\mathcal{C}$ can be considered as an extension of $D = D[0,1]$ in the classical case, where $X = [0,1]$, $\mathcal{C} = \{[0,t]: t \in [0,1]\}$, and μ is the uniform distribution on $[0,1]$ or any other distribution on $[0,1]$ with a strictly increasing distribution function; also, in the latter case, $\mathcal{U}^b(\mathcal{C},d_\mu)$ equals $C[0,1]$ after identifying $\varphi([0,t])$ with $x(t)$.

Having made this choice for S_o, S and d, in view of (46) the following problems still remain:

<u>PROBLEM ⓐ (MEASURABILITY):</u> Find conditions under which the β_n's can be viewed as random elements in $(S,\mathcal{A})$ for some σ-algebra $\mathcal{A}$ in S such that one meets the situation of Section 3, i.e.

(47) $$\mathcal{B}_b(S,\rho) \subset \mathcal{A} \subset \mathcal{B}(S,\rho)$$

(with $\mathcal{B}_b(S,\rho)$ being the σ-algebra generated by the open ρ-balls in S, and $\mathcal{B}(S,\rho)$ being the Borel σ-algebra in (S,ρ)).

Taking $\mathcal{A} := \sigma(\{\pi_C: C \in \mathcal{C}\})$, with $\pi_C: S \to \mathbb{R}$ being defined by

$\pi_C(\varphi) := \varphi(C)$, $C \in \mathcal{C}$,

<u>β_n is $\mathcal{F},\mathcal{A}$-measurable</u>

(since $\mathcal{F},\sigma(\{\pi_C: C \in \mathcal{C}\})$-measurability of β_n is equivalent with $\mathcal{F},\mathcal{B}$-measurability of $\pi_C(\beta_n) = \beta_n(C)$ for each fixed $C \in \mathcal{C}$, the latter being satisfied since $\beta_n(C)$ is a random variable (on $(\Omega,\mathcal{F},\mathbb{P})$) for each fixed C),

<u>but the first inclusion in (47) fails to hold, in general:</u>

in fact, looking back to (10) in Section 1, it follows that in the example considered there β_n is <u>not</u> even $\mathcal{F},\mathcal{B}_b(S,\rho)$-measurable.

So, we will restrict our consideration to cases where the following measurability condition

$$(M): \mathcal{B}_b(S,\rho) \subset \mathcal{A} := \sigma(\{\pi_C: C \in \mathcal{C}\})$$

is fulfilled, which turns out to be satisfied in important cases of interest; note that (M) implies (47), since the other inclusion there holds trivially due to the ρ-continuity of the π_C's for each fixed $C \in \mathcal{C}$.

LEMMA 20. Suppose that $\mathcal{C}$ fulfills the following condition

(SE): There exists a countable subclass $\mathcal{D}$ of $\mathcal{C}$ such that for any $C \in \mathcal{C}$ there exists a sequence $(D_n)_{n\in\mathbb{N}}$ in $\mathcal{D}$ with $1_{D_n}(x) \longrightarrow 1_C(x)$ for all $x \in X$;

then (M) holds true.

Proof. (SE) implies that for any $C \in \mathcal{C}$ there exists a sequence $(D_n)_{n\in\mathbb{N}}$ in $\mathcal{D}$ such that $\lim_{n\to\infty} d_\mu(D_n,C) = 0$ from which it follows that $\varphi_1(C) = \lim_{n\to\infty} \varphi_1(D_n)$ for every $\varphi_1 \in S_o$; on the other hand, since $1_{D_n}(x) \to 1_C(x)$ for all x is equivalent with $\lim_{n\to\infty} \varepsilon_x(D_n) = \varepsilon_x(C)$ for all x, we obtain $\varphi(C) = \lim_{n\to\infty} \varphi(D_n)$ for every $\varphi \in S$. But from this it follows that for any $\varphi_o \in S$ and any $r > 0$

$$\{\varphi \in S: \rho(\varphi,\varphi_o) \leq r\} = \bigcap_{D\in\mathcal{D}} \{\varphi \in S: |\varphi(D) - \varphi_o(D)| \leq r\} \in A,$$

since $\mathcal{D}$ is countable, implying (M). □

(48) EXAMPLES. (a) Let $(X,\mathcal{B}) = (\mathbb{R}^k,\mathcal{B}_k)$, $k \geq 1$, and let $\mathcal{C}$ be the class $\mathcal{J}_k$ of all lower left orthants or the class $\mathbb{B}_k$ of all closed Euclidean balls in $\mathbb{R}^k$, respectively; then (SE) and therefore (M) holds true for $\mathcal{C} = \mathcal{J}_k$ and $\mathcal{C} = \mathbb{B}_k$, respectively.

(b) If we consider instead e.g., the class $\mathcal{C} := \{C_o + z: z \in \mathbb{R}^k\}$, C_o being a fixed closed Euclidean ball in $\mathbb{R}^k$, then (SE) fails to hold:
in fact, no $\mathcal{D} = \{C_o + q: q \in R\}$ with countable $R \subset \mathbb{R}^k$ can serve as a countable subclass of $\mathcal{C}$ with the desired property stated in (SE), since for any fixed $z \in \mathbb{R}^k \setminus R$ and any $D_q \in \mathcal{D}$ there exists a $y_q \in \mathbb{R}^k$ such that
$1 = 1_{C_o+z}(y_q) \neq 1_{D_q}(y_q) = 0$

(cf. FIGURE 4).

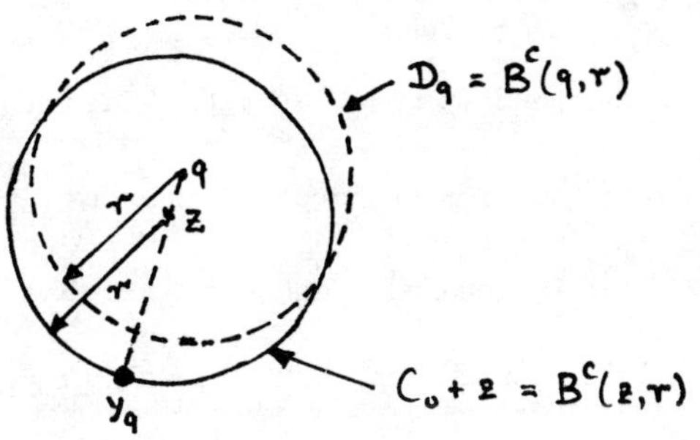

FIGURE 4

We shall see below how to cope also with examples where (SE) fails to hold. For this another measurability assumption (M_o) weaker than (M) will be needed.

It should be noticed (cf. the proof of Lemma 20) that in case of (SE) we have SEPARABILITY of the process $\beta_n \equiv (\beta_n(C))_{C \in \mathcal{C}}$ in the sense that each sample path of β_n is uniquely determined by its values on $\mathcal{D}$.

Let us make some further remarks at this place:

first, note that (M) implies

(49) $\mathcal{B}_b(T,\rho) = \sigma(\{\pi_C(T)\colon C \in \mathcal{C}\}) = \mathcal{B}(T,\rho)$ for <u>any</u> separable subspace T of S, with $\pi_C(T)\colon T \to \mathbb{R}$ being defined by $\pi_C(T)(\varphi) := \varphi(C)$.

In fact, the same reasoning which gave us (39) in Section 3 yields

(50) $\mathcal{B}_b(T,\rho) = T \cap \mathcal{B}_b(S,\rho)$ for any separable subspace T of S,

whence (cf. Lemma 11 (iv))

$$\mathcal{B}_b(T,\rho) = T \cap \mathcal{B}_b(S,\rho) \underset{(M)}{\subset} T \cap \mathcal{A} = \sigma(\{\pi_C(T)\colon C \in \mathcal{C}\}) \subset \mathcal{B}(T,\rho) = \mathcal{B}_b(T,\rho),$$

which proves (49).

Next, <u>concerning $S_o \equiv \mathcal{U}^b(\mathcal{C},d_\mu)$</u>, it follows even without imposing (M) that

(49*) $\mathcal{B}_b(S_o,\rho) = \sigma(\{\pi_C(S_o)\colon C \in \mathcal{C}\}) = \mathcal{B}(S_o,\rho)$, <u>provided that $\mathcal{C}$ is totally bounded for d_μ.</u>

In fact, if $\mathcal{C}$ is totally bounded for d_μ, there exists a countable d_μ-dense subset $\mathcal{D}$ of $\mathcal{C}$ implying, due to the d_μ-continuity of functions belonging to S_o, that for any $\varphi_o \in S_o$ and any $r > 0$

$$\{\varphi \in S_o : \rho(\varphi,\varphi_o) \leq r\} = \bigcap_{D \in \mathcal{D}} \{\varphi \in S_o : |\varphi(D) - \varphi_o(D)| \leq r\}$$

$\in \sigma(\{\pi_C(S_o): C \in \mathcal{C}\})$, whence $\mathcal{B}_b(S_o,\rho) \subset \sigma(\{\pi_C(S_o): C \in \mathcal{C}\}) \subset \mathcal{B}(S_o,\rho)$;

on the other hand, using the Stone-Weierstraß theorem, it can be shown that

(51) $\quad S_o \equiv \mathcal{U}^b(\mathcal{C},d_\mu)$ is separable and ρ-closed (i.e. $S_o^c = S_o$),

<u>provided that $\mathcal{C}$ is totally bounded for d_μ.</u>

This proves (49^*).

For later use it is important to note that (49^*) together with (50) and (51) imply

<u>LEMMA 21.</u> Let $\mathcal{C}$ be totally bounded for d_μ and suppose that $\mathbb{G}_\mu \equiv (G_\mu(C))_{C\in\mathcal{C}}$ has all its sample paths in $S_o \equiv \mathcal{U}^b(\mathcal{C},d_\mu)$; then $\mathbb{G}_\mu$ can be viewed as a random element in $(S,\mathcal{B}_b(S,\rho))$ with $\mathcal{L}\{\mathbb{G}_\mu\}(S_o) = 1$. Furthermore, $\mathcal{L}\{\mathbb{G}_\mu\}$ as well as any other law $\nu \in M_b^1(S)$ with $\nu(S_o) = 1$ is uniquely determined by its fidis (which are the image measures that $\pi_{C_1,\ldots,C_k}(S_o): S_o \to \mathbb{R}^k$ induce on $\mathcal{B}_k$ from ν when ν is viewed as defined on $S_o \cap \mathcal{B}_b(S,\rho) = \mathcal{B}_b(S_o,\rho) = \sigma(\{\pi_C(S_o): C \in \mathcal{C}\})$, where $\pi_{C_1,\ldots,C_k}(S_o)(\varphi) := (\varphi(C_1),\ldots,\varphi(C_k))$.)

This leads us to the next

<u>PROBLEM ⓑ:</u> <u>(EXISTENCE OF A VERSION OF $\overline{\mathbb{G}}_\mu \equiv (\overline{G}_\mu(C))_{C\in\mathcal{C}}$ in $S_o \equiv \mathcal{U}^b(\mathcal{C},d_\mu)$):</u>

Let $\overline{\mathbb{G}}_\mu \equiv (\overline{G}_\mu(C))_{C\in\mathcal{C}}$ be a mean-zero Gaussian process with covariance structure (cf. Section 1, (4))

$$\mathrm{cov}(\overline{G}_\mu(C_1), \overline{G}_\mu(C_2)) = \mu(C_1 \cap C_2) - \mu(C_1)\mu(C_2), \; C_1,C_2 \in \mathcal{C}.$$

Noticing that the fidis of β_n (viewed as a random element in $(S,\mathcal{A})$ with $\mathcal{A} := \sigma(\{\pi_C: C \in \mathcal{C}\})$) are well defined, we have according to (4) of Section 1

(52) $\quad \beta_n \xrightarrow[\text{f.d.}]{\mathcal{L}} \overline{\mathbb{G}}_\mu$, $\overline{\mathbb{G}}_\mu$ being viewed as the coordinate process on

$$(\overline{\Omega},\overline{F},\overline{\mathbb{P}}) = (\mathbb{R}^{\mathcal{C}},\mathcal{B}_{\mathcal{C}},\mathcal{L}\{\overline{\mathbb{G}}_\mu\})$$

(where $\mathcal{L}\{\overline{\mathbb{G}}_\mu\}$ is uniquely determined by the fidis of $\overline{\mathbb{G}}_\mu$ (Kolmogorov's theorem)).

Now, the problem is to find suitable conditions under which there exists a version $\mathbb{G}_\mu$ of $\overline{\mathbb{G}}_\mu$ having all its sample paths in S_o, where here VERSION is to be understood in the sense that $\mathbb{G}_\mu$ and $\overline{\mathbb{G}}_\mu$ have the same fidis (denoted by $\mathbb{G}_\mu \overset{L}{\underset{f.d.}{=}} \overline{\mathbb{G}}_\mu$); in this connection $\mathbb{G}_\mu$ is allowed to be defined on a p-space $(\Omega',F',\mathbb{P}')$ different from $(\overline{\Omega},\overline{F},\overline{\mathbb{P}})$.

It turns out that in order to get a positive result, C is not allowed to be too "large"; cf. R.M. Dudley (1979 a) and also R.M. Dudley (1982). A proper condition on a class C being not too large to allow for a solution of problem ⓑ is in terms of the so-called metric entropy:

for this, let for any $\varepsilon>0$ $N(\varepsilon,C,\mu)$ be the smallest $n \in \mathbb{N}$ such that $C = \bigcup_{j=1}^{n} C_j$ for some classes C_j with $d_\mu\text{-diam}(C_j) := \sup\{d_\mu(C',C''): C',C''\in C_j\} \leq 2\varepsilon$ for each j;

$\log N(\varepsilon,C,\mu)$ is called a METRIC ENTROPY (of C w.r.t. μ).

Obviously, $N(\varepsilon,C,\mu) < \infty$ for each $\varepsilon>0$ iff C is totally bounded for d_μ (in which case $S_o \equiv U^b(C,d_\mu)$ is separable and ρ-closed, by (51)).

Now, as shown by R.M. Dudley (1967) and (1973), cf. p. 71,

(53) $\overline{\mathbb{G}}_\mu$ has a version $\mathbb{G}_\mu \equiv (G_\mu(C))_{C\in C}$ having all its sample paths in $S_o \equiv U^b(C,d_\mu)$ provided that

$$(E_o):\ \int_0^1 (\log N(x^2,C,\mu))^{1/2}\,dx < \infty.$$

But it turns out that (E_o) is not sufficient to ensure (46); in fact, disregarding for the moment measurability questions, the following example shows that (46), i.e. $\beta_n \xrightarrow{L_b} \mathbb{G}_\mu$, fails to hold although (E_o) is satisfied:

Let C be the collection of all finite subsets of $X = [0,1]$ and let μ be the uniform distribution (Lebesgue measure) on $B = [0,1] \cap \mathcal{B}$; then $d_\mu(C_1,C_2) = 0$

for all $C_1, C_2 \in \mathcal{C}$, whence $N(x^2,\mathcal{C},\mu) \equiv 1$ and therefore (E_o) obviously holds true; also $\mu(C) \equiv 0$ on $\mathcal{C}$ implies that $\mathbb{G}_\mu \equiv 0$, but still (46) fails to hold: (46) would imply $\sup_{C\in\mathcal{C}} |\beta_n(C)| \xrightarrow{\mathcal{L}} \sup_{C\in\mathcal{C}} |G_\mu(C)| = 0$ which cannot be true since for the present $\mathcal{C}$ $\sup_{C\in\mathcal{C}} |\beta_n(C)| \equiv n^{1/2} \to \infty$ as $n \to \infty$.

A proper strengthening of (E_o) which will yield (46) and hence also a solution to problem ⓑ is in terms of the so-called metric entropy with inclusion.

For this, let for any $\varepsilon>0$ $N_I(\varepsilon,\mathcal{C},\mu)$ be the smallest $n \in \mathbb{N}$ such that for some $A_1,\ldots,A_n \in \mathcal{B}$ (not necessarily in $\mathcal{C}$), for every $C \in \mathcal{C}$ there exist i,j with $A_i \subset C \subset A_j$ and $\mu(A_j \setminus A_i) < \varepsilon$; $\log N_I(\varepsilon,\mathcal{C},\mu)$ is called a METRIC ENTROPY WITH INCLUSION (of $\mathcal{C}$ w.r.t. μ).

Compared with $N(\varepsilon,\mathcal{C},\mu)$ we have for any $\mathcal{C} \subset \mathcal{B}$ and any μ

(54) $$N(\varepsilon,\mathcal{C},\mu) \leqq N_I(\varepsilon,\mathcal{C},\mu) \text{ for each } \varepsilon>0.$$

For, suppose w.l.o.g. that $n = N_I(\varepsilon,\mathcal{C},\mu) < \infty$; then there exist $A_1,\ldots,A_n \in \mathcal{B}$ such that for any $C \in \mathcal{C}$ there exist i,j with $A_i \subset C \subset A_j$ and $\mu(A_j \setminus A_i) < \varepsilon$. But then, for $i=1,\ldots,n$, $\mathcal{C}_i := \{C \in \mathcal{C}\colon A_i \subset C \text{ and } d_\mu(A_i,C) < \varepsilon\} \neq \emptyset$, d_μ-diam $(\mathcal{C}_i) \leqq 2\varepsilon$, and $\mathcal{C} = \bigcup_{i=1}^{n} \mathcal{C}_i$ (since for each $C \in \mathcal{C}$ there exist i,j such that $A_i \subset C \subset A_j$ and $\mu(A_j \setminus A_i) < \varepsilon$ which implies $d_\mu(A_i,C) \leqq \mu(A_j \setminus A_i) < \varepsilon$, i.e., $C \in \mathcal{C}_i$). This proves (54).

Now, as shown by R.M. Dudley (1978), Theorem 5.1, the following result holds true:

<u>THEOREM A.</u> (M) together with

$$(E_1)\colon \int_0^1 (\log N_I(x^2,\mathcal{C},\mu))^{1/2}\, dx < \infty$$

imply that $\beta_n \xrightarrow{\mathcal{L}_b} \mathbb{G}_\mu$.

The proof of Theorem A is based on the following fundamental characterization theorem (cf. R.M. Dudley (1978)):

THEOREM B. Let $(X,\mathcal{B})$ be an arbitrary measurable space considered as sample space for a given sequence $\xi_1,\xi_2,\ldots$ of i.i.d. random elements ξ_i in $(X,\mathcal{B})$, where the ξ_i's are viewed as coordinate projections of $(\Omega,\mathcal{F},\mathbb{P}) = (X^{\mathbb{N}}, \mathcal{B}_{\mathbb{N}}, \times_{\mathbb{N}} \mu)$ onto X with law $\mathcal{L}\{\xi_i\} \equiv \mu$ on $\mathcal{B}$. Suppose, given some subclass $\mathcal{C}$ of $\mathcal{B}$ together with the empirical $\mathcal{C}$-process $\beta_n \equiv (\beta_n(C))_{C\in\mathcal{C}}$ based on $\xi_1,\ldots,\xi_n$, that (M) is fulfilled.

Then $\beta_n \xrightarrow{\mathcal{L}_b} \mathbb{G}_\mu$ (in which case $\mathcal{C}$ will be called a μ-DONSKER CLASS) if and only if both

(a) $\mathcal{C}$ is totally bounded for d_μ, and

(b) for any $\varepsilon,\eta > 0$ there exists a $\delta = \delta(\varepsilon,\eta)$, $0 < \delta < 1$, and there exists an $n_o = n_o(\varepsilon,\eta,\delta) \in \mathbb{N}$ such that for $n \geq n_o$

$$\mathbb{P}^*(\omega_{\beta_n}(\delta) > \varepsilon) < \eta,$$

where $\omega_\varphi(\delta) := \sup\{|\varphi(C_1) - \varphi(C_2)|: d_\mu(C_1,C_2) < \delta,\ C_1,C_2 \in \mathcal{C}\}$

for $\varphi \in S \equiv D_o(\mathcal{C},\mu)$.

(55) REMARK. A comparison with (45) shows the complete analogy with the classical situation $X = [0,1]$, $\mathcal{B} = [0,1] \cap \mathbb{B}$, μ = uniform distribution on $\mathcal{B}$, $\mathcal{C} = \{[0,t]: t \in [0,1]\}$, where β_n can be identified with the uniform empirical process α_n; note that, due to the compactness of the unit interval, $\mathcal{C} = \{[0,t]: t \in [0,1]\}$ is totally bounded for d_μ: given any $\varepsilon>0$ let

$$n_o := \inf\{n: \tfrac{1}{n} \leq 2\varepsilon\} \text{ and } C_j := \{[0,t]: \tfrac{j-1}{n_o} \leq t < \tfrac{j}{n_o}\};$$

then d_μ-diam $(C_j) \leq 2\varepsilon$ and $\mathcal{C} = \bigcup_{j=1}^{n_o} C_j$.

Before proving Theorem B we will show two auxiliary results:

PROPOSITION B_1 (cf. Problem Ⓑ above). Suppose that (a) and (b) of Theorem B are fulfilled; then $\overline{\mathbb{G}}_\mu = (\overline{G}_\mu(C))_{C\in\mathcal{C}}$ has a version in $S_o \equiv \mathcal{U}^b(\mathcal{C},d_\mu)$, i.e., there exists a Gaussian process $\mathbb{G}_\mu \equiv (G_\mu(C))_{C\in\mathcal{C}}$ having all its sample paths in S_o and such that $\mathbb{G}_\mu \overset{\mathcal{L}}{\underset{\text{f.d.}}{=}} \overline{\mathbb{G}}_\mu$.

Thus, by Lemma 21, $\mathbb{G}_\mu$ can be viewed as a random element in $(S,\mathcal{B}_b(S,\rho))$ with $\mathcal{L}\{\mathbb{G}_\mu\}(S_o) = 1$, where, by (51), S_o is separable and ρ-closed.

<u>Proof of Proposition B_1.</u> As already remarked in connection with problem (b) above, the process $\overline{\mathbb{G}}_\mu$ is viewed as the coordinate process on $(\mathbb{R}^{\mathcal{C}},\mathcal{B}_{\mathcal{C}},\mathcal{L}\{\overline{\mathbb{G}}_\mu\})$. According to (a), for every $n \in \mathbb{N}$ there exist $m_n \in \mathbb{N}$ and $C_{n,1},\ldots,C_{n,m_n} \in \mathcal{C}$ such that $\mathcal{C} = \bigcup_{i=1}^{m_n} B^c_{d_\mu}(C_{n,i},\frac{1}{n})$, where $B^c_{d_\mu}(C_{i,n},\frac{1}{n}) := \{C \in \mathcal{C}: d_\mu(C_{i,n},C) \leq \frac{1}{n}\}$; therefore, $\mathcal{D} := \bigcup_{n\in\mathbb{N}} \bigcup_{i=1}^{m_n} \{C_{n,i}\}$ is a countable and d_μ-dense subset of $\mathcal{C}$. Let

$\mathcal{U}(\mathcal{D},d_\mu) := \{\varphi: \mathcal{D} \to \mathbb{R},\ \varphi \text{ uniformly } d_\mu\text{-continuous}\}$, and let

$\overline{\mathbb{G}}_{\mu,\mathcal{D}} \equiv (\overline{G}_\mu(D))_{D\in\mathcal{D}}$, viewed as the coordinate process on

$(\overline{\Omega},\overline{F},\overline{\mathbb{P}}_{\mathcal{D}}) = (\mathbb{R}^{\mathcal{D}},\mathcal{B}_{\mathcal{D}},\mathcal{L}\{\overline{\mathbb{G}}_{\mu,\mathcal{D}}\})$. Then it suffices to show

> (+) There exists a Gaussian process $\mathbb{G}_{\mu,\mathcal{D}} \equiv (G_\mu(D))_{D\in\mathcal{D}}$ on some p-space $(\Omega',F',\mathbb{P}')$ having all its sample paths in $\mathcal{U}(\mathcal{D},d_\mu)$ and such that $\mathbb{G}_{\mu,\mathcal{D}} \overset{\mathcal{L}}{\underset{\text{f.d.}}{=}} \overline{\mathbb{G}}_{\mu,\mathcal{D}}$.

In fact, once (+) is shown, we can define for each $\omega' \in \Omega'$ $\mathbb{G}_\mu(\omega')$ as the uniquely determined uniformly d_μ-continuous extension on $\mathcal{C}$ of $\mathbb{G}_{\mu,\mathcal{D}}(\omega')$ (i.e., for each $C \in \mathcal{C}$ $G_\mu(C,\omega') = \lim_{n\to\infty} G_\mu(D_n,\omega')$, $(D_n)_{n\in\mathbb{N}} \subset \mathcal{D}$ being such that $d_\mu(C,D_n) \to 0$ as $n \to \infty$). It follows that

(*) $\mathbb{G}_\mu(\omega')$ is bounded for each ω', whence $\mathbb{G}_\mu(\omega') \in S_o$ for all ω',

and (**) $\mathbb{G}_\mu \overset{\mathcal{L}}{\underset{\text{f.d.}}{=}} \overline{\mathbb{G}}_\mu$.

<u>ad (*):</u> By (a), for every $\varepsilon>0$ there exist an $n_o = n_o(\varepsilon) \in \mathbb{N}$ and $\mathcal{C}_j \subset \mathcal{C}$, $j=1,\ldots,n_o$, such that d_μ-diam $(\mathcal{C}_j) \leq 2\varepsilon$ and $\mathcal{C} = \bigcup_{j=1}^{n_o} \mathcal{C}_j$.

Let $\omega' \in \Omega'$ be arbitrary but fixed; since $\mathbb{G}_\mu(\omega')$ is uniformly continuous on $\mathcal{C}$, for each $\delta>0$ there exists an $\varepsilon = \varepsilon(\delta,\omega') > 0$ such that

$$|G_\mu(C_1,\omega') - G_\mu(C_2,\omega')| < \delta \text{ whenever } d_\mu(C_1,C_2) \leq 2\varepsilon \text{ for } C_1,C_2 \in \mathcal{C}.$$

Now, given an arbitrary $C \in \mathcal{C}$, there exists a $j \in \{1,\ldots,n_o\}$ and a $C_j \in \mathcal{C}_j$ such that $d_\mu(C,C_j) \leq 2\varepsilon$, and therefore

$$|G_\mu(C,\omega')| \leq |G_\mu(C,\omega') - G_\mu(C_j,\omega')| + |G_\mu(C_j,\omega')| \leq \delta + |G_\mu(C_j,\omega')|, \text{ whence}$$

$$\sup_{C\in\mathcal{C}} |G_\mu(C,\omega')| \leq \delta + \sup_{1\leq j\leq n_o} |G_\mu(C_j,\omega')| < \infty.$$

ad (**): Let us confine here to show that $\mathcal{L}\{G_\mu(C)\} = \mathcal{L}\{\bar{G}_\mu(C)\}$ for each fixed $C \in \mathcal{C}$; concerning the higher-dimensional fidis the proof runs in a similar way.

Now, given any $C \in \mathcal{C}$, let $(D_n)_{n\in\mathbb{N}} \subset \mathcal{D}$ be such that $d_\mu(C,D_n) \to 0$ as $n \to \infty$, whence, by construction,

$$G_\mu(C,\omega') = \lim_{n\to\infty} G_\mu(D_n,\omega') \quad \text{for all } \omega' \in \Omega',$$

implying $G_\mu(D_n) \xrightarrow{\mathcal{L}} G_\mu(C)$. Now, by $\oplus$, $\mathcal{L}\{G_\mu(D_n)\} = \mathcal{L}\{\bar{G}_\mu(D_n)\} = N(0,\mu(D_n)(1 - \mu(D_n)))$ (cf. (3) of Section 1) for each $n \in \mathbb{N}$, where $\mu(D_n) \to \mu(C)$ as $n \to \infty$, since $\lim_{n\to\infty} d_\mu(C,D_n) = 0$;

therefore $\mathcal{L}\{G_\mu(C)\} = N(0,\mu(C)(1 - \mu(C))) = \mathcal{L}\{\bar{G}_\mu(C)\}$.

So it remains to show $\oplus$:

According to Lemma 7.2.31 and Satz 7.1.18 in Gaenssler-Stute (1977) $\oplus$ is equivalent with

$$(\text{++}) \qquad \bar{\mathbb{P}}_{\mathcal{D}}(\{\varphi \in \mathbb{R}^{\mathcal{D}} : \varphi \in \mathcal{U}(\mathcal{D},d_\mu)\}) = 1,$$

where $\varphi \in \mathcal{U}(\mathcal{D},d_\mu)$ iff $\lim_{\delta\downarrow 0} w_\varphi^{\mathcal{D}}(\delta) = 0$ with

$$w_\varphi^{\mathcal{D}}(\delta) := \sup \{|\varphi(D_1) - \varphi(D_2)| : d_\mu(D_1,D_2) < \delta,\ D_1,D_2 \in \mathcal{D}\}$$

being $\mathcal{B}_{\mathcal{D}},\mathcal{B}$-measurable as a function in φ.

Note that for any $\varphi \in \mathbb{R}^{\mathcal{D}}$ and any $\delta>0$

$$w_\varphi^{\mathcal{D}_n}(\delta) \uparrow w_\varphi^{\mathcal{D}}(\delta) \quad \text{as } \mathcal{D}_n \uparrow \mathcal{D},$$

whence for any $\varepsilon>0$ we have

(c) $$\{\varphi \in \mathbb{R}^{\mathcal{D}}: w_{\varphi}^{\mathcal{D}}(\delta) > \varepsilon\} \subset \bigcup_{n\in\mathbb{N}} \{\varphi \in \mathbb{R}^{\mathcal{D}}: w_{\varphi}^{\mathcal{D}_n}(\delta) > \varepsilon\} \text{ as } \mathcal{D}_n \uparrow \mathcal{D}.$$

We are going to show next that (++) is implied by

(R_o): For any $\varepsilon,\eta > 0$ there exists a $\delta = \delta(\varepsilon,\eta)$, $0 < \delta < 1$, such that

$$\bar{\mathbb{P}}_{\mathcal{D}}(\{\varphi \in \mathbb{R}^{\mathcal{D}}: w_{\varphi}^{\mathcal{D}}(\delta) > \varepsilon\}) < \eta.$$

In fact, (R_o) implies that for each fixed $\varepsilon>0$

$$\sum_{n\in\mathbb{N}} \bar{\mathbb{P}}_{\mathcal{D}}(\{\varphi \in \mathbb{R}^{\mathcal{D}}: w_{\varphi}^{\mathcal{D}}(\delta_n) > \varepsilon\}) < \infty$$

for some suitable sequence $\delta_n \downarrow 0$, whence, by the Borel-Cantelli lemma, for $\bar{\mathbb{P}}_{\mathcal{D}}$-almost all $\varphi \in \mathbb{R}^{\mathcal{D}}$ there exists an $n(\varphi) \in \mathbb{N}$ such that for all $n \geqq n(\varphi)$ $w_{\varphi}^{\mathcal{D}}(\delta_n) \leqq \varepsilon$ which implies, by repeating the argument for a sequence of ε's tending to zero, that for $\bar{\mathbb{P}}_{\mathcal{D}}$-almost all $\varphi \in \mathbb{R}^{\mathcal{D}}$

$$\lim_{\delta\downarrow 0} w_{\varphi}^{\mathcal{D}}(\delta) = 0, \text{ i.e. } \varphi \in \mathcal{U}(\mathcal{D},d_{\mu}),$$

which proves (++).

So far we only made use of assumption (a); now, the proof of Proposition B_1 will be concluded by showing that the other assumption (b) implies (R_o): for this, remembering that $\mathcal{D}$ is countable, let $\mathcal{D}_n \subset \mathcal{D}$, $n \in \mathbb{N}$, with $|\mathcal{D}_n| < \infty$ $\mathcal{D}_n \uparrow \mathcal{D}$; then, according to (c) it suffices to show:

(d) For any $\varepsilon,\eta > 0$ there exists a $\delta = \delta(\varepsilon,\eta)$, $0 < \delta < 1$, such that for any $\mathcal{D}' \subset \mathcal{D}$ with $|\mathcal{D}'| < \infty$

$$\bar{\mathbb{P}}_{\mathcal{D}}(\{\varphi \in \mathbb{R}^{\mathcal{D}}: w_{\varphi}^{\mathcal{D}'}(\delta) > \varepsilon\}) < \eta,$$

where, for $\mathcal{D}' = \{D_1,\ldots,D_\ell\}$, $w_{\varphi}^{\mathcal{D}'}(\delta) > \varepsilon$ iff $(\varphi(D_1),\ldots,\varphi(D_\ell)) \in G$ with $G = G_{\varepsilon,\delta}$ being some <u>open</u> subset of $\mathbb{R}^{\ell}$.

Now, given an arbitrary $\varepsilon>0$ and an arbitrary $\eta>0$ choose $\delta = \delta(\varepsilon,\eta)$, $0 < \delta < 1$ according to (b) such that for all $n \geqq n_o(\varepsilon,\eta,\delta)$

(e) $$\mathbb{P}^*(w_{\beta_n}(\delta) > \varepsilon) < \eta.$$

Then it follows that for each $\mathcal{D}' = \{D_1,\dots,D_\ell\} \subset \mathcal{D}$ $(\subset \mathcal{C})$

$$\bar{\mathbb{P}}_{\mathcal{D}}(\{\varphi \in \mathbb{R}^{\mathcal{D}}: w_\varphi^{\mathcal{D}'}(\delta) > \varepsilon\}) = \bar{\mathbb{P}}_{\mathcal{D}}(\{\varphi \in \mathbb{R}^{\mathcal{D}}: (\varphi(D_1),\dots,\varphi(D_\ell)) \in G\})$$

$$= \bar{\mathbb{P}}_{\mathcal{D}} \circ \pi^{-1}_{D_1,\dots,D_\ell}(G) = L\{\mathbb{G}_\mu\} \circ \pi^{-1}_{D_1,\dots,D_\ell}(G)$$

$$\leq \liminf_{n\to\infty} L\{\beta_n\} \circ \pi^{-1}_{\{D_1,\dots,D_\ell\}}(G) = \liminf_{n\to\infty} \mathbb{P} \circ (\pi_{\{D_1,\dots,D_\ell\}} \circ \beta_n)^{-1}(G)$$

$$= \liminf_{n\to\infty} \mathbb{P}(w_{\beta_n}^{\mathcal{D}'}(\delta) > \varepsilon) \leq \liminf_{n\to\infty} \mathbb{P}^*(w_{\beta_n}(\delta) > \varepsilon) \underset{(e)}{\leq} \eta,$$

where for the first inequality above we made use of (28) and the fact that according to (52) and (**) $\beta_n \xrightarrow[\text{f.d.}]{L} \mathbb{G}_\mu$.

This proves Proposition B_1. □

(56) <u>REMARK.</u> The proof just given of Proposition B_1 shows that in order to get a result like (53), it suffices to show that an entropy condition like (E_o) implies (R_o). This was nicely demonstrated by D. Pollard (1982) in one of his Seminar talks at Seattle using an analogue of the chaining argument of R.M. Dudley ((1978), pp. 915, 924); cf. also D. Pollard (1981), pp. 191-192.

<u>PROPOSITION B_2.</u> Suppose that (a) and (b) of Theorem B are fulfilled and also (M); then $(L\{\beta_n\})_{n\in\mathbb{N}}$ is δ-tight w.r.t. $S_o \equiv \mathcal{U}^b(\mathcal{C},d_\mu)$.

(Note again that $L\{\beta_n\} \in M_a^1(S)$, $S \equiv D_o(\mathcal{C},\mu)$.)

For the proof of Proposition B_2 we will make use of the <u>Kirszbraun-McShane-Theorem</u> (cf. M.D. Kirszbraun (1934) and McShane (1934)): let $S = (S,d)$ be a metric space, $A \subset S$, and let φ be a real-valued function defined on A such that

$$\sup\{|\varphi(x) - \varphi(y)|/d(x,y): x,y \in A,\ x \neq y\} =: K < \infty;$$

then φ can be extended to a function ψ on all of S with

$$\sup\{|\psi(x) - \psi(y)|/d(x,y): x,y \in S,\ x \neq y\} = K.$$

<u>Proof of Proposition B_2 (cf. R.M. Dudley (1978), Lemma (1.3)).</u>

For any $\varepsilon,\delta > 0$ let

$B_{\delta,\varepsilon} := \{\varphi \in D_o(\mathcal{C},\mu)\colon \exists C_1,C_2 \in \mathcal{C} \text{ s.t. } d_\mu(C_1,C_2) < \delta \text{ and } |\varphi(C_1) - \varphi(C_2)| > \varepsilon\}.$

Note that $\varphi \in B_{\delta,\varepsilon}$ iff $\omega_\varphi(\delta) > \varepsilon$.

We have to show:

for any $0 < \varepsilon < 1$ there exists a compact set $K \subset \mathcal{U}^b(\mathcal{C},d_\mu)$ such that for each $\gamma>0$ $\mathcal{L}\{\beta_n\}(K^\gamma) > 1 - \varepsilon$ for n large enough.

(Note that $K^\gamma \in \mathcal{B}_b(S,\rho) \subset \mathcal{A}$ by (M).)

Let $0 < \varepsilon < 1$ be given; by (b) take $\delta = \delta(\varepsilon)$, $0 < \delta < 1$, such that

ⓐ $$\mathbb{P}^*(\beta_n \in B_{\delta,\varepsilon/2}) < \varepsilon/4 \text{ for all } n \geq n_o(\varepsilon,\delta(\varepsilon)).$$

According to (a) there exists a finite $\mathcal{C}_o = \mathcal{C}_o(\delta) \subset \mathcal{C}$ such that for all $C \in \mathcal{C}$, $d_\mu(C,C_o) < \delta$ for some $C_o \in \mathcal{C}_o$.

Let $k := |\mathcal{C}_o|$; then $k = k(\delta(\varepsilon)) \in \mathbb{N}$.

Take $M = M(\varepsilon)$ large enough so that $(M - 1)^{-2} < \varepsilon/k$; then

ⓑ $$\mathbb{P}(\sup_{C\in\mathcal{C}} |\beta_n(C)| > M) < \varepsilon/2 \text{ for all } n \geq n_o(\varepsilon) \equiv n_o(\varepsilon,\delta(\varepsilon)).$$

<u>ad ⓑ:</u> Note that $\{\omega\colon \sup_{C\in\mathcal{C}} |\beta_n(C,\omega)| > M\} \in \mathcal{F}$ according to (M);

now, for each $C_o \in \mathcal{C}_o$, $\mathbb{P}(|\beta_n(C_o)| > M - 1) < \varepsilon/4k$ by Chebyshev's inequality (and the choice of M), whence

(b_o) $$\mathbb{P}(\sup_{C\in\mathcal{C}_o} |\beta_n(C_o)| > M - 1) < \varepsilon/4.$$

Next, $\sup_{C\in\mathcal{C}} |\beta_n(C,\omega)| > M$ and $|\beta_n(C_1,\omega) - \beta_n(C_2,\omega)| \leq \varepsilon/2$

for all $C_1,C_2 \in \mathcal{C}$ with $d_\mu(C_1,C_2) < \delta$ together imply (due to the choice of $\mathcal{C}_o$) that there exists a $C_o \in \mathcal{C}_o$ such that

$|\beta_n(C_o,\omega)| > M - \varepsilon/2 > M - 1$, whence

$$\{\sup_{C\in\mathcal{C}} |\beta_n(C)| > M\} \subset \{\beta_n \in B_{\delta,\varepsilon/2}\} \cup \{\sup_{C_o\in\mathcal{C}_o} |\beta_n(C_o)| > M - 1\}$$

which implies ⓑ according to ⓐ and (b_o).

Now, for any $j \in \mathbb{N}$, let $\varepsilon(j) := \varepsilon \cdot 2^{-j}$; then by (b) there exists a sequence $\delta(j) = \delta(j,\varepsilon) > 0$, $j \in \mathbb{N}$, such that

(i) $\delta(j+1) < \delta(j)/2$, and

(ii) $\mathbb{P}^*(\beta_n \in B_{\delta(j),\varepsilon(j)}) < \varepsilon(j)$ for all $n \geq n_0(\varepsilon,j)$.

Let $A_j := B_{\delta(j),\varepsilon(j)}$ and $\delta_j := \dfrac{\delta(j)\varepsilon}{2^{j+1}M} = \dfrac{\delta(j)\varepsilon(j)}{2M}$;

then, by (i), we have

(iii) $\delta_{j+1} < \delta_j/4$ and $\dfrac{\varepsilon(j)}{\delta_j}$ is increasing with j.

Furthermore, for $m \geq 2$, let

$$F_m := \{\varphi \in D_o(\mathcal{C},\mu): \sup_{C\in\mathcal{C}} |\varphi(C)| \leq M \text{ and s.t. for all } C_1,C_2 \in \mathcal{C}$$

$$|\varphi(C_1) - \varphi(C_2)| \leq \varepsilon(j)\cdot \max\left(1, \frac{d_\mu(C_1,C_2)}{\delta_j}\right) \text{ for } j=2,\ldots,m\};$$

then

ⓒ $\sup_{C\in\mathcal{C}} |\varphi(C)| \leq M$ for some $\varphi \in D_o(\mathcal{C},\mu)$ and $\varphi \in \complement A_j$ for $j=2,\ldots,m$

together imply that $\varphi \in F_m$.

ad ⓒ: $\sup_{C\in\mathcal{C}} |\varphi(C)| \leq M$ implies that for all $C_1,C_2 \in \mathcal{C}$

$$|\varphi(C_1) - \varphi(C_2)| \leq 2M = \frac{\delta(j)\varepsilon(j)}{\delta_j} \leq \varepsilon(j)\,\frac{d_\mu(C_1,C_2)}{\delta_j}, \text{ if}$$

$d_\mu(C_1,C_2) \geq \delta(j)$ for all $C_1,C_2 \in \mathcal{C}$; on the other hand,

$d_\mu(C_1,C_2) < \delta(j)$ for some $C_1,C_2 \in \mathcal{C}$ together with $\varphi \in \complement A_j$

imply $|\varphi(C_1) - \varphi(C_2)| \leq \varepsilon(j)$, which proves ⓒ.

We will show next that (ii) together with ⓑ and ⓒ imply

ⓓ For each $m \geq 2$ there exists an $n_1 = n_1(\varepsilon,m) \in \mathbb{N}$ such that for all $n \geq n_1$ there exists an $E_{nm} \in \mathcal{F}$ with $\mathbb{P}(E_{nm}) > 1-\varepsilon$ and $\beta_n(\cdot,\omega) \in F_m$ for all $\omega \in E_{nm}$.

ad ⓓ: According to (ii), let $n_0(\varepsilon,m)$ be large enough such that for all $n \geq n_0(\varepsilon,m)$ and each $j=2,\ldots,m$ there exist $E'_{nj} \in \mathcal{F}$ with

$\{\beta_n \in A_j\} \subset E'_{nj}$ and $\mathbb{P}(E'_{nj}) < \varepsilon(j) = \varepsilon \cdot 2^{-j}$,

whence $\mathbb{P}(\complement \bigcup_{j=2}^{m} E'_{nj}) > 1 - \varepsilon/2$ and $\complement \bigcup_{j=2}^{m} E'_{nj} \subset \bigcap_{j=2}^{m} \{\beta_n \in \complement A_j\}$;

thus, for $E_{nm} := (\complement \bigcup_{j=2}^{m} E'_{nj}) \cap \{\sup_{C \in \mathcal{C}} |\beta_n(C)| \leq M\} \in \mathcal{F}$,

we obtain together with (b) and (c) that for $n \geq n_1 := \max(n_o(\varepsilon,m), n_o(\varepsilon))$

$\mathbb{P}(E_{nm}) > 1 - \varepsilon$ and $\beta_n(\cdot,\omega) \in F_m$ for all $\omega \in E_{nm}$.

This proves (d).

Now let

$$K := \{\varphi \in \ell^\infty(\mathcal{C}) \colon \sup_{C \in \mathcal{C}} |\varphi(C)| \leq M \text{ and s.t. for all } j \in \mathbb{N}$$

$$d_\mu(C_1,C_2) < \delta_j/2 \text{ implies } |\varphi(C_1) - \varphi(C_2)| \leq 3\varepsilon(j)\}.$$

Then $K \subset \mathcal{U}^b(\mathcal{C},d_\mu)$. Now, $(\mathcal{C},d_\mu)$ is totally bounded and K is a uniformly bounded and equicontinuous family of functions being ρ-closed in the Banach space $(\ell^\infty(\mathcal{C}),\rho)$ whence, by the Arzelà-Ascoli theorem (applied to the completion of $(\mathcal{C},d_\mu)$) it follows that K is compact.

So, it remains to show that for each $\gamma > 0$

$$\mathcal{L}\{\beta_n\}(K^\gamma) > 1 - \varepsilon \quad \text{for n large enough.}$$

For this it suffices to prove

(e) For each $\gamma > 0$ there exists an $m = m(\varepsilon,\gamma)$ such that $F_m \subset K^\gamma$.

In fact, (e) together with (d) imply $\mathcal{L}\{\beta_n\}(K^\gamma) \geq \mathbb{P}^*(\beta_n \in F_m) \geq \mathbb{P}(E_{nm}) > 1 - \varepsilon$ for $n \geq n_1(\varepsilon, m(\varepsilon,\gamma))$, which concludes the proof of Proposition B_2.

<u>ad (e):</u> Given $\gamma > 0$, choose $m = m(\varepsilon,\gamma)$ such that $\varepsilon(m) < \gamma/2$ and take a <u>maximal</u> set $\mathcal{C}_m \subset \mathcal{C}$ such that

$$d_\mu(C_1,C_2) \geq \delta_m \text{ for all } C_1 \neq C_2 \text{ in } \mathcal{C}_m.$$

Then $\mathcal{C}_m$ is finite by (a) and for all $C \in \mathcal{C}$, $d_\mu(C,C') < \delta_m$ for some $C' \in \mathcal{C}_m$ (by the maximality of $\mathcal{C}_m$).

Now, if $\varphi \in F_m$ and $C_1, C_2 \in \mathcal{C}_m$, then (since $\frac{d_\mu(C_1,C_2)}{\delta_m} \geq 1$ for $C_1 \neq C_2$) we obtain (cf. the definition of F_m)

$$|\varphi(C_1) - \varphi(C_2)| \leq \varepsilon(m) \frac{d_\mu(C_1,C_2)}{\delta_m}.$$

Applying the Kirszbraun-McShane Theorem, $\text{rest}_{\mathcal{C}_m} \varphi$ can be extended to a function ψ on $\mathcal{C}$ with

$$\text{(iv)} \qquad |\psi(C_1) - \psi(C_2)| \leq \varepsilon(m) \frac{d_\mu(C_1,C_2)}{\delta_m} \quad \text{for all } C_1, C_2 \in \mathcal{C}.$$

In addition, w.l.o.g. we may assume that $\sup_{C \in \mathcal{C}} |\psi(C)| \leq M$.

Let us show that $\psi \in K$, i.e.,

for all $j \in \mathbb{N}$ $\quad d_\mu(C_1,C_2) < \delta_j/2$ implies $|\psi(C_1) - \psi(C_2)| \leq 3\varepsilon(j)$.

For $j \geq m$, since $\frac{\varepsilon(j)}{\delta_j} \geq \frac{\varepsilon(m)}{\delta_m}$ by (iii), we obtain from (iv)

$$|\psi(C_1) - \psi(C_2)| \leq \varepsilon(j) \text{ if } d_\mu(C_1,C_2) \leq \delta_j;$$

for $j < m$, given $C_i \in \mathcal{C}$, $i=1,2$, with $d_\mu(C_1,C_2) < \delta_j/2$, choose $C_i' \in \mathcal{C}_m$ such that $d_\mu(C_i,C_i') < \delta_m$, $i=1,2$;

then $d_\mu(C_1',C_2') < 2\delta_m + \delta_j/2 \underset{\text{(iii)}}{\leq} \delta_j$, and so by (iv) (note that $\text{rest}_{\mathcal{C}_m} \psi = \text{rest}_{\mathcal{C}_m} \varphi$, $\varphi \in F_m$)

$$|\psi(C_1) - \psi(C_2)| \leq |\psi(C_1) - \psi(C_1')| + |\varphi(C_1') - \varphi(C_2')|$$
$$+ |\psi(C_2') - \psi(C_2)| \leq \varepsilon(m) + \varepsilon(j) + \varepsilon(m) \leq 3\varepsilon(j).$$

Thus $\psi \in K$.

Now, we have $\rho(\varphi,\psi) < \gamma$ since for any $C \in \mathcal{C}$ there exists a $C' \in \mathcal{C}_m$ such that $d_\mu(C,C') < \delta_m$, whence (since $\varphi \in F_m$ and by (iv))

$$|\varphi(C) - \psi(C)| \leq |\varphi(C) - \varphi(C')| + |\psi(C') - \psi(C)|$$
$$\leq 2\varepsilon(m) < \gamma.$$

So $F_m \subset K^\gamma$ which concludes the proof of ⓔ. □

We are now in a position to give the

Proof of Theorem B. First assume (a) and (b). Then, by Proposition B_1, we can view $\mathbb{G}_\mu \equiv (G_\mu(C))_{C\in\mathcal{C}}$ as a random element in $(S,\mathcal{B}_b(S,\rho))$ with $\mathcal{L}\{\mathbb{G}_\mu\}(S_o) = 1$, $S_o \equiv \mathcal{U}^b(\mathcal{C},d_\mu)$ being ρ-closed and separable; furthermore, as mentioned at the end of the proof of Proposition B_1, we have

(1) $$\beta_n \xrightarrow[\text{f.d.}]{\mathcal{L}} \mathbb{G}_\mu.$$

Now, by Proposition B_2, $(\mathcal{L}\{\beta_n\})_{n\in\mathbb{N}}$ is δ-tight w.r.t. S_o, whence it follows from Theorem 11^* that

for every subsequence $(\mathcal{L}\{\beta_{n'}\})$ of $(\mathcal{L}\{\beta_n\})$ there exists a further subsequence $(\mathcal{L}\{\beta_{n''}\})$ of $(\mathcal{L}\{\beta_{n'}\})$ and a $\nu = \nu_{(n'),(n'')} \in \mathcal{M}_b^1(S)$ with $\nu(S_o) = 1$ such that

(2) $$\mathcal{L}\{\beta_{n''}\} \xrightarrow[b]{} \nu.$$

Since each projection $\pi_{C_1,\ldots,C_k} : S \to \mathbb{R}^k$ is $\mathcal{A},\mathcal{B}_k$-measurable and ρ-continuous and since (M) is assumed, we obtain from (2) by Theorem 3 that

(3) $$\mathcal{L}\{\beta_{n''}\}\circ\pi^{-1}_{C_1,\ldots,C_k} \xrightarrow[b]{} \nu\circ\pi^{-1}_{C_1,\ldots,C_k}$$

for each $C_1,\ldots,C_k \in \mathcal{C}$.

Together with (1) this implies that ν and $\mathcal{L}\{\mathbb{G}_\mu\}$ must have the same fidis; thus $\nu = \mathcal{L}\{\mathbb{G}_\mu\}$ on $\mathcal{B}_b(S,\rho)$ (cf. Lemma 21) and therefore

$$\mathcal{L}\{\beta_n\} \xrightarrow[b]{} \mathcal{L}\{\mathbb{G}_\mu\}, \text{ i.e. } \beta_n \xrightarrow{\mathcal{L}_b} \mathbb{G}_\mu.$$

Conversely if $\mathcal{C}$ is a μ-Donsker class, then (a) holds (cf. Proposition 3.4 in R.M. Dudley (1967)). So it remains to prove (b) (where it suffices to prove the assertion there by taking $\eta = \varepsilon$).

Now, by Theorem 12 there exists a sequence $\hat\beta_n$, $n \in \mathbb{N}$, of random elements in $(S,\mathcal{A})$ and a random element $\hat{\mathbb{G}}_\mu$ in $(S,\mathcal{B}_b(S,\rho))$, all defined on an appropriate p-space $(\hat\Omega,\hat{\mathcal{F}},\hat{\mathbb{P}})$, such that

(4) $L\{\hat{\beta}_n\} = L\{\beta_n\}$ (on A) for all $n \in \mathbb{N}$, $L\{\hat{\mathbb{G}}_\mu\} = L\{\mathbb{G}_\mu\}$ (on $\mathcal{B}_b(S,\rho)$)

and

(5) $\rho(\hat{\beta}_n(\hat{\omega}), \hat{\mathbb{G}}_\mu(\hat{\omega})) = \sup_{C\in\mathcal{C}} |\hat{\beta}_n(C,\hat{\omega}) - \hat{G}_\mu(C,\hat{\omega})| \to 0$ as $n \to \infty$

for all $\hat{\omega} \in \hat{\Omega}_o \in \hat{F}$ with $\hat{\mathbb{P}}(\hat{\Omega}_o) = 1$.

Since $L\{\hat{\mathbb{G}}_\mu\}(S_0) \underset{(4)}{=} L\{\mathbb{G}_\mu\}(S_0) = 1$, we may assume w.l.o.g. that $\hat{\mathbb{G}}_\mu(\hat{\omega}) \in S_0$ for all $\hat{\omega} \in \hat{\Omega}$, whence for any $\varepsilon>0$ there exists a $\delta = \delta(\varepsilon) > 0$ such that

(6) $\hat{\mathbb{P}}(w_{\hat{\mathbb{G}}_\mu}(\delta) > \varepsilon/2) < \varepsilon/2.$

(Note that $\{\hat{\omega} \in \hat{\Omega}: w_{\hat{\mathbb{G}}_\mu(\hat{\omega})}(\delta) > \varepsilon/2\} \in \hat{F}$ if, as just assumed, $\hat{\mathbb{G}}_\mu(\hat{\omega}) \in S_0$ for all $\hat{\omega} \in \hat{\Omega}$.)

Now, since S_0 is separable, take a sequence $\{\varphi_m: m \in \mathbb{N}\}$ dense in $S_0 \cap \complement B_{\delta,\varepsilon/2}$ (with $B_{\delta,\varepsilon/2} := \{\varphi \in S: \exists C_1,C_2 \in \mathcal{C}$ s.t. $d_\mu(C_1,C_2) < \delta$ and $|\varphi(C_1)-\varphi(C_2)| > \varepsilon/2\}$).

Let

$T_0 := \bigcup_{m\in\mathbb{N}} B_\rho(\varphi_m,\varepsilon/4)$ ($B_\rho(\varphi_m,\varepsilon/4)$ denoting the open ρ-ball with center φ_m and radius $\varepsilon/4$);

then $T_0 \in \mathcal{B}_b(S,\rho)$ whence, by (M), $\{\beta_n \notin T_0\} \in F$ as well as $\{\hat{\beta}_n \notin T_0\} \in \hat{F}$ for each n.

Furthermore we have

$$T_0 \cap B_{\delta,\varepsilon} = \emptyset:$$

in fact, $\varphi \in T_0$ implies that $\rho(\varphi_m,\varphi) < \varepsilon/4$ for some $m \in \mathbb{N}$, and since $\varphi_m \in \complement B_{\delta,\varepsilon/2}$, we have for any $C_1,C_2 \in \mathcal{C}$

$$\text{either } d_\mu(C_1,C_2) \geq \delta \quad \text{or} \quad |\varphi_m(C_1) - \varphi_m(C_2)| \leq \varepsilon/2,$$

implying in the latter case that $|\varphi(C_1) - \varphi(C_2)| \leq |\varphi(C_1) - \varphi_m(C_1)| + |\varphi_m(C_1) - \varphi_m(C_2)| + |\varphi_m(C_2) - \varphi(C_2)| < \varepsilon$, whence $\varphi \in \complement B_{\delta,\varepsilon}$.

We thus obtain for each $n \in \mathbb{N}$

$$\mathbb{P}^*(\omega_{\beta_n}(\delta) > \varepsilon) = \mathbb{P}^*(\beta_n \in B_{\delta,\varepsilon}) \leq \mathbb{P}^*(\beta_n \notin T_o) = \mathbb{P}(\beta_n \notin T_o) = \hat{\mathbb{P}}(\hat{\beta}_n \notin T_o),$$

and so it remains to show

⑦ $\hat{\mathbb{P}}(\hat{\beta}_n \notin T_o) < \varepsilon$ for n sufficiently large.

This will follow now easily from ⑤ together with ⑥:

At first ⑤ implies that there exists an $n_o = n_o(\varepsilon) \in \mathbb{N}$ such that

⑧ $\hat{\mathbb{P}}^*(\rho(\hat{\beta}_n, \hat{\mathbb{G}}_\mu) > \varepsilon/8) < \varepsilon/2$ for all $n \geq n_o$.

Next, if $\hat{\beta}_n(\hat{\omega}) \notin T_o$ then $\rho(\varphi_m, \hat{\beta}_n(\hat{\omega})) \geq \varepsilon/4$ for all $m \in \mathbb{N}$, whence

either $\rho(\hat{\beta}_n(\hat{\omega}), \hat{\mathbb{G}}_\mu(\hat{\omega})) > \varepsilon/8$

or $\rho(\varphi_m, \hat{\mathbb{G}}_\mu(\hat{\omega})) \geq \varepsilon/8$ for all $m \in \mathbb{N}$

(note that $\rho(\hat{\beta}_n(\hat{\omega}), \hat{\mathbb{G}}_\mu(\hat{\omega})) \leq \varepsilon/8$ implies $\rho(\varphi_m, \hat{\mathbb{G}}_\mu(\hat{\omega})) \geq \rho(\varphi_m, \hat{\beta}_n(\hat{\omega})) - \rho(\hat{\beta}_n(\hat{\omega}), \hat{\mathbb{G}}_\mu(\hat{\omega})) \geq \varepsilon/4 - \varepsilon/8 = \varepsilon/8$ for all $m \in \mathbb{N}$).

But since $\rho(\varphi_m, \hat{\mathbb{G}}_\mu(\hat{\omega})) \geq \varepsilon/8$ for all $m \in \mathbb{N}$ implies $\omega_{\hat{\mathbb{G}}_\mu(\hat{\omega})}(\delta) > \varepsilon/2$ (note that $\omega_{\hat{\mathbb{G}}_\mu(\hat{\omega})}(\delta) \leq \varepsilon/2$ would imply $\hat{\mathbb{G}}_\mu(\hat{\omega}) \in H := S_o \cap \complement B_{\delta,\varepsilon/2}$, whence $\rho(\varphi_m, \hat{\mathbb{G}}_\mu(\hat{\omega})) < \varepsilon/8$ for some $m \in \mathbb{N}$ since $\{\varphi_m : m \in \mathbb{N}\}$ is dense in H),

it follows from ⑥ together with ⑧ that ⑦ holds true.

This concludes the proof of Theorem B. □

After having taken great care in proving the fundamental characterization theorem for μ-Donsker classes[1)], we can confine ourselves now to giving Dudley's

<u>Proof of Theorem A.</u>

In view of (E_1) and (54) we have $N(\varepsilon, \mathcal{C}, \mu) < \infty$ for each $\varepsilon > 0$, i.e. $\mathcal{C}$ is totally bounded for d_μ, and therefore by Theorem B it suffices to prove

---

1) By the way, if instead of Theorem 12 the Portmanteau theorem (cf. (b) there) is used, the last part of the proof becomes much simpler.

(+): (E_1) implies that for any $0 < \varepsilon < 1$ there exists a $\delta_o = \delta_o(\varepsilon)$, $0 < \delta_o < 1$, and there exists an $n_o = n_o(\varepsilon,\delta_o)$ such that for each $n > n_o$

$$\mathbb{P}^*(w_{\beta_n}(\delta_o) > \varepsilon) < \varepsilon.$$

Let $0 < \varepsilon < 1$ be arbitrary but fixed and $N_I(x) \equiv N_I(x,\mathcal{C},\mu)$.

Suppose that δ_k, $k=0,1,2,\ldots$ is a sequence of nonnegative real numbers tending to zero (δ_k will be specified below).

According to the definition of $N_I(\delta_k,\mathcal{C},\mu)$ take sets

$$A_{k1},\ldots,A_{km(k)} \in \mathcal{B}, \quad m(k) := N_I(\delta_k),$$

such that for each $C \in \mathcal{C}$ and $k=0,1,2,\ldots$ there exist

$$i(k) = i(k,C) \text{ and } j(k) = j(k,C),\ i(k),j(k) \in \{1,\ldots,m(k)\},$$

with $A_{ki(k)} \subset C \subset A_{kj(k)}$ and $\mu(A_{kj(k)} \setminus A_{ki(k)}) < \delta_k$.

Since $\{w_{\beta_n}(\delta_o) > \varepsilon\} = \{\sup[|\beta_n(C) - \beta_n(D)|: C,D \in \mathcal{C},\ \mu(C \Delta D) < \delta_o] > \varepsilon\}$

$$\subset \{\sup_{C\in\mathcal{C}} |\beta_n(C) - \beta_n(A_{oj(o,C)})| > \varepsilon/2\}$$

$$\cup \{\sup [|\beta_n(A_{or}) - \beta_n(A_{os})|,\ \mu(A_{or} \Delta A_{os}) < 3\delta_o,\ r,s \in \{1,\ldots,m(0)\}] > \varepsilon/2\}$$

$$= E_1(\varepsilon,\delta_o,n) \cup E_2(\varepsilon,\delta_o,n), \text{ say,}$$

it suffices to show that $\mathbb{P}^*(E_i(\varepsilon,\delta_o,n)) < \varepsilon/2$, $i=1,2$, for an appropriate $\delta_o = \delta_o(\varepsilon)$ and n sufficiently large.

STEP ①: Let us consider first E_2 replacing (in view of STEP ② below) ε by $\varepsilon/2$, i.e. we will show that

$P_2 := \mathbb{P}^*(E_2(\varepsilon/2,\delta_o,n)) = \mathbb{P}(E_2(\varepsilon/2,\delta_o,n)) < \varepsilon/4$ for a proper choice of $\delta_o = \delta_o(\varepsilon)$ and n sufficiently large.

Applying Lemma 4 (i) of Section 1 we get

$$P_2 \leq 2\,[m(0)]^2 \exp\left(-\frac{\varepsilon^2/16}{6\delta_o + \frac{4}{3} n^{-1/2} \frac{\varepsilon}{4}}\right) \leq 2\,[m(0)]^2 \exp\left(-\frac{\varepsilon^2}{192\,\delta_o}\right)$$

for $n > n_o := \varepsilon^2/(256\,\delta_o^2)$;

now, as to m(0), it follows from (E_1) together with $N_I(x) \uparrow$ as $x \downarrow 0$ that

$x \log N_I(x) \to 0$ as $x \to 0$, whence there is a $\gamma = \gamma(\varepsilon) > 0$ such that

(1) $$N_I(x) \leq \exp(\varepsilon^2/(800\, x)) \quad \text{for all } 0 < x \leq \gamma.$$

Thus, for $\delta_0 \leq \gamma$ and $n > n_0$, $P_2 \leq 2 \exp\left(\frac{\varepsilon^2}{400\delta_0} - \frac{\varepsilon^2}{192\delta_0}\right) = 2 \exp\left(-\frac{\varepsilon^2}{1600\delta_0}\right)$.

But since

(2) $$\exp\left(-\frac{\varepsilon^2}{1600\alpha}\right) < \varepsilon/8 \text{ for } \alpha \text{ small enough,}$$

we obtain for $\delta_0 \leq \min(\gamma,\alpha)$ that $P_2 < \varepsilon/4$ for all $n > n_0$.

STEP (2): To cope with the other event E_1 a certain chaining argument will be used: for this we note first that the entropy condition (E_1) is equivalent to

$$\int_0^1 y^{-1/2}(\log N_I(y))^{1/2}\, dy < \infty \text{ and to } \sum_{i \in \mathbb{N}} (2^{-i} \log N_I(2^{-i}))^{1/2} < \infty;$$

therefore, there exists a $u = u(\varepsilon)$ so that

(3) $$\sum_{i \geq u} (2^{-i} \log N_I(2^{-i}))^{1/2} < \varepsilon/96 \quad \text{and}$$

(4) $$\sum_{\ell \geq 0} \exp(-2^{\ell+u}\, \varepsilon^2/(9000(\ell+1)^4)) < \varepsilon/32.$$

Now, let $\delta_0 = \delta_0(\varepsilon) := 2^{-r}$ with $r \geq u$ and r large enough so that also $\delta_0 \leq \min(\gamma,\alpha)$ (cf. STEP (1)).

For $k=1,2,\ldots$ let $\delta_k := \delta_0 \cdot 2^{-k} = 2^{-(r+k)}$ and $b_k := (2^{-k} \log m(k))^{1/2}$,

i.e. $b_k \delta_0^{1/2} = (2^{-(r+k)} \log N_I(2^{-(r+k)}))^{1/2}$ so that by (3) we have

(3*) $$\sum_{k \geq 0} b_k \delta_0^{1/2} < \varepsilon/96.$$

Next, let $B_k = B_k(C) := A_{kj(k,C)} \setminus A_{k+1,j(k+1,C)}$ and

$D_k = D_k(C) := A_{k+1,j(k+1,C)} \setminus A_{kj(k,C)}$; then $\mu(B_k) < \delta_k$

and $\mu(D_k) < \delta_{k+1} < \delta_k$ (cf. STEP (1)).

As in STEP (1) we choose $n_0 := \varepsilon^2/(256\, \delta_0^2)$. (Note that $\delta_o \leq \alpha \underset{(2)}{<} \varepsilon^2/1600$, so that $n_0 > 10.000/\varepsilon^2 \to \infty$ as $\varepsilon \to 0$.)

Then, for each $n > n_0$ there is a unique $k = k(n)$ such that

(5) $$1/2 < 8\delta_k n^{1/2}/\varepsilon \leq 1.$$

Now, for each $n > n_o$ and each $C \in \mathcal{C}$ we obtain (with $k = k(n)$, $i(k) = i(k,C)$ and $j(k) = j(k,C)$)

(6) $$\beta_n(A_{ki(k)}) - \varepsilon/8 \leq \beta_n(A_{ki(k)}) - \delta_k n^{1/2} \leq \beta_n(C)$$
$$\leq \beta_n(A_{kj(k)}) + \varepsilon/8.$$

Also

(7) $$|\beta_n(A_{kj(k)}) - \beta_n(A_{oj(o)})| \leq \sum_{0\leq \ell<k} |\beta_n(A_{\ell j(\ell)}) - \beta_n(A_{\ell+1,j(\ell+1)})|$$
$$\leq \sum_{0\leq \ell<k} [|\beta_n(B_\ell)| + |\beta_n(D_\ell)|].$$

Let $\mathcal{S}_\ell$ be the collection of sets $B = A_{\ell j} \setminus A_{\ell+1,m}$ or $A_{\ell+1,m} \setminus A_{\ell j}$ with $j \in \{1,\dots,m(\ell)\}$ and $m \in \{1,\dots,m(\ell+1)\}$, respectively, and so that $\mu(B) < \delta_\ell$. Then, for each $C \in \mathcal{C}$, $B_\ell(C)$ and $D_\ell(C) \in \mathcal{S}_\ell$.

The number of sets in $\mathcal{S}_\ell$ is bounded by

(8) $$|\mathcal{S}_\ell| \leq 2m(\ell)m(\ell+1).$$

For later use, note that (by the definition of b_ℓ)

$$m(\ell) = \exp(2^\ell b_\ell^2).$$

Let $d_\ell := \max((\ell+1)^{-2}\varepsilon/32,\ 6\, b_{\ell+1}\delta_o^{1/2})$; then by (3*)

(9) $$\sum_{\ell\geq 0} d_\ell < \varepsilon/8.$$

For each $\ell \leq k = k(n)$, $n > n_o$, we have $n^{1/2}\delta_\ell \geq n^{1/2}\delta_k \underset{(5)}{>} \varepsilon/16$; thus by (9)

$$d_\ell \leq 2n^{1/2}\delta_\ell.$$

Now, by Lemma 4 (ii) of Section 1 we obtain for each $B \in \mathcal{S}_\ell$

$$P_{\ell nB} := \mathbb{P}(|\beta_n(B)| > d_\ell) \leq 2\exp\left(-\frac{d_\ell^2}{2\mu(B)(1-\mu(B))+d_\ell n^{-1/2}}\right).$$

Thus, since $\mu(B) < \delta_\ell$ and $d_\ell n^{-1/2} \leq 2\delta_\ell$, we have

(10) $$P_{\ell nB} \leq 2 \exp\left(-\frac{d_\ell^2}{4\delta_\ell}\right).$$

Let $M_\ell := 4\, m(\ell)m(\ell+1) \leq 4[m(\ell+1)]^2 = 4 \exp(2^{\ell+2} b_{\ell+1}^2)$.

Then, using (8) and (10) we obtain

$$P_{\ell n} := \mathbb{P}(|\beta_n(B)| > d_\ell \text{ for some } B \in \mathcal{S}_\ell)$$

$$\leq M_\ell \exp\left(-\frac{d_\ell^2}{4\delta_\ell}\right) = M_\ell \exp\left(-\frac{2^\ell d_\ell^2}{4\delta_o}\right)$$

$$\leq 4 \exp[2^\ell(4\, b_{\ell+1}^2 - d_\ell^2/(4\,\delta_o))].$$

Now, by definition of d_ℓ, $4\, b_{\ell+1}^2 \leq d_\ell^2/(8\,\delta_o)$ and

$-2^{-\ell+r}\, d_\ell^2/8 \leq -2^{-\ell+r}\, \varepsilon^2/(8 \cdot (32)^2(\ell+1)^4)$ and so

$$P_{\ell n} \leq 4 \exp(-2^\ell d_\ell^2/(8\,\delta_o)) \leq 4 \exp(-2^{\ell+r}\, \varepsilon^2/(8\cdot(32)^2(\ell+1)^4))$$

$$\leq 4 \exp(-2^{\ell+r}\, \varepsilon^2/(9000(\ell+1)^4)).$$

Thus, by (4), for each $k = k(n)$ $(n > n_o)$ we have

(11) $$\sum_{0\leq\ell<k} P_{\ell n} < 4\cdot\varepsilon/32 = \varepsilon/8.$$

Next, again for $k = k(n)$, $n > n_o$, let

$V_n := \sup\{|\beta_n(A_{kj}) - \beta_n(A_{ki})| : A_{ki} \subset A_{kj},\ \mu(A_{kj} \setminus A_{ki}) < \delta_k,\ i,j=1,\dots,m(k)\}$

and $Q_n := \mathbb{P}(V_n > \varepsilon/8)$.

Then by Lemma 4 (i) of Section 1 and (5) (according to which $\frac{4}{3}\, n^{-1/2}\, \frac{\varepsilon}{8} \leq 3\, \delta_k$)

$$Q_n \leq [m(k)]^2 \cdot 2 \exp\left(-\frac{\varepsilon^2/64}{2\delta_k + \frac{4}{3}\, n^{-1/2}\, \frac{\varepsilon}{8}}\right) \leq [m(k)]^2 \cdot 2 \exp\left(-\frac{\varepsilon^2}{64\cdot 5\, \delta_k}\right)$$

$$= \exp(2 \cdot 2^k b_k^2) \cdot 2 \exp\left(-\frac{\varepsilon^2 2^k}{320\, \delta_o}\right) = 2 \exp\left[2^k\left(2b_k^2 - \frac{\varepsilon^2 2^r}{320}\right)\right].$$

Now, for $s := k+r$,

$$2b_k^2 = 2^{1-k} \log m(k) = 2^{1-k} \log N_I(\delta_k) = 2^{1-k} \log N_I(2^{-(k+r)})$$

$$= 2^{r+1-s}\log N_I(2^{-s}) \underset{①}{\leq} 2^{r+1-s}\,\frac{\varepsilon^2}{800\ 2^{-s}} = 2^r\,\frac{\varepsilon^2}{400}.$$

Thus $Q_n \leq 2\exp\left[2^{k+r}\left(\frac{\varepsilon^2}{400} - \frac{\varepsilon^2}{320}\right)\right] = 2\exp\left(-2^{k+r}\,\frac{\varepsilon^2}{1600}\right)$

$$\leq 2\exp\left(-\frac{\varepsilon^2}{1600\alpha}\right) \underset{②}{<} \varepsilon/4.$$

Now, if $V_n \leq \varepsilon/8$ then by ⑥ $|\beta_n(C) - \beta_n(A_{kj(k,C)})| \leq \varepsilon/4$ for all $C \in \mathcal{C}$, and therefore

$$E_1 \equiv E_1(\varepsilon,\delta_o,n) := \{\sup_{C\in\mathcal{C}} |\beta_n(C) - \beta_n(A_{oj(o,C)})| > \varepsilon/2\}$$

$$= (E_1 \cap \{V_n > \varepsilon/8\}) \cup (E_1 \cap \{V_n \leq \varepsilon/8\}) \subset \{V_n > \varepsilon/8\} \cup W_n$$

with $W_n := \{\sup_{C\in\mathcal{C}} |\beta_n(A_{kj(k,C)}) - \beta_n(A_{oj(o,C)})| > \varepsilon/4\}$.

Now $W_n \underset{⑦}{\subset} W'_n := \{\sup_{C\in\mathcal{C}}[\sum_{0\leq\ell<k} |\beta_n(B_\ell(C))|] > \varepsilon/8\} \cup \{\sup_{C\in\mathcal{C}}[\sum_{0\leq\ell<k} |\beta_n(D_\ell(C))|] > \varepsilon/8\}$,

where according to ⑨ (note that $B_\ell(C),\ D_\ell(C) \in \mathcal{S}_\ell$)

$$\mathbb{P}(W'_n) \leq \sum_{0\leq\ell<k} P_{\ell n} + \sum_{0\leq\ell<k} P_{\ell n} \underset{⑪}{<} \varepsilon/4;$$

thus, together with $\mathbb{P}(V_n > \varepsilon/8) = Q_n < \varepsilon/4$ it follows that

$$\mathbb{P}^*(E_1(\varepsilon,\delta_o,n)) < \varepsilon/2 \text{ for } n > n_o.$$

This proves (+) and concludes the proof of Theorem A. □

<u>(57) REMARK.</u> The above proof shows that the two conditions (a) and (b) of Theorem B are implied by (E_1) <u>without imposing (M)</u>. I.S. Borisov (1981) has shown that (E_1) cannot be weakened, being necessary in case $\mathcal{C}$ is the collection of all subsets of a countable set X, where (E_1) is equivalent to $\sum_{x\in X} (\mu(\{x\}))^{1/2} < \infty$; cf. also M. Durst and R.M. Dudley (1980).

<u>(58) EXAMPLE.</u> As an illustration of the applicability of Theorem A we will show that in $(X,\mathcal{B}) = (\mathbb{R}^k,\mathbb{B}_k)$, $k \geq 1$, the class $\mathcal{C} = \mathbb{J}_k$ of all lower left orthants is a μ-Donsker class for any p-measure μ on $\mathbb{B}_k$ (proved by M.D. Donsker (1952) for k = 1 and by R.M. Dudley (1966) for $k \geq 1$).

As remarked in (48) (a), condition (M) holds true for $\mathcal{J}_k$; so, by Theorem A, we must show that (E_1) is fulfilled:

a) For $k = 1$, consider for any $0 < \varepsilon \leq 1$ the partition

$-\infty =: t_o < t_1 < \ldots < t_{m-1} < t_m := \infty$ of $\mathbb{R}$, where

$$t_{i+1} := \sup \{t \in \mathbb{R}: \mu((t_i,t]) \leq \varepsilon/2\}.$$

Since $\mu((t_i,t_{i+1}]) \geq \varepsilon/2$ and $\mu(\mathbb{R}) = 1$, we have $m - 1 \leq 2/\varepsilon$.

Then, taking as A_i's in the definition of $N_I(\varepsilon,\mathcal{J}_1,\mu)$ all sets of the form $\emptyset$, $(-\infty,t_1),(-\infty,t_1],(-\infty,t_2),(-\infty,t_2],\ldots,(-\infty,t_{m-1}),(-\infty,t_{m-1}]$, $\mathbb{R}$ we obtain

$$\min \{n \in \mathbb{N}: \exists A_1,\ldots,A_n \in \mathcal{B} \text{ s.t. for all } C \in \mathcal{J}_1 \text{ there exist } i,j \text{ with }$$
$$A_i \subset C \subset A_j \text{ and } \mu(A_j \setminus A_i) < \varepsilon\}$$
$$\leq 2(m-1) + 2 = 2m \leq 4/\varepsilon + 2 \leq 6/\varepsilon.$$

This implies that $\log N_I(\varepsilon^2,\mathcal{J}_1,\mu) \leq \log 6/\varepsilon^2$ showing that (E_1) is fulfilled for $k = 1$.

b) For $k > 1$ the result is an immediate consequence of a) and the inequality (59) of the following lemma (formulated in greater generality as needed in the present case).

LEMMA. Let $(X,\mathcal{B})$ be a measurable space and let μ be a probability measure on the product σ-algebra $\bigotimes_1^k \mathcal{B}$ in X^k, $k \geq 1$, with marginal laws $\pi_i\mu$ on $\mathcal{B}$, $i=1,\ldots,k$. Let $\mathcal{C}_i \subset \mathcal{B}$, $i=1,\ldots,k$, be given classes of sets and

$$\mathcal{C} := \{ \times_{i=k}^{k} C_i : C_i \in \mathcal{C}_i,\ i=1,\ldots,k\}.$$

Then

(59) $$N_I(\varepsilon,\mathcal{C},\mu) \leq \prod_{i=1}^{k} N_I(\varepsilon/k,\mathcal{C}_i,\pi_i\mu).$$

Proof. We may and do assume that $n_i := N_I(\varepsilon/k,\mathcal{C}_i,\pi_i\mu) < \infty$ for each $i=1,\ldots,k$. Then there exist $A_{i1},\ldots,A_{in_i} \in \mathcal{B}$ such that for any $C_i \in \mathcal{C}_i$ there exist $r_i,s_i \in \{1,\ldots,n_i\}$ with

$$A_{ir_i} \subset C_i \subset A_{is_i} \text{ and } \pi_i\mu(A_{is_i} \setminus A_{ir_i}) < \varepsilon/k,$$

i=1,...,k. This implies that

$$\mathop{\times}_{i=1}^{k} A_{ir_i} \subset \mathop{\times}_{i=1}^{k} C_i \subset \mathop{\times}_{i=1}^{k} A_{is_i} \quad \text{and} \quad \mu(\mathop{\times}_{i=1}^{k} A_{is_i} \setminus \mathop{\times}_{i=1}^{k} A_{ir_i})$$

$$\leqq \sum_{i=1}^{k} \mu(B_i) \text{ (with } B_i := X \times \ldots \times X \times (A_{is_i} \setminus A_{ir_i}) \times X \times \ldots \times X)$$

$$= \sum_{i=1}^{k} \pi_i\mu(A_{is_i} \setminus A_{ir_i}) < \varepsilon.$$

Since there are at most $n_1 \cdot n_2 \cdot \ldots \cdot n_k$ approximating sets of the form

$\mathop{\times}_{i=1}^{k} A_{it_i} \in \bigotimes_1^k \mathcal{B}$, (59) follows. □

SOME REMARKS ON OTHER MEASURABILITY ASSUMPTIONS AND FURTHER RESULTS:

Instead of (M) Dudley (1978) used the following measurability assumption (M_o) (again w.r.t. the canonical model $(\Omega, F, \mathbb{P}) = (X^{\mathbb{N}}, \mathcal{B}_{\mathbb{N}}, \times_{\mathbb{N}} \mu)$):

(M_o): $\beta_n : \Omega \to S \equiv D_o(\mathcal{C}, \mu)$ is $\tilde{F}, \mathcal{B}_b(S, \rho)$-measurable,

where $\tilde{F}$ denotes the measure-theoretic completion of F w.r.t. $\mathbb{P} = \times_{\mathbb{N}} \mu$.

Imposing (M), it follows that β_n is $F, \mathcal{B}_b(S,\rho)$-measurable, whence

(M) implies (M_o).

On the other hand, replacing $A = \sigma(\{\pi_C : C \in \mathcal{C}\})$ by

$$A_o := \sigma(\{\pi_C : C \in \mathcal{C};\ \rho(\cdot, \varphi) : \varphi \in S\})$$

and imposing (M_o) instead of (M), it follows that

$$\beta_n \text{ is } \tilde{F}, A_o\text{-measurable},$$

where $\mathcal{B}_b(S,\rho) \subset A_o \subset \mathcal{B}(S,\rho)$ (cf. (47)), which means that also under (M_o) one meets the basic model of Section 3.

Thus, Theorem A and Theorem B hold as well (with the same proof) if (M) is replaced by (M_o).

Besides (M_o) Dudley (1978) introduced a second measurability assumption

(M_1) (called a $\mu\in$ Suslin property for $\mathcal{C}$),

stronger that (M_o), which turned out to be verifiable in cases of interest where (M) or (SE) fails to hold (cf. (48) (b)).

As shown in Gaenssler (1983), based on Theorem A (with (M) replaced by (M_o)) one obtains a functional central limit theorem for empirical $\mathcal{C}$-processes indexed by classes $\mathcal{C}$ allowing a finite-dimensional parametrization in the sense of the following theorem:

THEOREM C. Let X be a locally compact, separable metric space, $\mathcal{B} = \mathcal{B}(X)$ be the σ-algebra of Borel sets in X, and let K be a compact subset of $\mathbb{R}^\ell$, $\ell \geq 1$. Suppose that

$$f: X \times K \to \mathbb{R}$$

is a function satisfying the following conditions (i) - (iii) ((iii) with respect to a given probability measure μ on $\mathcal{B}$):

(i) $f_z := f(\cdot,z): X \to \mathbb{R}$ is continuous for each $z \in K$

(ii) $f.(x): K \to \mathbb{R}$ is "uniformly Lipschitz", i.e.,

$$M := \sup_{x\in X} \sup\{|f_z(x) - f_{z'}(x)| / |z - z'|, z \neq z', z,z' \in K\} < \infty$$

(where $|z - z'|$ denotes the Euclidean distance between z and z')

(iii) $\mu(\{f_z \in [-\varepsilon,\varepsilon)\}) = \mathcal{O}(\varepsilon)$ uniformly in $z \in K$.

Let $\mathcal{C} \subset \mathcal{B}$ be defined by $\mathcal{C} := \{\{f_z \geq 0\}: z \in K\}$.

Then $\mathcal{C}$ is a μ-Donsker class; furthermore, (M_1) (and therefore also (M_o)) is satisfied for $\mathcal{C}$ and μ.

(60) EXAMPLES. (a): Let $(X,\mathcal{B},\mu) = ([0,1]^k,[0,1]^k \cap \mathcal{B}_k,\lambda_k)$, $k \geq 1$, λ_k being the k-dimensional Lebesgue measure on $[0,1]^k \cap \mathcal{B}_k$, and let $\mathcal{C} \subset \mathcal{B}$ be the class of all closed Euclidean balls in $[0,1]^k$. Then $\mathcal{C}$ is a λ_k-Donsker class and (M_1) is satisfied for $\mathcal{C}$ and λ_k.

In fact, take

$K := \{z = (y,r): y \in [0,1]^k,\ 0 \leq r \leq r_y := \sup\{r: B^c(y,r) \subset [0,1]^k\}\}$,

where $B^c(y,r) := \{x \in \mathbb{R}^k: e(x,y) \leq r\}$ (e denoting the Euclidean distance in $[0,1]^k$), and define $f: [0,1]^k \times K \to \mathbb{R}$ by

$$f(x,z) := e(x, \complement B^o(y,r)) - e(x, B^c(y,r)),\quad z = (y,r) \in K$$
$$(= r - e(x,y))$$

where $B^o(y,r) := \{x \in \mathbb{R}^k: e(x,y) < r\}$.

Then $\{\{f_z \geq 0\}: z \in K\}$ is the class of all closed Euclidean balls in $X = [0,1]^k$ and it is easy to verify (i) - (iii) of Theorem C giving the result.

(b) (cf. (48)(b)): consider the same p-space $(X, \mathcal{B}, \mu)$ as in (a) and let

$$\mathcal{C} := \{(C + z) \cap [0,1]^k: z \in [0,1]^k\},$$

C being a fixed closed and convex subset of $X = [0,1]^k$, $k \geq 1$, (cf. R. Pyke (1979)). As in (a) let $f(x,z) := e(x, \complement C_z^o) - e(x, C_z)$, $x,z \in [0,1]^k$, with $C_z := C + z$ and C_z^o denoting the interior of C_z.

Then $\mathcal{C}$ is a λ_k-Donsker class and (M_1) is satisfied for $\mathcal{C}$ and λ_k. This follows again from Theorem C; for this we have to verify the conditions (i) - (iii) there and also that

$$\mathcal{C} = \{\{f_z \geq 0\}: z \in [0,1]^k\},\ \text{i.e., that}$$

(+) $$C_z = \{f_z \geq 0\}\quad \text{for each } z \in [0,1]^k.$$

<u>ad (+):</u> $x \in C_z$ implies that $e(x, C_z) = 0$ whence $f_z(x) = e(x, \complement C_z^o) \geq 0$; on the other hand, if $x \in \complement C_z$ then $e(x, C_z) > 0$, since C_z is closed, and $e(x, \complement C_z^o) = 0$ whence $f_z(x) = -e(x, C_z) < 0$; this shows (+).

<u>ad (i):</u> follows immediately from the fact that for any $\emptyset \neq A \subset X$

$$|e(x_1, A) - e(x_2, A)| \leq e(x_1, x_2)\ \text{for each } x_1, x_2 \in X.$$

<u>ad (ii):</u> let $f_z'(x) := e(x, \complement C_z^o)$ and $f_z''(x) := e(x, C_z)$, i.e., $f_\cdot(x) = f_\cdot'(x) - f_\cdot''(x)$ for all $x \in [0,1]^k$. Then it suffices to show that both

$f_{\cdot}'(x)$ and $f_{\cdot}''(x)$ are uniformly Lipschitz:

as to $f_{\cdot}'(x)$ this follows from

$$\textcircled{1}\ \forall x \in [0,1]^k: |e(x,\complement C_z^{\circ}) - e(x,\complement C_{z'}^{\circ})| \leq e(z,z')\ \forall z,z' \in [0,1]^k.$$

ad ①: we use the following fact which is easy to prove:

(+) For any closed $F \subset [0,1]^k$ and any $x \in F^{\circ}$ there exists a $w \in \partial F$ such that $e(x,w) = e(x,\complement F^{\circ})$.

Now, given any $x \in [0,1]^k$ let w.l.o.g. z and z' be such that $x \in C_z^{\circ} \cap C_{z'}^{\circ}$; applying then (+) for $F = C_z$ and $F = C_{z'}$, respectively, we obtain $e(x,\complement C_z^{\circ}) = e(x,w_{x,z})$ and $e(x,\complement C_{z'}^{\circ}) = e(x,w_{x,z'})$ for some $w_{x,z} \in \partial C_z$ and $w_{x,z'} \in \partial C_{z'}$, respectively.

Furthermore, since C_z and $C_{z'}$ are closed,

$$w_{x,z} = c_{x,z} + z \quad \text{and} \quad w_{x,z'} = c_{x,z'} + z'$$

for some $c_{x,z} \in C$ and $c_{x,z'} \in C$, respectively, and

$$\text{(++)} \quad e(x,c_{x,z} + z) \leq e(x,c_{x,z'} + z) \text{ and } e(x,c_{x,z'} + z') \leq e(x,c_{x,z} + z'), \text{ respectively.}$$

Thus

$$e(x,\complement C_z^{\circ}) - e(x,\complement C_{z'}^{\circ}) = e(x,c_{x,z} + z) - e(x,c_{x,z'} + z')$$

$$\underset{(++)}{\leq} e(x,c_{x,z'} + z) - e(x,c_{x,z'} + z') \leq e(c_{x,z'} + z,c_{x,z'} + z') = e(z,z').$$

This proves ①.

That also $f_{\cdot}''$ is uniformly Lipschitz follows from

$$\textcircled{2}\quad \forall x \in [0,1]^k: |e(x,C_z) - e(x,C_{z'})| \leq e(z,z')\ \forall z,z' \in [0,1]^k.$$

ad ②: Given any $x \in [0,1]^k$ and any $\varepsilon>0$ there exists a $c = c(x,\varepsilon) \in C$ such that for all $z,z' \in [0,1]^k$, $e(x,c + z) \leq e(x,C_z) + \varepsilon$ and thus

$$e(x,C_{z'}) \leq e(x,c + z') \leq e(x,c + z) + e(c + z,c + z')$$

$$= e(x,c + z) + e(z,z') \leq e(x,C_z) + \varepsilon + e(z,z') \text{ for any } \varepsilon>0,$$

whence $e(x,C_{z'}) - e(x,C_z) \leq e(z,z')$ yielding ② by symmetry.

Before proving (iii), let us remark that so far we have only used that C is a closed subset of $[0,1]^k$; for proving (iii), in addition, some smoothness of the boundary of C is needed. So we will now use that C is convex.

ad (iii): We must show that

$$\lambda_k(\{f_z \in [-\varepsilon,\varepsilon)\}) = \mathcal{O}(\varepsilon) \text{ uniformly in } z \in K.$$

For this it suffices to prove

(3) $\{f_z \in [-\varepsilon,\varepsilon)\} \subset C_z^\varepsilon \setminus {}_\varepsilon C_z$ for all $z \in [0,1]^k$, and

(4) $\sup_{z\in[0,1]^k} \lambda_k(C_z^\varepsilon \setminus {}_\varepsilon C_z) \leq c_k\varepsilon$ for $\varepsilon \downarrow 0$ with some constant c_k depending only on k.

(Here $A^\varepsilon := \{x: e(x,A) \leq \varepsilon\}$ and ${}_\varepsilon A := \{x: e(x,\complement A) > \varepsilon\}$.)

ad (3): Suppose that $-\varepsilon \leq f_z(x) < \varepsilon$, where $f_z(x) = e(x,\complement C_z^o) - e(x,C_z)$, $x \in X$, whence

(a) $f_z(x) = -e(x,C_z)$ iff $x \in \complement C_z^o$,

(b) $f_z(x) = e(x,\complement C_z^o)$ iff $x \in C_z$, and

(c) $f_z(x) = 0$ iff $x \in \partial C_z$.

Thus (note that $X = [(\complement C_z^o)\setminus\partial C_z] + (C_z\setminus\partial C_z) + \partial C_z$)

$$\left\{\begin{matrix} -\varepsilon \leq f_z(x) < \varepsilon \\ x \in (\complement C_z^o)\setminus\partial C_z \end{matrix}\right\} \underset{(a)}{\Leftrightarrow} \left\{\begin{matrix} -\varepsilon < e(x,C_z) \leq \varepsilon \\ x \in (\complement C_z^o)\setminus\partial C_z \end{matrix}\right\} \Rightarrow x \in C_z^\varepsilon \setminus {}_\varepsilon C_z,$$

$$\left\{\begin{matrix} -\varepsilon \leq f_z(x) < \varepsilon \\ x \in C_z\setminus\partial C_z \end{matrix}\right\} \underset{(b)}{\Leftrightarrow} \left\{\begin{matrix} -\varepsilon \leq e(x,\complement C_z^o) < \varepsilon \\ x \in C_z\setminus\partial C_z \end{matrix}\right\} \Rightarrow x \in C_z^\varepsilon \setminus {}_\varepsilon C_z, \text{ and}$$

$$\left\{\begin{matrix} -\varepsilon \leq f_z(x) < \varepsilon \\ x \in \partial C_z \end{matrix}\right\} \underset{(c)}{\Leftrightarrow} \left\{\begin{matrix} f_z(x) = 0 \\ x \in \partial C_z \end{matrix}\right\} \Rightarrow x \in C_z^\varepsilon \setminus {}_\varepsilon C_z.$$

This proves (3).

Ad (4): Due to the translation invariance of λ_k (4) is equivalent to

$$\lambda_k(C^\varepsilon \setminus {}_\varepsilon C) \leq c_k\varepsilon \text{ as } \varepsilon \downarrow 0.$$

Now, as shown in Gaenssler (1981) one has

(61) $\sup_{C\in\mathfrak{C}_k} \lambda_k(C^\varepsilon \setminus_\varepsilon C) \leq c_k\varepsilon$ as $\varepsilon \downarrow 0$,

where $\mathfrak{C}_k$ denotes the class of <u>all</u> convex Borel sets in $[0,1]^k$, $k \geq 1$.

This proves the assertion of Example (b). □

(62) <u>ADDITIONAL REMARKS.</u> (a): the above considerations show that the set of all translates of a fixed closed but not necessarily convex set C is a λ_k-Donsker class provided that C has a smooth boundary in the sense that $\lambda_k(C^\varepsilon \setminus_\varepsilon C) = \mathcal{O}(\varepsilon)$. Based on a result of E.M. Bronštein (1976) it was shown by Dudley (1981a) that for the class $\mathfrak{C}_k^c$ of all closed convex Borel sets in $[0,1]^k$, $k \geq 2$, the following inequality holds true:

(63) $N_I(\varepsilon, \mathfrak{C}_k^c, \lambda_k) \leq \exp(M/\varepsilon^{(k-1)/2})$ for $0 < \varepsilon \leq 1$

and some constant $M < \infty$ depending only on k.

For k = 2 this yields that (E_1) is fulfilled for $\mathfrak{C}_2^c$ and λ_2; in fact,

$$\int_0^1 (\log N_I(x^2, \mathfrak{C}_2^c, \lambda_2))^{1/2}\, dx \leq \int_0^1 M^{1/2}\, x^{-1/2}\, dx < \infty,$$

implying a result of Bolthausen (1978) according to which $\mathfrak{C}_2^c$ is a λ_2-Donsker class.

But, for $k \geq 3$, (63) does not yield (E_1) for $\mathfrak{C}_k^c$ and λ_k which is in accordance with a result of Dudley (1979a) showing that $\mathfrak{C}_k^c$ is <u>not</u> a λ_k-Donsker class for $k \geq 3$.

(b): let us reconsider the example in (60)(b) according to which for any fixed closed and convex set C in $X = [0,1]^k$, $k \geq 1$,

$$\mathcal{C} = \{(C + z) \cap [0,1]^k : z \in [0,1]^k\}$$

is a λ_k-Donsker class and also (M_1) (and therefore also (M_o)) is satisfied for $\mathcal{C}$ and λ_k. The way we derived this result from Theorem C shows that λ_k can be replaced by any p-measure μ on $[0,1]^k \cap \mathcal{B}_k$ having a bounded density w.r.t.

λ_k, whence, by Theorem 3 (using (M_o)),

$$n^{1/2} \sup_{C \in \mathcal{C}} |\mu_n(C) - \mu(C)| \xrightarrow{L} \sup_{C \in \mathcal{C}} |G_\mu(C)|$$

implying (note that w.l.o.g. $G_\mu(\cdot,\omega) \in S_o$ and therefore $\sup_{C\in\mathcal{C}} |G_\mu(C,\omega)| < \infty$ for each ω)

$$\sup_{C\in\mathcal{C}} |\mu_n(C) - \mu(C)| = D_n(\mathcal{C},\mu) \xrightarrow{\mathbb{P}} 0$$

being equivalent with

$$D_n(\mathcal{C},\mu) \to 0 \quad \mathbb{P}\text{-a.s.}$$

according to Lemma 6 in Section 1. (Note that the necessary measurability for $D_n(\mathcal{C},\mu)$ is implied by (M_o).)

Thus

$$\mathcal{C} = \{(C + z) \cap [0,1]^k : z \in [0,1]^k\}$$

is also a Glivenko-Cantelli class (compare this with our conjecture at the end of Section 2 stating that $\mathcal{C}$ is <u>not</u> a Vapnik-Chervonenkis class). Of course the above reasoning works in general, i.e. one gets

(64) Any μ-Donsker class $\mathcal{C}$ satisfying (M_o) is also a Glivenko-Cantelli class.

(c): Let $(X,\mathcal{B})$ be the Euclidean space $\mathbb{R}^k$, $k \geq 1$, with its Borel σ-algebra $\mathcal{B} = \mathbb{B}_k$ and let μ be any p-measure on $\mathbb{B}_k$. Let $\mathbb{B}_k$ be the class of all closed Euclidean balls in $\mathbb{R}^k$. As shown at the end of Section 2 $\mathbb{B}_k$ is a Vapnik-Chervonenkis class (VCC); we also know from (48)(a) that (M) holds true for $\mathbb{B}_k$. Furthermore, as pointed out in Gaenssler (1983), also (M_1) is satisfied for $\mathcal{C} = \mathbb{B}_k$ and any μ on $\mathbb{B}_k$. Thus, for any μ, $\mathbb{B}_k$ is a μ-Donsker class according to the following general result of R.M. Dudley ((1978), Theorem 7.1) stated here without proof (cf. also D. Pollard (1981):

<u>THEOREM D.</u> Let $(X,\mathcal{B},\mu)$ be an arbitrary sample space and $\mathcal{C} \subset \mathcal{B}$ be a VCC such that (M_1) is satisfied for $\mathcal{C}$ and μ; then $\mathcal{C}$ is a μ-Donsker class.

(d): A condition like (61) was also basic for the results of R. Pyke (1977 and 1982) on the Haar function construction of Brownian motion indexed by sets and on functional limit theorems for partial-sum processes indexed by sets (1982a). In fact, Pyke considers classes $\mathcal{C}$ of closed sets in $X = [0,1]^k$, $k \geq 1$, fulfilling (besides an entropy condition) the following two conditions:

A1. There is a constant $c > 0$ such that for all $\varepsilon > 0$ and $C \in \mathcal{C}$

$$\lambda_k(C^\varepsilon \setminus {}_\varepsilon C) \leq c\varepsilon.$$

A2. $\mathcal{C}$ is totally bounded with respect to the Hausdorff metric d_H defined by

$d_H(C,D) := \inf\{\varepsilon > 0\colon C \subset D^\varepsilon \text{ and } D \subset C^\varepsilon\}$ for $C,D \in \mathcal{C}$

(and $C^\varepsilon := \{x\colon e(x,C) \leq \varepsilon\}$).

In another very important and original contribution of T.G. Sun and R. Pyke (1982) on weak convergence of empirical processes, a certain index family $\mathcal{C}$ of closed sets in $[0,1]^k$, $k \geq 1$, closely related to one introduced by Dudley (1974) is studied and it is shown in particular that this class fulfills A1.

In contrary to Dudley's (1978) approach to functional central limit theorems for empirical measures (i.e., empirical $\mathcal{C}$-processes) the paper of Sun and Pyke (based on results of Sun's thesis (1977)) involves first the study of a SMOOTHED VERSION of the empirical processes obtained by replacing the unit point masses assigned to each observation by a uniform distribution of equal mass on a small ball (in the sample space $(X,\mathcal{B},\mu) = ([0,1]^k, [0,1]^k \cap \mathcal{B}_k, \lambda_k))$ of radius r centered at the observations (i.e. $\beta_n(C,\omega)$ is replaced by

$\beta_n^r(C,\omega) := n^{-1/2} \sum_{i=1}^n \zeta_i^r(C,\omega)$ with $\zeta_i^r(C,\omega) := \lambda_k(C \cap B^c(\xi_i(\omega),r))/\lambda_k(B^c(\xi_i(\omega),r))$ $-\lambda_k(C)$, where $B^c(\xi_i(\omega),r)$ denotes the closed ball of radius r centered at the observation $\xi_i(\omega)$).

This approach has the advantage that the smoothed version has continuous sample paths in the space of all d_H-continuous functions on $\mathcal{C}$. The remaining steps in the Sun-Pyke approach are then to show the uniform (w.r.t. $\mathcal{C}$) closeness of the smoothed and unsmoothed versions and to establish weak sequential compactness which amounts to verify a conditions like (b) in Theorem B on the uniform (w.r.t. n) behaviour of the modulus of continuity.

In this context the following mode of weak convergence is used (cf. R. Pyke and G. Shorack (1968)):

If η_n, $n \in \mathbb{N}$, and η are defined on some p-space $(\Omega,\mathcal{F},\mathbb{P})$ with values in a metric space $S = (S,d)$ (like e.g., $D_o(\mathcal{C},d_H)$), the η_n's and η being <u>not</u> assumed $\mathcal{F},\mathcal{A}$-measurable for some σ-algebra $\mathcal{A}$ in S (with $\mathcal{B}_b(S,d) \subset \mathcal{A} \subset \mathcal{B}(S)$), then η_n is said to converge weakly to η iff $\lim_{n\to\infty} \mathbb{E}(f(\eta_n)) = \mathbb{E}(f(\eta))$ for all $f \in C^b(S)$ which are, in addition, such that each $f(\eta_n)$, $n \in \mathbb{N}$, and $f(\eta)$ is a random variable, i.e., $\mathcal{F},\mathcal{B}$-measurable.

This concludes our remarks on the other measurability assumptions and further results. For other extensions the reader is referred to our concluding remarks at the end of Section 4.

At this place we prefer to present some of the interesting results obtained by G. Shorack (1979).

<u>FUNCTIONAL CENTRAL LIMIT THEOREMS FOR WEIGHTED EMPIRICAL PROCESSES:</u>

This part is concerned with some results on weak convergence of so-called weighted empirical processes supplementing in another way our earlier remarks in Section 2 on the a.s. behaviour of weighted discrepancies and giving at the same time a further illustration of the special results concerning the D[0,1]-case summarized at the end of Section 3. We will follow closely the presentation in Shorack's (1979) paper using some modifications due to W. Schneemeier in a first draft of his Diploma-Thesis, University of Munich, 1981/82.

Let $(\xi_{ni})_{1\leq i\leq n}$, $n \in \mathbb{N}$, be an array of row-wise independent random variables defined on some p-space $(\Omega,\mathcal{F},\mathbb{P})$ with distribution functions F_{ni}, $1\leq i\leq n$, $n \in \mathbb{N}$, being concentrated on [0,1] (i.e. $F_{ni}(0) = 0$ and $F_{ni}(1) = 1$ for all $1\leq i\leq n$, $n \in \mathbb{N}$).

Before introducing some weight functions q as in Section 2, let us start with the consideration of the following form of a WEIGHTED EMPIRICAL PROCESS W_n based on (ξ_{ni}) and on a given array of so-called scores $(c_{ni})_{1\leq i\leq n}$, $n \in \mathbb{N}$:

(65) $$W_n(t) := n^{-1/2} \sum_{i=1}^{n} c_{ni}[1_{[0,t]}(\xi_{ni}) - F_{ni}(t)], \quad t \in [0,1],$$

where the constant scores c_{ni} are assumed to satisfy

(66) $$n^{-1} \sum_{i=1}^{n} c_{ni}^2 = 1 \quad \text{for each } n.$$

Note that for $c_{ni} \equiv 1$ and for ξ_{ni} being uniformly distributed on $[0,1]$ W_n reduces to the uniform empirical process α_n considered at the end of Section 3. In the same way as α_n there, also W_n will be considered as a random element in $(D,\mathcal{B}_b(D,\rho))$ as well as in $(D,\mathcal{B}(D,s))$.

Generalizing Donsker's functional central limit theorem for α_n we are going to give sufficient conditions under which there exists a certain Gaussian stochastic process W being a random element in $(D,\mathcal{B}_b(D,\rho))$ with $\mathcal{L}\{W\}(C) = 1$ ($C \equiv C[0,1]$ being again the space of continuous functions on $[0,1]$) and such that $W_n \xrightarrow{\mathcal{L}_b} W$.

Before proving one of the main results of Shorack (1979), Theorem 1.1, we will mention some basic facts and preliminary results.

<u>(67) REMARKS.</u> (a) It follows from (66) that ν_n, defined by

$$\nu_n(t) := n^{-1} \sum_{i=1}^{n} c_{ni}^2 F_{ni}(t), \quad t \in [0,1],$$

is a distribution function on $[0,1]$ (with $\nu_n(0) = 0$ and $\nu_n(1) = 1$).

(b) For each $0 \leq s, t \leq 1$ we have $\mathbb{E}(W_n(t)) = 0$ and

$$K_n(s,t) := \operatorname{cov}(W_n(s),W_n(t)) = n^{-1} \sum_{i=1}^{n} c_{ni}^2[F_{ni}(s\wedge t) - F_{ni}(s)F_{ni}(t)],$$

whence

(68) $$\mathbb{E}(W_n^2(t)) \leq \nu_n(t) \quad \text{for all } t \in [0,1].$$

In the following, let $F_{ni}(s,t] := F_{ni}(t) - F_{ni}(s)$, $\nu_n(s,t] := \nu_n(t) - \nu_n(s)$, and $W_n(s,t] := W_n(t) - W_n(s)$ for $0 \leq s \leq t \leq 1$; then we have

LEMMA 22. (i) $\mathbb{E}(W_n^2(r,s] \cdot W_n^2(s,t]) \leq 3\nu_n(r,s] \cdot \nu_n(s,t]$, $0 \leq r \leq s \leq t \leq 1$;

(ii) $\mathbb{E}(W_n^4(s,t]) \leq 3\nu_n^2(s,t] + (\max_{1\leq i\leq n} \frac{c_{ni}^2}{n}) \cdot \nu_n(s,t]$, $0 \leq s \leq t \leq 1$.

Proof (cf. G. Shorack (1979), INEQUALITY 1.1). Writing c_i for $n^{-1/2}c_{ni}$ we have for $0 \leq r \leq s \leq 1$

(a) $W_n(r,s] = \sum_{i=1}^{n} c_i X_i(r,s)$ with $X_i(r,s) := 1_{(r,s]}(\xi_{ni}) - F_{ni}(r,s]$;

furthermore, for $0 \leq r \leq s \leq t \leq 1$,

(b1) $\mathbb{E}(X_i(r,s)) = 0$

(b2) $\mathbb{E}(X_i^2(r,s)) = F_{ni}(r,s](1 - F_{ni}(r,s]) \leq F_{ni}(r,s]$

(b3) $\mathbb{E}(X_i^4(r,s)) \leq F_{ni}(r,s]$

(b4) $\mathbb{E}(X_i(r,s)X_i(s,t)) = -F_{ni}(r,s] \cdot F_{ni}(s,t]$

(b5) $\mathbb{E}(X_i^2(r,s)\, X_i^2(s,t)) \leq F_{ni}(r,s] \cdot F_{ni}(s,t]$

(b6) If $\{i,j,k,\ell\} \subset \{1,\ldots,n\}$ such that $|\{i,j,k,\ell\}| \geq 3$, then assuming w.l.o.g. that $i \notin \{j,k,\ell\}$, we have (by independence)

$\mathbb{E}(X_i(r,s)X_j(r,s)X_k(s,t)X_\ell(s,t))$

$= \mathbb{E}(X_i(r,s))\, \mathbb{E}(X_j(r,s)X_k(s,t)X_\ell(s,t)) = 0.$

Therefore,

$$\mathbb{E}(W_n^2(r,s]W_n^2(s,t]) = \mathbb{E}((\sum_{i=1}^{n} c_i X_i(r,s))^2 (\sum_{i=1}^{n} c_i X_i(s,t))^2)$$

$$= \sum_{i,j,k,\ell=1}^{n} c_i c_j c_k c_\ell\, \mathbb{E}(X_i(r,s)X_j(r,s)X_k(s,t)X_\ell(s,t))$$

$$\underset{(b6)}{=} \sum_{\substack{i,j,k,\ell=1 \\ |\{i,j,k,\ell\}|\leq 2}}^{n} c_i c_j c_k c_\ell\, \mathbb{E}(X_i(r,s)X_j(r,s)X_k(s,t)X_\ell(s,t))$$

$$= \sum_{i=1}^{n} c_i^4\, \mathbb{E}(X_i^2(r,s)X_i^2(s,t)) + \sum_{\substack{i,j,k,\ell=1 \\ i=j\neq k=\ell}}^{n} c_i^2 c_k^2\, \mathbb{E}(X_i^2(r,s))\, \mathbb{E}(X_k^2(s,t))$$

$$+ \sum_{\substack{i,j,k,\ell=1 \\ i=k\neq j=\ell}}^{n} c_i^2 c_j^2 \, \mathbb{E}(X_i(r,s)X_i(s,t)) \, \mathbb{E}(X_j(r,s)X_j(s,t))$$

$$+ \sum_{\substack{i,j,k,\ell=1 \\ i=\ell\neq k=j}}^{n} c_i^2 c_k^2 \, \mathbb{E}(X_i(r,s)X_i(s,t)) \, \mathbb{E}(X_k(r,s)X_k(s,t))$$

$$\underset{(b5),(b2),(b4)}{\leq} \sum_{i=1}^{n} c_i^4 F_{ni}(r,s] \, F_{ni}(s,t] + 3 \sum_{\substack{i,k=1 \\ i\neq k}}^{n} c_i^2 c_k^2 F_{ni}(r,s] \, F_{nk}(s,t]$$

$$\leq 3\Big(\sum_{i=1}^{n} c_i^2 F_{ni}(r,s]\Big)\Big(\sum_{k=1}^{n} c_k^2 F_{nk}(s,t]\Big) = 3\nu_n(r,s]\nu_n(s,t] \text{ proving (i).}$$

As to (ii) we have $\mathbb{E}(W_n^4(s,t]) = \mathbb{E}((\sum_{i=1}^{n} c_i X_i(s,t))^4)$

$$= \sum_{i=1}^{n} c_i^4 \, \mathbb{E}(X_i^4(s,t)) + 3 \sum_{\substack{i,k=1 \\ i\neq k}}^{n} c_i^2 c_k^2 \, \mathbb{E}(X_i^2(s,t)X_k^2(s,t))$$

$$= 3\Big(\sum_{i=1}^{n} c_i^2 \, \mathbb{E}(X_i^2(s,t))\Big)^2 - 3 \sum_{i=1}^{n} c_i^4 (\mathbb{E}(X_i^2(s,t)))^2 + \sum_{i=1}^{n} c_i^4 \, \mathbb{E}(X_i^4(s,t))$$

$$\underset{(b2),(b3)}{\leq} 3\nu_n^2(s,t] + \Big(\max_{1\leq i\leq n} c_i^2\Big)\cdot \nu_n(s,t] \text{ proving (ii). } \square$$

<u>THEOREM 18 (G. Shorack (1979), Theorem 1.1).</u>

(i) If there exists a monotone increasing and continuous function

$G\colon [0,1] \to \mathbb{R}_+$ for which

either ⓐ $\nu_n(r,s] \leq G(r,s] := G(s) - G(r)$ for all $0 \leq r \leq s \leq 1$ and all $n \in \mathbb{N}$

or ⓑ $\lim_{n\to\infty} \nu_n(t) = G(t)$ for all $t \in [0,1]$,

then $(W_n)_{n\in\mathbb{N}}$ is relatively L-sequentially compact.

(ii) If further

$$\max_{1\leq i\leq n} \frac{c_{ni}^2}{n} \to 0 \quad \text{as} \quad n \to \infty,$$

then any possible limiting process, i.e., any random element W in $(D,\mathcal{B}(D,s)) = (D,\mathcal{B}_b(D,\rho))$ such that $W_{n'} \xrightarrow{L} W$ for some subsequence (n') of $\mathbb{N}$, satisfies $L\{W\}(C) = 1$;

thus (cf. Lemma 18) $(W_n)_{n\in\mathbb{N}}$ is relatively L_b-sequentially compact.

(iii) Suppose the hypotheses of (i) and (ii) hold. Then

there exists a random element W in $(D,\mathcal{B}_b(D,\rho))$ being a mean-zero Gaussian stochastic process with $\mathrm{cov}(W(s),W(t)) = K(s,t)$, $L\{W\}(C) = 1$ and such that $W_n \xrightarrow{L_b} W$ in (D,ρ)

if and only if

$\lim_{n\to\infty} K_n(s,t) = K(s,t)$ for all $0 \leqq s \leqq t \leqq 1$.

Proof. ad (i): We shall apply Theorem 14 in connection with our remarks (41) and (42). In view of this we have to verify the conditions (A), (B'), (C') and (D) for $\xi_n = W_n$ choosing $F_n := \sqrt{3}\,\nu_n$ and $F := \sqrt{3}\,G$.

ad (D): Follows immediately from the above assumptions (a) or (b) according to the choice of F_n and F in the present situation.

ad (C'): Follows from Lemma 22 (i) according to the choice of F_n.

ad (B'): Given any $\varepsilon > 0$ we have to show that

(+) $\limsup_{n\to\infty} \mathbb{P}(|W_n(\delta) - W_n(0)| \geqq \varepsilon) \to 0$ as $\delta \to 0$

and

(++) $\limsup_{n\to\infty} \mathbb{P}(|W_n(1) - W_n(\delta)| \geqq \varepsilon) \to 0$ as $\delta \to 1$.

ad (+):
$$\mathbb{P}(|W_n(\delta) - W_n(0)| \geqq \varepsilon) \leqq \varepsilon^{-2}\, \mathbb{E}(W_n^2(0,\delta])$$

$$\underset{(b1),(b2),L.22}{=} \varepsilon^{-2} n^{-1} \sum_{i=1}^{n} c_{ni}^2 [F_{ni}(0,\delta] - F_{ni}^2(0,\delta]] \leqq \varepsilon^{-2} n^{-1} \sum_{i=1}^{n} c_{ni}^2\, F_{ni}(0,\delta]$$

$= \varepsilon^{-2}\, \nu_n(0,\delta]$, whence by (a) or (b)

$$\limsup_{n\to\infty} \mathbb{P}(|W_n(\delta) - W_n(0)| \geqq \varepsilon) \leqq \varepsilon^{-2}(G(\delta) - G(0)) \to 0 \text{ as } \delta \to 0$$

since G was assumed to be continuous.

ad (++): Follows in the same way as (+).

ad (A): By (42) (C') implies (C) which together with (D) implies (C") by (41). According to (C"), given any $\eta > 0$ there exist $\delta = \delta(\eta) > 0$ and

$n_o = n_o(\delta(\eta)) \in \mathbb{N}$ such that for all $n \geq n_o$ $\mathbb{P}(\omega''_{W_n}(\delta) \geq 1) \leq \eta/2$.

Now, choose $k \in \mathbb{N}$ and $a > 0$ such that

$$k^{-1} < \delta \quad \text{and} \quad a^{-2} \leq \eta/2;$$

then

$$\mathbb{P}\Big(\bigcup_{i=1}^{k} \{|W_n(\tfrac{i-1}{k}, \tfrac{i}{k}]| \geq a\}\Big) \leq a^{-2} \sum_{i=1}^{k} \mathbb{E}(W_n^2(\tfrac{i-1}{k}, \tfrac{i}{k}])$$

$$\leq a^{-2} \sum_{i=1}^{k} \nu_n(\tfrac{i-1}{k}, \tfrac{i}{k}] \underset{(67)(a)}{\leq} a^{-2} \leq \eta/2.$$

Furthermore, for $n \geq n_o$, let

$$A_n := \bigcap_{i=1}^{k} \{|W_n(\tfrac{i-1}{k}, \tfrac{i}{k}]| < a\} \cap \{\omega''_{W_n}(\delta) < 1\} \cap \{W_n(0) = 0\};$$

then $\mathbb{P}(A_n) \geq 1 - \eta$ and for each $\omega \in A_n$ we have for any $t \in [0,1]$ and $1 \leq i \leq k$ so that $t \in [\frac{i-1}{k}, \frac{i}{k})$

$$|W_n(t,\omega) - W_n(\tfrac{i-1}{k},\omega)| \leq |W_n(\tfrac{i}{k},\omega) - W_n(\tfrac{i-1}{k},\omega)|$$

$$+ \min\{|W_n(\tfrac{i}{k},\omega) - W_n(t,\omega)|, |W_n(t,\omega) - W_n(\tfrac{i-1}{k},\omega)|\}$$

$$< a + \omega''_{W_n(\omega)}(k^{-1}) \leq a + \omega''_{W_n(\omega)}(\delta) < a + 1, \text{ whence}$$

$|W_n(t,\omega)| < ka + 1$, and therefore

$\mathbb{P}(\|W_n\| \leq ka + 1) \geq 1 - \eta$ for all $n \geq n_o$ which proves (A).

This concludes the proof of (i).

<u>ad (ii):</u> Suppose that for some random element W in $(D,\mathcal{B}(D,s)) = (D,\mathcal{B}_b(D,\rho))$ $W_{n'} \xrightarrow{L} W$ for some subsequence (n') of $\mathbb{N}$;

then for any $0 \leq s \leq t \leq 1$ such that

$$s,t \in T_W := \{r \in [0,1]: \pi_r \text{ is } L\{W\}\text{-a.e. } s\text{-continuous}\}$$

it follows from Theorem 5.1 in Billingsley (1968) that

$$(+) \qquad |W_{n'}(t) - W_{n'}(s)|^3 \xrightarrow{L} |W(t) - W(s)|^3;$$

on the other hand it follows from Lemma 22 (ii) that

(++) $\mathbb{E}(W_{n'}^4(s,t]) \leq 3\nu_{n'}^2(s,t] + (\max_{1\leq i\leq n'} \frac{c_{n'i}^2}{n'})\, \nu_{n'}(s,t] \leq 4$ for all n' (cf. (66) and (67)(a)).

But (+) together with (++) imply (cf. Gaenssler-Stute (1977), Exercise 1.14.4, p. 114) that

$$\mathbb{E}(|W(s,t]|^3) = \lim_{n'\to\infty} \mathbb{E}(|W_{n'}(s,t]|^3) \underset{(\text{Hölder})}{\leq} \limsup_{n'\to\infty} (\mathbb{E}(W_{n'}^4(s,t]))^{3/4}$$

$$\underset{(++)\text{ and ⓐ or ⓑ}}{\leq} (3G^2(s,t])^{3/4} \leq 3(G(s,t])^{3/2}.$$

Since T_W contains 0 and 1 and is dense in [0,1] (cf. Billingsley (1968)), it follows that

$$\mathbb{E}(|W(t) - W(s)|^3) \leq 3|G(t) - G(s)|^{3/2}$$

for <u>all</u> $0 \leq s \leq t \leq 1$,

whence by Lemma 19 $\mathbb{P}(W \in C) = 1$.

<u>ad (iii):</u> Assume first that

$$\lim_{n\to\infty} K_n(s,t) = K(s,t) \quad \text{for all } 0 \leq s \leq t \leq 1.$$

We are going to show that for any $\alpha_1,\ldots,\alpha_k \in \mathbb{R}$ and any $t_1,\ldots,t_k \in [0,1]$

(+++) $$\sum_{j=1}^{k} \alpha_j W_n(t_j) \xrightarrow{L} N(0,V) \text{ with } V := \sum_{r,s=1}^{k} \alpha_r\alpha_s K(t_r,t_s).$$

<u>ad (+++):</u> If V = 0, then for any $\varepsilon > 0$

$$\mathbb{P}(|\sum_{j=1}^{k} \alpha_j W_n(t_j)| \geq \varepsilon) \leq \varepsilon^{-2}\, \mathbb{E}(|\sum_{j=1}^{k} \alpha_j W_n(t_j)|^2)$$

$$\underset{(\text{cf.}(67)(\text{b}))}{=} \varepsilon^{-2} \sum_{r,s=1}^{k} \alpha_r\alpha_s K_n(t_r,t_s) \longrightarrow \varepsilon^{-2}\, V = 0$$ as $n \to \infty$ which proves (+++) in case V = 0.

If V > 0, consider

$$V^{-1/2} \sum_{j=1}^{k} \alpha_j W_n(t_j) = V^{-1/2} \sum_{j=1}^{k} \alpha_j [n^{-1/2} \sum_{i=1}^{n} c_{ni}(1_{[0,t_j]}(\xi_{ni}) - F_{ni}(t_j))]$$

$$= \sum_{i=1}^{n} (nV)^{-1/2}\, c_{ni}[\sum_{j=1}^{k} \alpha_j (1_{[0,t_j]}(\xi_{ni}) - F_{ni}(t_j))] =: \sum_{i=1}^{n} \zeta_{ni}, \text{ say.}$$

Then the ζ_{ni}'s form a triangular array of row-wise independent random variables with $\mathbb{E}(\zeta_{ni}) = 0$ and such that

$$\sum_{i=1}^{n} \mathbb{E}(\zeta_{ni}^2) = \mathbb{E}((\sum_{i=1}^{n} \zeta_{ni})^2) = V^{-1}\, \mathbb{E}((\sum_{j=1}^{k} \alpha_j W_n(t_j))^2)$$

$$= V^{-1} \sum_{r,s=1}^{k} \alpha_r \alpha_s K_n(t_r,t_s) \to 1 \quad \text{as } n \to \infty;$$

furthermore, for any $\delta > 0$ we have

$$\sum_{i=1}^{n} \mathbb{E}(\zeta_{ni}^2\, 1_{\{|\zeta_{ni}| > \delta\}}) \to 0 \quad \text{as} \quad n \to \infty:$$

in fact, given any $\varepsilon > 0$ let $p := 1 + \varepsilon/2$ and $q > 0$ be such that $1/p + 1/q = 1$; then, by Hölder's and Markov's inequality we obtain for any $\delta > 0$

$$\sum_{i=1}^{n} \mathbb{E}(\zeta_{ni}^2\, 1_{\{|\zeta_{ni}| > \delta\}}) \leq \sum_{i=1}^{n} \mathbb{E}(|\zeta_{ni}|^{2+\varepsilon})^{1/p}\, \mathbb{P}(|\zeta_{ni}| > \delta)^{1/q}$$

$$\leq \sum_{i=1}^{n} \mathbb{E}(|\zeta_{ni}|^{2+\varepsilon})^{1/p} (\delta^{-(2+\varepsilon)})^{1/q}\, \mathbb{E}(|\zeta_{ni}|^{2+\varepsilon})^{1/q} = \delta^{-2p/q} \sum_{i=1}^{n} \mathbb{E}(|\zeta_{ni}|^{2+\varepsilon})$$

$$\leq \delta^{-2p/q} \sum_{i=1}^{n} \left(\frac{|c_{ni}|}{(Vn)^{1/2}} \right)^{2+\varepsilon} \left(\sum_{j=1}^{k} |\alpha_j| \right)^{2+\varepsilon}$$

$$\leq \delta^{-2p/q}\, V^{-1-\varepsilon/2} \underbrace{\left(\max_{1 \leq i \leq n} \frac{|c_{ni}|}{n^{1/2}} \right)^{\varepsilon}}_{\to 0 \text{ as } n \to \infty} \underbrace{\left(\sum_{i=1}^{n} \frac{c_{ni}^2}{n} \right)}_{= 1} \left(\sum_{j=1}^{k} |\alpha_j| \right)^{2+\varepsilon} \to 0 \text{ as } n \to \infty.$$

Thus, it follows from the Central Limit Theorem (cf. Gaenssler-Stute (1977), 9.2.9) that

$$\sum_{i=1}^{n} \zeta_{ni} \xrightarrow{L} N(0,1) \quad \text{which proves (+++).}$$

Next, let $\overline{W}$ be a mean-zero Gaussian process with covariance structure given by K. Then, again for any $\alpha_1,\ldots,\alpha_k \in \mathbb{R}$ and any $t_1,\ldots,t_k \in [0,1]$

$$L\{\sum_{j=1}^{k} \alpha_j \overline{W}(t_j)\} = N(0,V) \quad \text{with } V \text{ defined as above.}$$

Therefore, by the Cramér-Wold Device (cf. Gaenssler-Stute (1977), 8.7.6) it follows together with (+++) that

$$W_n \xrightarrow[f.d.]{L} \overline{W}.$$

Now, by (ii), for any subsequence $(W_{n'})$ of (W_n) there exists a further subsequence $(W_{n''})$ and a random element $W_{(n')(n'')}$ in $(D,\mathcal{B}_b(D,\rho))$ such that $L\{W_{(n')(n'')}\}(C) = 1$ and

$$W_{n''} \xrightarrow{L_b} W_{(n')(n'')} \text{ in } (D,\rho).$$

Applying Theorem 3 and using the fact that each $W_{(n')(n'')}$ is uniquely determined by its fidis, it follows that

$$W_{(n')(n'')} \overset{L}{\equiv}: W \underset{f.d.}{\overset{L}{=}} \overline{W} \text{ and therefore}$$

$$W_n \xrightarrow{L_b} W \text{ in } (D,\rho).$$

To prove the other direction, suppose that $W_n \xrightarrow{L_b} W$ in (D,ρ) where W is a r.e. in $(D,\mathcal{B}_b(D,\rho))$ and is a mean-zero Gaussian process with covariance structure given by K (and such that $L\{W\}(C) = 1$). Then, by Theorem 3, for any $0 \leqq s \leqq t \leqq 1$

$$W_n(s)\cdot W_n(t) \xrightarrow{L} W(s)\cdot W(t) \quad \text{as} \quad n \to \infty,$$

and $\mathbb{E}(W_n^2(s)\cdot W_n^2(t)) \leqq \mathbb{E}(W_n^4(s))^{1/2}\,\mathbb{E}(W_n^4(t))^{1/2} \leqq 4$

for all $n \in \mathbb{N}$ (cf. (+++) above), whence (by the same reasoning as in the proof of (ii))

$$\mathbb{E}(W(s)\cdot W(t)) = \lim_{n\to\infty} \mathbb{E}(W_n(s)\cdot W_n(t)), \text{ i.e.,}$$

$$\lim_{n\to\infty} K_n(s,t) = K(s,t) \quad \text{for all } 0 \leqq s \leqq t \leqq 1. \quad \square$$

SOME GENERAL REMARKS ON WEAK CONVERGENCE OF RANDOM ELEMENTS IN $D \equiv D[0,1]$ w.r.t. ρ_q-METRICS:

Let q be any weight function belonging to the set

$\mathcal{Q}_2$:= {q: $[0,1] \to \mathbb{R}$, q continuous, $q(0) = q(1) = 0$ and $q(t) > 0$ for all $t \in (0,1)$, having the following additional properties (i_q) - (iii_q)}:

There exists a $\delta^* = \delta^*(q)$, $0 < \delta^* \leqq 1/2$, such that

(i_q) $q(t)$ and $q(1-t)$ are monotone increasing on $[0,\delta^*]$;

(ii_q) $\frac{q(t)}{\sqrt{t}}$ and $\frac{q(1-t)}{\sqrt{t}}$ are monotone decreasing on $[0,\delta^*]$;

(iii_q) $\int_0^{\delta^*} q^{-2}(u)du < \infty$ and $\int_{1-\delta^*}^1 q^{-2}(u)du < \infty$

(i.e. q^{-1} square integrable).

Here and in the following we make use of the convention $\frac{0}{0} := 0$.

REMARK. Let $q \in \mathcal{Q}_2$; then for any $t \leq \delta^*$

$\frac{\sqrt{t}}{q(t)} = (\frac{t}{q^2(t)})^{1/2} = (\int_0^t q^{-2}(t)du)^{1/2} \leq (\int_0^t q^{-2}(u)du)^{1/2}$, whence by ($iii_q$) one has

(iv_q) $\frac{\sqrt{t}}{q(t)} \to 0$ as $t \to 0$; similarly, by symmetry,

$\frac{\sqrt{1-t}}{q(t)} \to 0$ as $t \to 1$.

Now, let ξ_n, $n \geq 0$, be random elements in $(D,\mathcal{B}_b(D,\rho))$, defined on a common p-space $(\Omega,\mathcal{F},\mathbb{P})$, such that $\mathbb{P}(\xi_n(0) = 0, \xi_n(1) = 0) = 1$ and $\mathbb{P}(\xi_n/q \in D) = 1$ for all $n \geq 0$; in this case we shall assume w.l.o.g. that

$$\frac{\xi_n(\cdot,\omega)}{q(\cdot)} \in D \quad \text{for each } \omega \in \Omega \text{ and all } n \geq 0.$$

Then the ξ_n/q, $n \geq 0$, are also random elements in $(D,\mathcal{B}_b(D,\rho))$ (cf. (37)).

Let $q \in \mathcal{Q}_2$ and define

$$D_q := \{y = qx: x \in D\} \equiv qD, \text{ and } C_q := qC$$

with $C \equiv C[0,1]$, and define the ρ_q-METRIC on D_q by

$\rho_q(y_1,y_2) := \rho(x_1,x_2)$ if $y_i = qx_i \in D_q$, $i=1,2$, where we tacitly assume that $x(0) = x(1) = 0$ whenever $x \in D$ occurs.

Let $\mathcal{B}_b(D_q,\rho_q)$ be the σ-algebra in D_q generated by the open ρ_q-balls and consider the map

T_1: $D \to D_q$, defined by $T_1(x) := qx$ for $x \in D$;

then T_1 is $\mathcal{B}_b(D,\rho)$, $\mathcal{B}_b(D_q,\rho_q)$-measurable:

in fact, let $B_{\rho_q}(y,\varepsilon)$ be the open ρ_q-ball with center $y \in D_q$ and radius ε; then

$$T_1^{-1}(B_{\rho_q}(y,\varepsilon)) = \{x \in D: \rho_q(y,qx) < \varepsilon\} = \{x \in D: \rho(y/q,x) < \varepsilon\} \in \mathcal{B}_b(D,\rho).$$

In the same way

$T_2: D_q \to D$, defined by $T_2(y) := y/q$, is $\mathcal{B}_b(D_q,\rho_q)$, $\mathcal{B}_b(D,\rho)$-measurable.

This implies that

ξ/q is a random element in $(D,\mathcal{B}_b(D,\rho))$ iff

ξ is a random element in $(D_q,\mathcal{B}_b(D_q,\rho_q))$.

Note also (cf. (39)) that $C_q \in \mathcal{B}_b(D_q,\rho_q)$ and that (C_q,ρ_q) is a separable and closed subspace of (D_q,ρ_q).

Furthermore, one has the following

<u>LEMMA 23.</u> In the just described setting, the following two statements are equivalent:

(i) $\quad \xi_n/q \xrightarrow{L_b} \xi_o/q$ in (D,ρ) and $L\{\xi_o/q\}(C) = 1$

(ii) $\quad \xi_n \xrightarrow{L_b} \xi_o$ in (D_q,ρ_q) and $L\{\xi_o\}(C_q) = 1$.

<u>Proof.</u> (i) $\Rightarrow$ (ii): Note first that $L\{\xi_o\}(C_q) = \mathbb{P}(\xi_o \in C_q = qC)$ $= \mathbb{P}(\xi_o/q \in C) = L\{\xi_o/q\}(C)$.

Now, according to (28) (cf. (h') there) it remains to show

(+) $\quad \mathbb{E}(f(\xi_n)) \to \mathbb{E}(f(\xi_o))$ for every $f: D_q \to \mathbb{R}$ which is bounded, uniformly ρ_q-continuous and $\mathcal{B}_b(D_q,\rho_q)$, $\mathcal{B}$-measurable.

So, let $f: D_q \to \mathbb{R}$ be bounded, uniformly ρ_q-continuous and $\mathcal{B}_b(D_q,\rho_q)$, $\mathcal{B}$-measurable, and let $g: D \to \mathbb{R}$ be defined by $g(x) := f(qx)$, $x \in D$; then g is bounded, $\mathcal{B}_b(D,\rho)$, $\mathcal{B}$-measurable (since $g = f \circ T_1$) and uniformly ρ-continuous (since $\rho(x_1,x_2) = \rho_q(qx_1,qx_2)$ and $|g(x_1) - g(x_2)| = |f(qx_1) - f(qx_2)|$ for any $x_1,x_2 \in D$, i.e. $qx_1,qx_2 \in D_q$). Therefore, by (i) and (28) $\mathbb{E}(g(\xi_n/q)) \to \mathbb{E}(g(\xi_o/q))$ which implies (+) since $\mathbb{E}(g(\xi_n/q)) = \mathbb{E}(f(\xi_n))$ for all

$n \geq 0$.

(ii) $\Rightarrow$ (i): follows in the same way. □

FUNCTIONAL CENTRAL LIMIT THEOREMS FOR WEIGHTED EMPIRICAL PROCESSES w.r.t. ρ_q-METRICS:

As before let W_n be a weighted empirical process based on an array (ξ_{ni}) of row-wise independent random variables ξ_{ni}, $1 \leq i \leq n$, $n \in \mathbb{N}$, defined on some p-space $(\Omega, \mathcal{F}, \mathbb{P})$, and on an array (c_{ni}) of given scores (cf. (65)).
We assume again that the distribution functions F_{ni} of the ξ_{ni}'s are concentrated on $[0,1]$; here, in addition, we suppose that

(69) $$\text{for each } n \in \mathbb{N}: n^{-1} \sum_{i=1}^{n} F_{ni}(t) = t \quad \text{for all } t \in [0,1].$$

Then, for any $q \in \mathcal{Q}_2$, we have

LEMMA 24. $\mathbb{P}(W_n/q \in D) = 1$ for all n, whence we may and do assume w.l.o.g. that $W_n(\cdot,\omega)/q(\cdot) \in D$ for each $\omega \in \Omega$ and all $n \in \mathbb{N}$.

Proof. According to the definition of W_n, for $\mathbb{P}$-a.a. $\omega \in \Omega$ there exists a $t = t(\omega) \leq \delta^*$ such that by (69) and (iv_q)

$$\frac{|W_n(t,\omega)|}{q(t)} \leq n^{-1/2} \sum_{i=1}^{n} |c_{ni}| \frac{F_{ni}(t)}{q(t)} \leq (\max_{1\leq i\leq n} |c_{ni}|)\, n^{1/2} \frac{t}{q(t)} \to 0$$

as $t \to 0$; similarly, $\frac{|W_n(t,\omega)|}{q(t)} \to 0$ as $t \to 1$ for $\mathbb{P}$-a.a. ω which implies the assertion (imposing the convention $\frac{0}{0} := 0$). □

Now, for uniformly bounded scores, Shorack (1979) has shown:

THEOREM 19 (Shorack (1979), Theorem 1.2).

Suppose that

(70) $$\sup_{n\in\mathbb{N}} (\max_{1\leq i\leq n} |c_{ni}|) \leq M < \infty.$$

Then for all $q \in \mathcal{Q}_2$ we have

(i) $(W_n/q)_{n\in\mathbb{N}}$ is relatively L-sequentially compact (in (D,s)).

(ii) Any limiting process, i.e. any random element W in $(D,\mathcal{B}(D,s)) = (D,\mathcal{B}_b(D,\rho))$ such that $W_{n'}/q \xrightarrow{L} W$ for some subsequence (n') of $\mathbb{N}$, satisfies $L\{W\}(C) = 1$, whence, by Lemma 18, $(W_n/q)_{n\in\mathbb{N}}$ is relatively L_b-sequentially compact in (D,ρ) such that for any limiting process W $L\{W\}(C) = 1$,

and therefore, by Lemma 23,

$(W_n)_{n\in\mathbb{N}}$ is relatively L_b-sequentially compact in (D_q,ρ_q) such that for any limiting process W_o $L\{W_o\}(C_q) = 1$.

(iii) There exists a random element W_o in $(D_q,\mathcal{B}_b(D_q,\rho_q))$ being a mean-zero Gaussian stochastic process with

$\text{cov}(W_o(s), W_o(t)) = K_o(s,t)$, $L\{W_o\}(C_q) = 1$ and such that

$W_n \xrightarrow{L_b} W_o$ in (D_q,ρ_q)

if and only if (for $K_n(s,t) = \text{cov}(W_n(s), W_n(t))$)

$\lim_{n\to\infty} K_n(s,t) = K_o(s,t)$ for all $0 \leq s \leq t \leq 1$.

The proof of Theorem 19 (being based on Theorem 18 and Theorem 17) can be carried through along the lines presented in Shorack's (1979) paper with some slight modifications being necessary due to our choice of $\mathcal{Q}_2$; by the way, instead of (15) on p. 171 it suffices to impose (iv_q) and instead of $\mathbb{P}(A_N) \leq \exp(-1/a_N)$ one shows $\mathbb{P}(A_N) \geq 1 - 1/a_N$ to get (v) on p. 181. We are not going to give further details here. Instead, since the proof of Theorem 1.2 in Shorack (1979) seems not suited to carry over to give a proof of his Theorem 1, 3 as mentioned there on p. 182 (note that in the case of not uniformly bounded scores it is not possible to estimate

$$\left(\max_{1\leq i\leq n} \frac{c_{ni}^2}{n}\right)(t - s) \text{ by } M^2(t - s)^2 \text{ for } t - s > n^{-1},$$ which was essentially used

to get (c) on p. 179) we want to present here a completely different proof of the following result:

THEOREM 20 (Shorack (1979), Theorem 1.3).

If all ξ_{ni} are uniformly distributed on $[0,1]$ and if instead of (70)

$$\max_{1\leq i\leq n} \frac{c_{ni}^2}{n} \to 0 \quad \text{as} \quad n \to \infty, \tag{71}$$

then, for any $q \in \mathcal{Q}_2$, $W_n \xrightarrow{\mathcal{L}_b} B^o$ in (D_q,ρ_q) as $n \to \infty$ and $\mathcal{L}\{B^o\}(C_q) = 1$, where B^o denotes the Brownian bridge.

The proof of Theorem 20 is based on the following lemmata which may be of independent interest.

The first lemma is concerned with a martingale property of the weighted empirical process W_n based on ξ_{ni} which are uniformly distributed on $[0,1]$.

LEMMA 25. Let $n \in \mathbb{N}$ be arbitrary but fixed and write ξ_i and c_i instead of ξ_{ni} and c_{ni}, respectively. Suppose that $F_{ni}(t) = t$ for all $t \in [0,1]$. Then for any $(c_1,\ldots,c_n) \in \mathbb{R}^n$

$$\left(\frac{n^{1/2}W_n(t)}{1-t}\right)_{0\leq t<1} = \left(\frac{\sum_{i=1}^{n} c_i[1_{[0,t]}(\xi_i) - t]}{1-t}\right)_{0\leq t<1} \quad \text{is a}$$

martingale w.r.t. $\mathcal{F}_t := \sigma(\{\frac{n^{1/2}W_n(s)}{1-s} : s \leq t\})$, $0 \leq t < 1$.

Proof. We use the following auxiliary result which is easy to prove:

(72) Let $(\zeta_t)_{0\leq t<T}$ and $(\eta_t)_{0\leq t<T}$, $T \leq \infty$, be martingales w.r.t.

$(\mathcal{F}_t := \sigma(\{\zeta_s : s \leq t\}))_{0\leq t<T}$ and $(\mathcal{G}_t := \sigma(\{\eta_s : s \leq t\}))_{0\leq t<T}$,

respectively. Assume that $(\zeta_t)_{0\leq t<T}$ and $(\eta_t)_{0\leq t<T}$ are independent.

Then $(\zeta_t + \eta_t)_{0\leq t<T}$ is a martingale w.r.t.

$(\mathcal{H}_t := \sigma(\{\zeta_s,\eta_s : s \leq t\}))_{0\leq t<T}$ and therefore also w.r.t.

$(\sigma(\{\zeta_s + \eta_s : s \leq t\}))_{0\leq t<T}$.

Now, given any $(c_1,\ldots,c_{n+1}) \in \mathbb{R}^{n+1}$, put

$$\zeta_t = \zeta_t^{(n)} := \sum_{i=1}^{n} c_i[1_{[0,t]}(\xi_i) - t]/(1-t),$$

$$\eta_t := \zeta_t^{(n+1)} - \zeta_t^{(n)}, \quad 0 \leq t < 1,$$

and apply (72) to get the assertion of Lemma 25 by induction on n; for n = 1 cf. Lemma 3 in Section 1 (choosing $(X,\mathcal{B},\mu) = ([0,1],[0,1] \cap \mathbb{B},\lambda)$, λ = Lebesgue measure, and $\mathcal{C} := \{[0,t]: 0 \leq t < 1\}$ there).

LEMMA 26. Suppose that $F_{ni}(t) = t$ for all $t \in [0,1]$; let $q \in \mathcal{Q}_2$ and $\delta^* = \delta^*(q)$, $0 < \delta^* \leq 1/2$, be as in the definition of $\mathcal{Q}_2$.
Then, for any $n \in \mathbb{N}$, each $\varepsilon > 0$, and any $\delta \leq \delta^*$, one has

(i) $$\mathbb{P}\Big(\sup_{t\in[0,\delta]} \Big| \frac{W_n(t)}{q(t)} \Big| > \varepsilon\Big) \leq \varepsilon^{-2} \cdot 8 \int_0^\delta q^{-2}(u)du, \text{ and}$$

(ii) $$\mathbb{P}\Big(\sup_{t\in[1-\delta,1]} \Big| \frac{W_n(t)}{q(t)} \Big| > \varepsilon\Big) \leq \varepsilon^{-2} \cdot 8 \int_{1-\delta}^1 q^{-2}(u)du.$$

Proof. ad (i): let $n \in \mathbb{N}$ be arbitrary but fixed and for each $k \in \mathbb{N}$ and $i \in \{0,\ldots,2^k\}$ let

$$t_{ki} := i \cdot \delta/2^k.$$

Then, due to the path properties of W_n/q (cf. Lemma 24), it suffices to show that for each $\varepsilon > 0$ and any $k \in \mathbb{N}$ one has

(+) $$\mathbb{P}\Big(\sup_{1\leq i\leq 2^k} \Big| \frac{W_n(t_{ki})}{q(t_{ki})} \Big| > \varepsilon\Big) \leq \varepsilon^{-2} \cdot 8 \int_0^\delta q^{-2}(u)du.$$

For later use note that

(++) $$1 \leq (1 - t_{ki})^{-2} \leq 4 \quad \text{for each } k \text{ and } i.$$

ad (+): let $\varepsilon > 0$ and $k \in \mathbb{N}$ be arbitrary but fixed.
Since, by Lemma 25, for any fixed $n \in \mathbb{N}$

$\left(\frac{W_n(t)}{1-t} \right)_{0\leq t<1}$ is a martingale, we can apply Chow's inequality (cf. Gaenssler-Stute (1977), (6.6.2)) on the submartingale

$\left(\left(\frac{W_n(t)}{1-t} \right)^2\right)_{0\leq t<1}$ to obtain

$$\varepsilon^2\, \mathbb{P}\Big(\max_{1\leq i\leq 2^k} \Big|\frac{W_n(t_{ki})}{q(t_{ki})}\Big| > \varepsilon\Big) \underset{(++)}{\leq} \varepsilon^2\, \mathbb{P}\Big(\max_{1\leq i\leq 2^k} [q^{-2}(t_{ki})\Big(\frac{W_n(t_{ki})}{1-t_{ki}} \Big)^2] > \varepsilon^2\Big)$$

$$\leq q^{-2}(t_{k1})\ \mathbb{E}((\frac{W_n(t_{k1})}{1-t_{k1}})^2) + \sum_{i=2}^{2^k} q^{-2}(t_{ki})\ \mathbb{E}((\frac{W_n(t_{ki})}{1-t_{ki}})^2 - (\frac{W_n(t_{k,i-1})}{1-t_{k,i-1}})^2).$$

Now, since $\mathbb{E}(W_n^2(t)) = n^{-1}\sum_{i=1}^{n} c_{ni}^2[F_{ni}(t) - F_{ni}^2(t)] = n^{-1}\sum_{i=1}^{n} c_{ni}^2(t - t^2)$

$= t(1-t) \leq t$, we get by the second inequality in (++)

(66)

$$q^{-2}(t_{k1})\ \mathbb{E}((\frac{W_n(t_{k1})}{1-t_{k1}})^2) \leq 4\ q^{-2}(t_{k1})t_{k1} \underset{(i_q)}{\leq} 4 \int_0^{t_{k1}} q^{-2}(u)du \leq 4\int_0^{\delta} q^{-2}(u)du;$$

on the other hand

$$\sum_{i=2}^{2^k} q^{-2}(t_{ki})\ \mathbb{E}((\frac{W_n(t_{ki})}{1-t_{ki}})^2 - (\frac{W_n(t_{k,i-1})}{1-t_{k,i-1}})^2)$$

$$= \sum_{i=2}^{2^k} q^{-2}(t_{ki})\ [\frac{t_{ki}}{1-t_{ki}} - \frac{t_{k,i-1}}{1-t_{k,i-1}}] \underset{(\text{cf.}(++))}{\leq} 4\sum_{i=2}^{2^k} q^{-2}(t_{ki})(t_{ki} - t_{k,i-1})$$

$$\leq 4\int_{t_{k1}}^{\delta} q^{-2}(u)du \leq 4\int_0^{\delta} q^{-2}(u)du.$$

So, in summary we have

$$\mathbb{P}(\max_{1\leq i\leq 2^k} |\frac{W_n(t_{ki})}{q(t_{ki})}| > \varepsilon) \leq \varepsilon^{-2}\cdot 8\int_0^{\delta} q^{-2}(u)du$$

which proves (+).

<u>ad (ii):</u> by symmetry this follows in the same way. □

<u>LEMMA 27.</u> For any $q \in \mathcal{Q}_2$ we have $\mathbb{P}(B^o/q \in C) = 1$, where B^o denotes the Brownian bridge and C is the space of all continuous functions on [0,1].

<u>Proof.</u> We have to show that B^o/q is $\mathbb{P}$-a.s. continuous at 0 (and also at 1 which is shown similarly). For this, according to Lemma 19, it suffices to show that for some constants $a > 1$, $b > 0$ and some continuous function $F: [0,1] \to \mathbb{R}$

(+) $\quad \mathbb{E}(|\bar{B}^o(t) - \bar{B}^o(s)|^b) \leq |F(t) - F(s)|^a$

for all $0 \leq s \leq t \leq 1$, where (using again the convention $\frac{0}{0} := 0$)

$$\bar{B}^o(t) := \frac{B^o(t)}{q(t)} 1_{[0,\delta^*]}(t) + \frac{B^o(\delta^*)}{q(\delta^*)} 1_{(\delta^*,1]}(t),\ t \in [0,1]$$

($\delta^* = \delta^*(q)$ as in the definition of $\mathcal{Q}_2$).

ad (+): since, for any $0 \leq s \leq t \leq 1$, $B^o(t) - B^o(s)$ is normally distributed with mean zero and variance $(t - s)(1 - (t - s))$, we have

$$\text{(a)} \qquad \mathbb{E}\left(\frac{(B^o(t) - B^o(s))^4}{q^4(t)} \right) = \frac{3(t - s)^2(1 - (t - s))^2}{q^4(t)}, \quad 0 \leq s \leq t \leq 1.$$

On the other hand, for any $0 < s \leq t \leq \delta^*$, we have

$$\mathbb{E}((B^o(s))^4[\frac{1}{q(s)} - \frac{1}{q(t)}]^4) = [\frac{1}{q(s)} - \frac{1}{q(t)}]^4 \cdot 3\, s^2(1 - s)^2,$$

where

$$s^2[\frac{1}{q(s)} - \frac{1}{q(t)}]^4 = [\frac{\sqrt{s}}{q(s)} (1 - \frac{q(s)}{q(t)})]^4$$

$$\leq [\frac{\sqrt{t}}{q(t)} (1 - \frac{\sqrt{s}}{t})]^4 \quad (\text{since } \frac{\sqrt{t}}{q(t)} \uparrow \text{ on } [0,\delta^*] \text{ by } (ii_q))$$

$$= [\frac{\sqrt{t} - \sqrt{s}}{q(t)}]^4 \leq (\frac{t - s}{q^2(t)})^2, \text{ whence}$$

$$\text{(b)} \qquad \mathbb{E}((B^o(s))^4[\frac{1}{q(s)} - \frac{1}{q(t)}]^4) \leq \frac{3(t - s)^2(1 - s)^2}{q^4(t)}, \quad 0 < s \leq t \leq \delta^*.$$

Now, it follows from (a) and (b) that for $0 < s \leq t \leq \delta^*$

$$\mathbb{E}(| \frac{B^o(t)}{q(t)} - \frac{B^o(s)}{q(s)} |^4) = \mathbb{E}((\frac{B^o(t) - B^o(s)}{q(t)} + B^o(s)[\frac{1}{q(t)} - \frac{1}{q(s)}])^4)$$

$$\leq 2^4[\mathbb{E}(\frac{(B^o(t) - B^o(s))^4}{q^4(t)}) + \mathbb{E}((B^o(s))^4[\frac{1}{q(t)} - \frac{1}{q(s)}]^4)]$$

$$\leq 2^4[\frac{3(t-s)^2(1-(t-s))^2 + 3(t-s)^2(1-s)^2}{q^4(t)}]$$

$$\leq 2^4 \cdot 6(q^{-2}(t)(t - s))^2 \underset{(i_q)}{\leq} (4\sqrt{6} \int_s^t q^{-2}(u)du)^2.$$

Thus, taking $F(t) := 4\sqrt{6} \int_0^t q^{-2}(u)du$, we get (+) (with $b = 4$, $a = 2$) for all $0 < s \leq t \leq 1$.

It remains to consider the case $s = 0$ and $0 < t \leq \delta^*$; but, by (a),

$$\mathbb{E}(| \frac{B^o(t)}{q(t)} |^4) \leq 3\, q^{-4}(t)t^2 \underset{(i_q)}{\leq} (\sqrt{3} \int_0^t q^{-2}(u)du)^2$$

$$\leq F^2(t) = |F(t) - F(0)|^2. \text{ This proves (+).} \quad \square$$

Proof of Theorem 20. In the setting of Theorem 18 and its preceding remarks (67) we have in the present situation (where $F_{ni}(t) = t$ for all $t \in [0,1]$) that (cf. (66))

$$\nu_n(t) = t \quad (=: G(t)) \text{ for all } t \in [0,1]$$

and $$K_n(s,t) \equiv K(s,t) = s \wedge t - st = \operatorname{cov}(B^{\circ}(s), B^{\circ}(t)).$$

Therefore, by Theorem 18 (iii), we have

(a) $$W_n \xrightarrow{L_b} B^{\circ} \quad \text{in } (D,\rho).$$

Furthermore, by Lemma 24 and Lemma 27, for any $q \in \mathcal{Q}_2$ we have

(b) $$\mathbb{P}(W_n/q \in D) = 1 \text{ for all } n \in \mathbb{N} \text{ and } \mathbb{P}(B^{\circ}/q \in C) = 1.$$

We are thus in a situation where our general remarks on weak convergence of random elements in $D = D[0,1]$ w.r.t. ρ_q-metrics can be applied.

So, by Lemma 23, it remains to show

(c) $$W_n/q \xrightarrow{L_b} B^{\circ}/q \quad \text{in } (D,\rho).$$

ad (c): let $q_o :\equiv 1$ and for $m \geq 1$ let

$$q_m := q\, 1_{(\frac{1}{m}, 1-\frac{1}{m})} + q(\tfrac{1}{m})\, 1_{[0,\frac{1}{m}]} + q(1-\tfrac{1}{m})\, 1_{[1-\frac{1}{m},1]}.$$

Since q_m is continuous and $q_m > 0$ on $[0,1]$

(d) $$W_n/q_m \xrightarrow{L_b} B^{\circ}/q_m \quad \text{in } (D,\rho) \text{ as } n \to \infty.$$

Now, according to (28), (c) holds if we show that

$$\lim_{n\to\infty} \mathbb{E}(f(W_n/q)) = \mathbb{E}(f(B^{\circ}/q)) \quad \text{for all } f \in U_b^b(D,\rho).$$

But, again by (28) and (d), we have for each m that

$$\lim_{n\to\infty} \mathbb{E}(f(W_n/q_m)) = \mathbb{E}(f(B^{\circ}/q_m)) \text{ for all } f \in U_b^b(D,\rho);$$

furthermore, by Lebesgue's theorem

$$\lim_{m\to\infty} \mathbb{E}(f(B^{\circ}/q_m)) = \mathbb{E}(f(B^{\circ}/q)) \text{ for all } f \in U_b^b(D,\rho),$$

since, by Lemma 27, $\mathbb{P}(B^{\circ}/q \in C) = 1$ and therefore $\lim_{m\to\infty} \rho(B^{\circ}/q_m, B^{\circ}/q) = 0$ $\mathbb{P}$-a.s.

Thus, given any $f \in U_b^b(D,\rho)$, choosing for each $m \in \mathbb{N}$ $k_m > k_{m-1}$ (with $k_o := 0$) such that

$$|\mathbb{E}(f(W_n/q_m)) - \mathbb{E}(f(B^o/q_m))| \leq \frac{1}{m} \text{ for } n \geq k_m,$$

and putting for each $n \in \mathbb{N}$ $i_n := m$ if $n \in \{k_m, \ldots, k_{m+1}-1\}$, we obtain

$$\lim_{n\to\infty} \mathbb{E}(f(W_n/q_{i_n})) = \mathbb{E}(f(B^o/q)).$$

So, it remains to show

(e) $$\lim_{n\to\infty} |\mathbb{E}(f(W_n/q_{i_n})) - \mathbb{E}(f(W_n/q))| = 0.$$

For this, let $\varepsilon > 0$ be arbitrary and $\delta = \delta(\varepsilon) > 0$ be such that $\rho(x,y) \leq \delta$ implies $|f(x) - f(y)| \leq \varepsilon$. (Note also that $||f|| := \sup_{x\in D} |f(x)| < \infty$.) Then for n sufficiently large (i.e. such that $i_n^{-1} \leq \delta^*$)

$$|\mathbb{E}(f(W_n/q_{i_n})) - \mathbb{E}(f(W_n/q))| \leq \mathbb{E}(|f(W_n/q_{i_n}) - f(W_n/q)|)$$

$$\leq \varepsilon + 2\,||f|| \cdot \mathbb{P}(\rho(W_n/q_{i_n}, W_n/q) > \delta)$$

$$\leq \varepsilon + 2\,||f|| \cdot [\mathbb{P}(\sup_{t\in[0,\frac{1}{i_n}]} |\frac{W_n(t)}{q(t)}| > \delta/2) + \mathbb{P}(\sup_{t\in[1-\frac{1}{i_n},1]} |\frac{W_n(t)}{q(t)}| > \delta/2)],$$

whence it follows from Lemma 26 that

$$|\mathbb{E}(f(W_n/q_{i_n})) - \mathbb{E}(f(W_n/q))|$$

$$\leq \varepsilon + 2\,||f|| \cdot [(\delta/2)^{-2} \cdot 8(\int_0^{\frac{1}{i_n}} q^{-2}(u)du + \int_{1-\frac{1}{i_n}}^{1} q^{-2}(u)du)],$$

and therefore, by (iii_q),

$$\limsup_{n\to\infty} |\mathbb{E}(f(W_n/q_{i_n})) - \mathbb{E}(f(W_n/q))| \leq \varepsilon .$$

Since $\varepsilon > 0$ was arbitrary, this proves (e) and therefore (c) is shown. □

(73) REMARKS. (a) W. Schneemeier (1982) has given an example showing that Theorem 19 fails to hold if the uniform boundedness condition (70) on the scores is replaced by the condition

$$\max_{1\le i\le n} \frac{c_{ni}^2}{n} \to 0 \quad \text{as} \quad n \to \infty$$

which was imposed in Theorem 18. Thus, the assumption in Theorem 20 of ξ_{ni} being uniformly distributed on $[0,1]$ cannot be weakened to the assumption that for every $n \in \mathbb{N}$ $n^{-1} \sum_{i=1}^{n} F_{ni}(t) = t$ for all $t \in [0,1]$ (cf. (69)) without strengthening the condition on the scores.

(b) As to the L_b-statements in Theorem 18 and Theorem 19 it is possible by making use of Theorem 11 a) (or Theorem 11^*) to modify the given proofs such that they operate totally within our theory of L_b-convergence.

Note, for example, that along the same lines as in the proof of Proposition B_2 together with an application of Theorem 11^* one obtains (within the theory of L_b-convergence) that any sequence $(\xi_n)_{n\in\mathbb{N}}$ of random elements in $(D,\mathcal{B}_b(D,\rho))$ which satisfies the following two conditions

(i) $\lim_{\delta\downarrow 0} \limsup_{n\to\infty} \mathbb{P}(\omega_{\xi_n}(\delta) > \varepsilon) = 0$ for each $\varepsilon > 0$

and

(ii) $\lim_{M\to\infty} \limsup_{n\to\infty} \mathbb{P}(\|\xi_n\| > M) = 0$

is relatively L_b-sequentially compact and such that for any limiting random element ξ_o one has $L\{\xi_o\}(C) = 1$.

Further results in this direction will be contained in a forthcoming paper by P. Gaenssler, E. Haeusler and W. Schneemeier (1983).

CONCLUDING REMARKS ON FURTHER RESULTS FOR EMPIRICAL PROCESSES INDEXED BY CLASSES OF SETS OR CLASSES OF FUNCTIONS:

(a) FUNCTIONAL LAWS OF THE ITERATED LOGARITHM

(cf. Gaenssler-Stute (1979), Section 1.3, concerning results for the uniform empirical process α_n).

One of the main theorems in Kuelbs and Dudley (1980) states that for any p-space $(X,\mathcal{B},\mu)$ the following holds true:

(74) If (M_1) is satisfied for a class $\mathcal{C} \subset \mathcal{B}$ and μ, and if $\mathcal{C}$ is a μ-Donsker class, then $\mathcal{C}$ is a STRASSEN LOG LOG CLASS for μ, i.e., with probability one the set

$$\{(\frac{\beta_n(C)}{(2\log\log n)^{1/2}})_{C\in\mathcal{C}}: n \geqq n_0\} \text{ is relatively compact}$$

(w.r.t. the supremum metric ρ in $D_o(\mathcal{C},\mu)$) with limit set

$B_{\mathcal{C}} := \{\varphi: C \mapsto \int_C f d\mu,\ C \in \mathcal{C};\ f \in B\}$, where

$B := \{f \in L^2(X,\mathcal{B},\mu): \int_X f d\mu = 0 \text{ and } \int_X |f|^2 d\mu \leqq 1\}$.

(Note that $B_{\mathcal{C}} \subset \mathcal{U}^b(\mathcal{C},d_\mu) \subset D_o(\mathcal{C},\mu)$.)

Now, as pointed out in Gaenssler (1983), since for $(X,\mathcal{B},\mu) = (\mathbb{R}^k,\mathcal{B}_k,\mu)$, $k \geqq 1$, the class $\mathcal{C} = \mathcal{J}_k$ of all lower left orthants satisfies (M_1) and is a μ-Donsker class for any μ by (58), one obtains by (74) the results of Finkelstein (1971) and Richter (1974), namely

(75) $\mathcal{J}_k$ is a Strassen log log class for every p-measure μ on $\mathcal{B}_k$, $k \geqq 1$.

That the same holds true for $\mathcal{C} = \mathbb{B}_k$ (the class of all closed Euclidean balls in $\mathbb{R}^k$, $k \geqq 1$) is a consequence of our remarks preceding Theorem D and of Corollary 2.4 in Kuelbs and Dudley (1980) according to which one has

(76) If (M_1) is satisfied for μ and a Vapnik-Chervonenkis class $\mathcal{C}$, then $\mathcal{C}$ is a Strassen log log class for μ.

(b) DONSKER CLASSES OF FUNCTIONS.

Let α_n be the uniform empirical process (cf. the end of Section 3) and let q be some weight function considered above in connection with weak convergence of random elements in $D \equiv D[0,1]$ w.r.t. ρ_q-metrics. For any $q \in \mathcal{Q}_2$ we know from Theorem 20 (with $c_{ni} \equiv 1$) that

$$\alpha_n \xrightarrow{\mathcal{L}_b} B^o \text{ in } (D_q,\rho_q)$$

or, equivalently by Lemma 23, that

(77) $$\alpha_n/q \xrightarrow{\mathcal{L}_b} B^o/q \quad (\text{in } (D,\rho)).$$

Now, from a different point of view, taking for each $t \in [0,1]$ the functions $f_t\colon [0,1] \to \mathbb{R}$ defined by

$$f_t(s) := q^{-1}(t)\, 1_{[0,t]}(s),\ s \in [0,1],$$

α_n/q can be considered as an empirical process indexed by a class of functions; in fact, let

$$\mathcal{F}_o := \{f_t\colon t \in [0,1]\},$$

then for each $t \in [0,1]$

$$\alpha_n(t)/q(t) = \int_0^1 f_t(s)\, d\alpha_n(s) =: \alpha_n(f_t).$$

Also the limiting process in (77) can be viewed as a mean-zero Gaussian process $\mathbb{G}_\mu$ (μ being here Lebesgue measure on $X = [0,1]$) indexed by $\mathcal{F}_o$, i.e., $\mathbb{G}_\mu \equiv (G_\mu(f))_{f\in\mathcal{F}_o}$, with covariance structure

(78) $$\operatorname{cov}(G_\mu(f_{t_1}), G_\mu(f_{t_2})) = \int_0^1 f_{t_1} f_{t_2}\, d\mu - \int_0^1 f_{t_1}\, d\mu \cdot \int_0^1 f_{t_2}\, d\mu;$$

note that $\operatorname{cov}(q^{-1}(t_1)\, B^o(t_1),\ q^{-1}(t_2)\, B^o(t_2))$

$$= q^{-1}(t_1)q^{-1}(t_2)[t_1 \wedge t_2 - t_1t_2] = \int_0^1 f_{t_1} f_{t_2}\, d\mu - \int_0^1 f_{t_1}\, d\mu \cdot \int_0^1 f_{t_2}\, d\mu.$$

Hence (77) is equivalent to

(79) $$(\alpha_n(f))_{f\in\mathcal{F}_o} \xrightarrow{\mathcal{L}_b} \mathbb{G}_\mu \equiv (G_\mu(f))_{f\in\mathcal{F}_o}.$$

This leads to the problem of generalizing Dudley's central limit theory from empirical $\mathcal{C}$-processes to the case of

EMPIRICAL $\mathcal{F}$-PROCESSES $\beta_n \equiv (\beta_n(f))_{f\in\mathcal{F}}$,

defined by

$$\beta_n(f) := n^{1/2}\, (\mu_n(f) - \mu(f)),\ f \in \mathcal{F},$$

where $\mathcal{F}$ is a given class of measurable functions defined on an arbitrary sample space $(X,\mathcal{B},\mu)$, and where

$$\mu_n(f) := \int f d\mu_n,\quad \mu(f) := \int f d\mu,\ f \in \mathcal{F},$$

μ_n being the empirical measure based on i.i.d. ξ_i's with values in X and distribution μ on $\mathcal{B}$.

For uniformly bounded classes of functions such an extension is more or less straightforward, but this does of course not meet the special case mentioned before (note that q^{-1} is approaching ∞ at the endpoints of $[0,1]$). For possibly unbounded classes $\mathfrak{F}$ the present knowledge is by recent work of R.M. Dudley (1981a), R.M. Dudley (1981b) and D. Pollard (1981a) as follows: let $(X,\mathcal{B},\mu)$ be an arbitrary p-space and $\beta_n \equiv (\beta_n(f))_{f\in\mathfrak{F}}$ be an empirical $\mathfrak{F}$-process with $\mathfrak{F} \subset L^2(X,\mathcal{B},\mu)$. It turns out that there are proper extensions of the spaces $S_o \equiv \mathcal{U}^b(\mathcal{C},d_\mu)$ and $S \equiv D_o(\mathcal{C},\mu)$ considered at the beginning of Section 4 (corresponding to the special situation $\mathfrak{F} = 1_{\mathcal{C}} := \{1_C: C \in \mathcal{C}\}$) to the present case with d_μ on $\mathcal{C}$ being replaced by

$$e_\mu(f_1,f_2) := (\int_X (f_1 - f_2)^2 d\mu)^{1/2}, \; f_1,f_2 \in \mathfrak{F},$$

$$\text{(or better } \rho_\mu(f_1,f_2) := (\int_X (f_1 - f_2 - \int_X (f_1 - f_2)d\mu)^2 d\mu)^{1/2}, \; f_1,f_2 \in \mathfrak{F}),$$

leading to certain spaces $S_o = S_o(\mathfrak{F},e_\mu)$ and $S = S(\mathfrak{F},\mu)$ of functions $\varphi: \mathfrak{F} \to \mathbb{R}$ which can be chosen in such a way that under certain conditions on $\mathfrak{F}$ $S_o(\mathfrak{F},e_\mu)$ becomes a separable subspace of $(S(\mathfrak{F},\mu),\rho)$ and such that $(\beta_n(f))_{f\in\mathfrak{F}}$ has all its sample paths in $S(\mathfrak{F},\mu)$; here as before ρ denotes the supremum metric, i.e.,

$$\rho(\varphi_1,\varphi_2) := \sup_{f\in\mathfrak{F}} |\varphi_1(f) - \varphi_2(f)| \quad \text{for } \varphi_1,\varphi_2 \in S(\mathfrak{F},\mu).$$

Now, again under certain measurability assumptions (like (M) or (M_o) imposed in the case of empirical $\mathcal{C}$-processes) the setting of a functional limit theorem for empirical $\mathfrak{F}$-processes $\beta_n \equiv (\beta_n(f))_{f\in\mathfrak{F}}$ in the sense of $\mathcal{L}_b$-convergence for random elements in $(S(\mathfrak{F},\mu), \mathcal{B}_b(S(\mathfrak{F},\mu),\rho))$ applies, i.e., one can speak of

(80) $\beta_n \xrightarrow{\mathcal{L}_b} \mathbb{G}_\mu$, where $\mathbb{G}_\mu \equiv (G_\mu(f))_{f\in\mathfrak{F}}$ is a mean-zero Gaussian process with covariance structure (cf. (78))

$$\operatorname{cov}(G_\mu(f_1), G_\mu(f_2)) = \int_X f_1 f_2 d\mu - \int_X f_1 d\mu \cdot \int_X f_2 d\mu.$$

If (80) holds true, $\mathcal{F}$ is called a μ-DONSKER CLASS OF FUNCTIONS.

Generalizing Theorem A from classes of sets to classes of functions the main result of R.M. Dudley (1981a) is:

(81) Suppose (M_o) (which means here that $\beta_n : X^{\mathbb{N}} \to S(\mathcal{F},\mu)$ is measurable from the measure-theoretic completion of $(X^{\mathbb{N}}, \mathcal{B}_{\mathbb{N}}, \times_{\mathbb{N}} \mu)$ to $(S(\mathcal{F},\mu), \mathcal{B}_b(S(\mathcal{F},\mu),\rho)))$ and suppose that $F := \sup\{|f| : f \in \mathcal{F}\} \in \mathcal{L}^p(X,\mathcal{B},\mu)$ for some $p > 2$; assume further that for γ with $0 < \gamma < 1 - 2/p$ and some $M < \infty$

(E_2) $N_I(\varepsilon,\mathcal{F},\mu) \leqq \exp(M\,\varepsilon^{-\gamma})$ for ε small enough.

Then $\mathcal{F}$ is a μ-Donsker class.

In this connection, $N_I(\varepsilon,\mathcal{F},\mu)$, a natural extension of $N_I(\varepsilon,\mathcal{C},\mu)$, is defined as the smallest $m \in \mathbb{N}$ such that for some $f_1,\dots,f_m \in \mathcal{L}^2(X,\mathcal{B},\mu)$ (not necessarily in $\mathcal{F}$), for every $f \in \mathcal{F}$ there exist $j,k \leqq m$ with $f_j(x) \leqq f(x) \leqq f_k(x)$ for all $x \in X$ and such that $\int_X (f_k - f_j)d\mu < \varepsilon$.

Note that for $\mathcal{F} = 1_{\mathcal{C}}$ with $\mathcal{C} \subset \mathcal{B}$ one has for any μ

(82) $$N_I(\varepsilon,1_{\mathcal{C}},\mu) \leqq N_I(\varepsilon,\mathcal{C},\mu) \leqq 2\, N_I(\varepsilon,1_{\mathcal{C}},\mu).$$

In fact, as to the first inequality, suppose that $n := N_I(\varepsilon,\mathcal{C},\mu) < \infty$; then there exist $A_1,\dots,A_n \in \mathcal{B}$ such that for every $C \in \mathcal{C}$ there exist i,j with $A_i \subset C \subset A_j$ and $\mu(A_j \setminus A_i) < \varepsilon$. Take $f_i := 1_{A_i}$, $i=1,\dots,n$, to obtain $f_i \in \mathcal{L}^2(X,\mathcal{B},\mu)$ so that for every $f = 1_C$ $f_i \leqq f \leqq f_j$ and $\int(f_j - f_i)d\mu = \mu(A_j \setminus A_i) < \varepsilon$. To verify the second inequality, let $m := N_I(\varepsilon,1_{\mathcal{C}},\mu) < \infty$; then there exist $f_1,\dots,f_m \in \mathcal{L}^2(X,\mathcal{B},\mu)$ such that for every $f = 1_C \in 1_{\mathcal{C}}$ there exist $j,k \leqq m$ with $f_j \leqq 1_C \leqq f_k$ and $\int(f_k - f_j)d\mu < \varepsilon$. Taking as $A_1,\dots,A_{2m}$ all sets of the form $\{f_i > 0\}$ and $\{f_i \geqq 1\}$, $i=1,\dots,m$, we obtain that for every $C \in \mathcal{C}$ there exist $j,k \leqq 2m$ such that $A_j \subset C \subset A_k$ and $\mu(A_k \setminus A_j) < \varepsilon$; in fact, $A_j := \{f_j > 0\}$ and $A_k := \{f_k \geqq 1\}$ serves for this.

(83) (R.M. Dudley (1981a)): as $p \to \infty$ the condition on γ in (81) approaches $\gamma < 1$; if $\mathcal{F}$ is a collection of indicator functions of sets, i.e.,

$\mathcal{F} = 1_C$ for some $C \subset \mathcal{B}$, then (E_2) does imply (E_1) for C (cf. (82)). For $\gamma = 1$ it appears that (81) fails, specifically it fails when $\mathcal{F}$ is the collection of indicator functions of convex sets in $\mathbb{R}^3$ and μ is Lebesgue measure on the unit cube (cf. (63) and its consequences).

Now, if one would try to infer (79) from (81), there is the problem of verifying (E_2); on the other hand the condition on the envelope function F imposed in (81) is rather restrictive since this forces q^{-1} to be in $L^p(X,\mathcal{B},\mu)$ for some $p > 2$ (cf. instead the condition (iii_q) imposed in the definition of $\mathcal{Q}_2$). But, from another point of view, the class

$\mathcal{F}_o = \{q^{-1}(t)\, 1_{[0,t]}: t \in [0,1]\}$ considered in (79) is of the following special form:

$$\mathcal{F}_o = \{f_o \cdot g_t: t \in [0,1]\} \text{ with } f_o = q^{-1} \text{ and } g_t(s) := \frac{q(s)}{q(t)}\, 1_{[0,t]}(s),\ s \in X = [0,1],$$

where $\frac{q(s)}{q(t)} \to 0$ as $s \to 0$.

Thus, restricting our attention at this place to weight functions q for which q^{-1} is continuous, monotone decreasing on $(0,1/2)$, symmetric around $s = 1/2$ and such that $q^{-1}(s) \geq \delta > 0$ for all $s \in [0,1]$, then there exists some $M < \infty$ such that for each $t \in [0,1]$ $\sup_{s\in[0,1]} |g_t(s)| \leq M$ and such that

$$\{g_t^{-1}((a,b]): a < b\} \text{ forms a Vapnik-Chervonenkis class,}$$

since for each $a < b$ $g_t^{-1}((a,b])$ consists of one or at most two disjoint intervals $(c,d]$ in $[0,1]$ (cf. FIGURE 5).

Thus, the following result of R.M. Dudley (1981b) gives another way to obtain (79) (for proper weight functions q):

(84) Suppose $\mathcal{F} = \{f_o \cdot g: g \in \mathcal{G}\}$ where for some constant $M < \infty$ and some (suitably measurable) Vapnik-Chervonenkis class C

a) $\mathcal{G} = \{g: X \to [-M,M],\ g^{-1}((a,b]) \in C\ \forall a < b\}$ and

b) $f_o \geq 0$, f_o is measurable and $\mu(\{f_o > t\}) = o(t^{-2}(\log t)^{-\beta})$ as $t \to \infty$ for some $\beta > 4$,

then $\mathcal{F}$ is a μ-Donsker class.

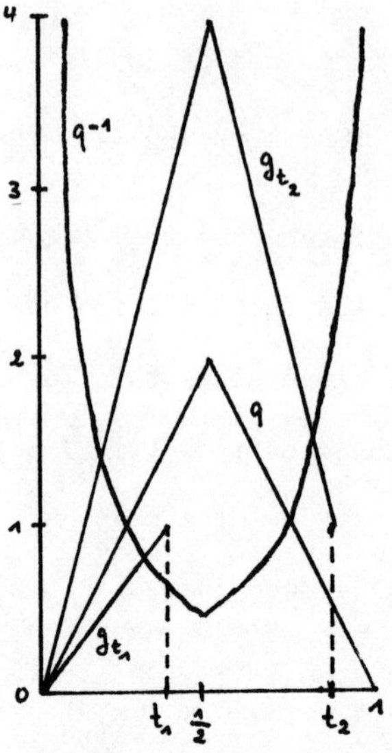

FIGURE 5

Note that b), even for $\beta > 1$, implies $f_o \in L^2(X,\mathcal{B},\mu)$. Conversely, the condition on $\mu(\{f_o > t\})$ is implied by $f_o \in L^p(X,\mathcal{B},\mu)$ for some $p > 2$.

Note also that by taking $f_o \equiv 1$ one obtains Theorem D as a corollary of (84). In this context the following result of D. Pollard (1981a) extends a special case of (84) to the case where only $f_o \in L^2(X,\mathcal{B},\mu)$ is assumed:

(85) If $f \in L^2(X,\mathcal{B},\mu)$ and if $\mathcal{C}$ is a Vapnik-Chervonenkis class of sets, then (for a separable version of $\beta_n \equiv (\beta_n(f))_{f\in\mathcal{F}}$), $\mathcal{F} := \{f_o \cdot 1_C : C \in \mathcal{C}\}$ is a μ-Donsker class.

(c) STRONG APPROXIMATIONS (cf. Gaenssler-Stute (1979), Section 3, concerning results for the uniform empirical process α_n).

In a recent paper by R.M. Dudley and W. Philipp (1983) almost sure and probability invariance principles are established for sums of independent not necessarily (Borel-)measurable random elements with values in a not necessarily separable Banach space like the closure of $D_o(\mathcal{C},\mu)$ in $(\ell^\infty(\mathcal{C}),\rho)$ fitting readily into the theory of empirical $\mathcal{C}$-processes $\beta_n \equiv (\beta_n(C))_{C\in\mathcal{C}}$ being now viewed as partial sum processes

$$\beta_n = n^{-1/2} \sum_{i=1}^{n} \zeta_i$$

with $\zeta_i \equiv (\zeta_i(C))_{C\in\mathcal{C}}$ defined by $\zeta_i(C) := 1_C(\xi_i) - \mu(C)$

(for a given sequence $(\xi_i)_{i\in\mathbb{N}}$ of random elements in $(X,\mathcal{B})$ with distribution μ on $\mathcal{B}$) having its values in $D_o(\mathcal{C},\mu)$.

In an analogous way the same viewpoint applies for empirical $\mathfrak{F}$-processes.

This approach of getting strong resp. weak invariance principles has the advantage that one can bypass most of the problems of measurability and topological characteristics which occurred in our theory of L_b-convergence where it was essential to choose proper sample spaces S and S_o for the processes β_n and $\mathbb{G}_\mu$, respectively, together with suitable σ-algebras in S and S_o on which the laws of β_n and $\mathbb{G}_\mu$ could be defined.

On the other hand, we think that the availability of the presented theory of weak convergence of empirical processes is at the least necessary to support Dudley's and Philipp's claim that strong approximation results are strengthened versions of functional central limit theorems.

REFERENCES

ANDERSON, T.W. and DARLING, D.A. (1952). Asymptotic theory of certain 'goodness of fit' criteria based on stochastic processes. Ann. Math. Statist. 23 193-212.

BAUER, H. (1978). Wahrscheinlichkeitstheorie und Grundzüge der Maßtheorie, 3. Auflage. Walter de Gruyter, Berlin - New York.

BENNETT, G. (1962). Probability inequalities for the sum of independent random variables. J. Amer. Statist. Assoc. 57 33-45.

BILLINGSLEY, P. (1968). Convergence of Probability Measures. Wiley, New York.

BILLINGSLEY, P. (1971). Weak Convergence of Measures. Applications in Probability. Regional Conference Series in Appl. Math., No. 5. SIAM, Philadelphia.

BOLTHAUSEN, E. (1978). Weak convergence of an empirical process indexed by the closed convex subsets of I^2. Z. Wahrscheinlichkeitstheorie und verw. Gebiete 43 173-181.

BORISOV, I.S. (1981). Some limit theorems for empirical distributions; Abstract of Reports, Third Vilnius Conference on Probability Theory and Math. Statistics I 71-72.

BREIMAN, L. (1968). Probability. Addison-Wesley, Reading.

BRONŠTEIN, E.M. (1976). ε-entropy of convex sets and functions. Siberian Math. J. (English translation) 17 393-398.

CHERNOFF, H. (1964). Estimation of the mode. Ann. Inst. Statist. Math. 16 31-41.

CHIBISOV, D.M. (1965). An investigation of the asymptotic power of tests of fit. Theor. Probability Appl. 10 421-437.

COVER, T.M. (1965). Geometric and statistical properties of systems of linear inequalities with applications to pattern recognition. IEEE Trans. Elec. Comp. EC-14 326-334.

DEVROYE, L. (1982). Bounds for the uniform deviation of empirical measures. J. Multiv. Anal. 12 72-79.

DONSKER, M.D. (1952). Justification and extension of Doob's heuristic approach to the Kolmogorov-Smirnov theorems. Ann. Math. Statist. 23 277-281.

DOOB, J.L. (1949). Heuristic approach to the Kolmogorov-Smirnov theorems. Ann. Math. Statist. 20 393-403.

DUDLEY, R.M. (1966). Weak convergence of probabilities on nonseparable metric spaces and empirical measures on Euclidean spaces. Illinois J. Math. 10 109-126.

DUDLEY, R.M. (1967). The sizes of compact subsets of Hilbert space and continuity of Gaussian processes. J. Functional Analysis 1 290-330.

DUDLEY, R.M. (1968). Distances of probability measures and random variables. Ann. Math. Statist. 39 1563-1572.

DUDLEY, R.M. (1973). Sample functions of the Gaussian process. Ann. Probability 1 66-103.

DUDLEY, R.M. (1974). Metric entropy of some classes of sets with differentiable boundaries. J. Approximation Theory 10 227-236.

DUDLEY, R.M. (1976). Probabilities and Metrics. Convergence of laws on metric spaces, with a view to statistical testing. Aarhus Lecture Notes Series No. 45.

DUDLEY, R.M. (1978). Central Limit Theorems for Empirical Measures. Ann. Probability 6 899-929.

DUDLEY, R.M. (1979). Balls in $\mathbb{R}^k$ Do Not Cut All Subsets of $k+2$ Points. Adv. in Math. 31 306-308.

DUDLEY, R.M. (1979a). Lower layers in $\mathbb{R}^2$ and convex sets in $\mathbb{R}^3$ are not GB classes. Springer Lecture Notes in Math. 709 97-102.

DUDLEY, R.M. (1981a). Donsker classes of functions; Statistics and Related

Topics (Proc. Symp. Ottawa, 1980), North Holland, New York - Amsterdam, 341-352.

DUDLEY, R.M. (1981b). Vapnik-Chervonenkis-Donsker classes of functions, Aspects Statistiques et aspects physiques des processus gaussiens (Proc. Colloque C.N.R.S. St. Flour, 1980), C.N.R.S. Paris, 251-269.

DUDLEY, R.M. (1982). Empirical and Poisson processes on classes of sets or functions too large for central limit theorems. Z. Wahrscheinlichkeitstheorie verw. Gebiete 61 355-368.

DUDLEY, R.M. and PHILIPP, W. (1983). Invariance principles for sums of Banach space valued random elements and empirical processes. Z. Wahrscheinlichkeitstheorie verw. Gebiete 62 509-552.

DURBIN, J. (1973). Distribution Theory for Tests based on the Sample Distribution Function. Regional Conference Series in Appl. Math., No. 9. SIAM, Philadelphia.

DURST, M. and DUDLEY, R.M. (1980). Empirical Processes, Vapnik-Chervonenkis classes and Poisson Processes. Probability and Mathematical Statistics (Wrocław) 1, Fasc. 2, 109-115.

FINKELSTEIN, H. (1971). The law of the iterated logarithm for empirical distributions. Ann. Math. Statist. 42 607-615.

GAENSSLER, P. and STUTE, W. (1977). Wahrscheinlichkeitstheorie. Springer, Berlin-Heidelberg-New York.

GAENSSLER, P. and STUTE, W. (1979). Empirical Processes: A Survey of Results for independent and identically distributed random variables. Ann. Probability 7 193-243.

GAENSSLER, P. (1981). On certain properties of convex sets in Euclidean spaces with probabilistic implications. Unpublished manuscript.

GAENSSLER, P. and WELLNER, J.A. (1981). Glivenko-Cantelli Theorems. To appear in the Encyclopedia of Statistical Sciences, Volume 3.

GAENSSLER, P. (1983). Limit Theorems for Empirical Processes indexed by classes of sets allowing a finite-dimensional parametrization. Probability and Mathematical Statistics (Wrocław), Vol. IV, Fasc. 1.

HARDING, E.F. (1967). The number of partitions of a set of N points in k dimensions induced by hyperplanes, Proc. Edinburgh Math. Soc. (Ser. II) 15 285-298.

HEWITT, E. (1947). Certain Generalizations of the Weierstraß Approximation Theorem. Duke Math. J. 14 419-427.

HOEFFDING, W. (1963). Probability inequalities for sums of bounded random variables. J. Amer. Statist. Assoc. 58 13-30.

KELLEY, J.L. (1961). General Topology. D. van Nostrand Comp., Inc. Princeton N.J.

KIRSZBRAUN, M.D. (1934). Über die zusammenziehende und Lipschitzsche Transformationen. Fund. Math. 22 77-108.

KUELBS, J. and DUDLEY, R.M. (1980). Log log laws for empirical measures. Ann. Probability 8 405-418.

McSHANE, E.J. (1934). Extension of range of functions. Bull, Amer. Math. Soc. 40 837-842.

POLLARD, D. (1979). Weak convergence on non-separable metric spaces. J. Austral. Math. Soc. (Ser. A) 28 197-204.

POLLARD, D. (1981). Limit theorems for empirical processes. Z. Wahrscheinlichkeitstheorie und verw. Gebiete 57 181-195.

POLLARD, D. (1981a). A central limit theorem for empirical processes. To appear in J. Austral. Math. Soc.

PROHOROV, Yu.V. (1956). Convergence of random processes and limit theorems in probability theory. Theor. Probability Appl. 1 157-214.

PYKE, R. and SHORACK, G. (1968). Weak convergence of a two sample empirical process and a new approach to Chernoff-Savage theorems. Ann. Math. Statist. 39 755-771.

PYKE, R. (1977). The Haar-function construction of Brownian motion indexed by sets. Technical Report 35, Dept. of Mathematics, University of Washington, Seattle.

PYKE, R. (1979). Recent developments in empirical processes. Adv. Appl. Prob.

11 267-268.

PYKE, R. (1982). The Haar-function construction of Brownian motion indexed by sets. Technical Report 18, Dept. of Statistics, University of Washington, Seattle.

PYKE, R. (1982a). A uniform central limit theorem for partial-sum processes indexed by sets. Technical Report 17, Dept. of Statistics, University of Washington, Seattle.

RICHTER, H. (1974). Das Gesetz vom iterierten Logarithmus für empirische Verteilungsfunktionen im $\mathbb{R}^k$. Manuscripta Math. 11 291-303.

SAUER, N. (1972). On the density of families of sets. J. Comb. Theory (A), 13 145-147.

SCHLÄFLI, L. (1901, posth.). Theorie der vielfachen Kontinuität, in Gesammelte Math. Abhandlungen I; Birkhäuser, Basel, 1950.

SERFLING, R.J. (1974). Probability Inequalities for the Sum in Sampling without Replacement. Ann. Statist. 2 39-48.

SHORACK, G.R. (1979). The weighted empirical process of row independent random variables with arbitrary distribution functions. Statistica Neerlandica 33 169-189.

SKOROKHOD, A.V. (1956). Limit theorems for stochastic processes. Theor. Probability Appl. 1 261-290.

STEELE, M. (1975). Combinatorial Entropy and Uniform Limit Laws. Ph. D. dissertation. Stanford University.

STEELE, M. (1978). Empirical discrepancies and subadditive processes. Ann. Probability 6 118-127.

STEINER, J. (1826). Einige Gesetze über die Theilung der Ebene und des Raumes. J. Reine Angew. Math. 1 349-364.

STUTE, W. (1982). The oscillation behavior of empirical processes. Ann. Probability 10 86-107.

SUN, T.G. (1977). Ph. D. dissertation, Dept. of Mathematics, University of Washington, Seattle.

SUN, T.G. and PYKE, R. (1982). Weak convergence of empirical processes. Technical Report 19, Dept. of Statistics, University of Washington, Seattle.

TALAGRAND, M. (1978). Les boules peuvent elles engendrer la tribu borélienne d'un espace métrisable non séparable? Communication au Séminaire Choquet (Paris.)

VALENTINE, F.A. (1964). Convex Sets. McGraw-Hill, New York.

VAPNIK, V.N. and CHERVONENKIS, A.Ya. (1971). On uniform convergence of the frequencies of events to their probabilities. Theor. Probability Appl. 16 264-280.

WATSON, D. (1969). On partitions of n points. Proc. Edinburgh Math. Soc. 16 263-264.

WEGMAN, E.J. (1971). A note on the estimation of the mode. Ann. Math. Statist. 42 1909-1915.

WELLNER, J.A. (1977). A Glivenko-Cantelli theorem and strong laws of large numbers for functions of order statistics. Ann. Statist. 5 473-480; Correction, ibid. 6 1394.

WENOCUR, R.S. and DUDLEY, R.M. (1981). Some special Vapnik-Chervonenkis classes. Disrete Math. 33 313-318.

WICHURA, M.J. (1968). On the weak convergence of non-Borel probabilities on a metric space. Ph. D. dissertation, Columbia University.

WICHURA, M.J. (1970). On the construction of almost uniformly convergent random variables with given weakly convergent image laws. Ann. Math. Statist. 41 284-291.

NOTATION INDEX

USED ABBREVIATIONS:

ad(·): = as to the proof of (·):

a.e. = almost everywhere

CLT = Central Limit Theorem

df = distribution function

fidis = finite dimensional distributions

GCC = Glivenko-Cantelli class

$\xrightarrow{L^1}$ = convergence in the mean

$\xrightarrow{\mathbb{P}}$ = convergence in probability

$\mathbb{P}$-a.s. = $\mathbb{P}$-almost surely

$\text{rest}_A f$ = restriction of f on A

r.h.s. = right hand side

SLLN = Strong Law of Large Numbers

w.r.t. = with respect to

VCC = Vapnik-Chervonenkis class

SUBJECT INDEX